MARTIAL ARTS

MARTIAL ARTS
A Critical Analysis of Orissa

Shyam Sundar Rath

Publications

KALPAZ PUBLICATIONS
DELHI - 110 052

Martial Arts: A Critical Analysis of Orissa

Rs. 750

ISBN : 81-7835-282-6

Published in 2005 in India by
Kalpaz Publications
C-30, Satyawati Nagar,
Delhi-110 052
Email : kalpaz@hotmail.com

Lasertype Setting by: Tact Computer Graphics, Delhi
Printed at: Mehra Offset Press, Delhi

To My

Father, Mother and Wife

Contents

Preface

The history of the martial arts is as old as the history of human race. It is the history concerning not only of the whole strategy of war science but the history of development of mans instinct for survival. The search for food and the necessity to defend his territory against wild animal and other enemies, were the founding needs of the development of the varieties of missiles, projectiles and throwing weapons. Enormous efforts have been put throughout the ages to develop various types of weapons and the using skills. In every culture, warriors have appreciated the importance of practice of the successful handling of weaponry and also welcomed the development and perfection of new combat techniques. Through the trial and error method various attacking and defensive techniques have been incorporated with and without weapons. This is the root of the martial arts. Martial art is the art concerned with the waging of war. Many of the martial arts presently seen, are stemed from ancient war skills. So also, the Orissan martial arts, popularly known as '*Paika Akheda*', represents one of the ancient war skill and happens to be one of the very old martial arts of the world.

In the course of the history of weaponry, weapons are divided into two categories, namely, indirect and direct weapons. The indirect weapons contain projectiles such as bows and arrows, throwing sticks, spears, stones, catapults, light and heavy artillery, and finally rockets and bombs. The second is direct weapons such as sword, shield, knife, clubs, sticks, flails, which is normally handled by the individual in a close combat. Both are practiced by the warriors as per the demand occur. According to Hindu mythology weapons generally used in fighting are categorised into five classes viz. weapon thrown or projected with a machine, those thrown with hands, those cast with hands and retained after use, those which are permanently retained with hand and the combative skills such as wrestling. Many skills of the weapon have become obsolete in modern times. Few combative skills are revived and introduced in sports such as judo, wrestling, tai kendo, karate. So also the weapons of the then period like pistol, rifle, bows and arrows have been introduced in sports in National and International level.

The book **Martial Arts: 'A Critical Analysis of Orissa'** is translated from the Ph.D thesis of the author. The original research work as titled "A Critical Analysis of Orissan Martial Arts" submitted to Utkal University in the year 2000 for the degree of Doctor of Philosophy in Physical Education. The book divided into five chapters, in which the first part deals with the introduction. The second part is review of related literature devoted to military tradition of Vedic period, Epic age, from the period of Ashoka to British period, important strongholds, martial arts of various states in India and abroad. The Orissan martial arts competition organised in different years by the Government is also elaborated. In the third chapter details of the Orissan martial arts and the descriptions of the weapons explained. Various photographs of weapons, war scene of the temple and photographs of present Orissan martial arts are also depicted. The various data collected through interview, questionnaire and observation are explained in the fourth chapter. The fifth chapter consists of Summary, Conclusion and Recommendations.

In the study of the martial arts of a region of a country, due emphasis is generally given to its political, cultural and military history. It has evidently the relation with the rise and fall of the royal dynasties, the military glories, literature, art and architecture, forts or strongholds in a chronological sequence. An attempt has been taken to give details of references of the political and the administrative history of Orissa, military glory and tradition, and also the origin and importance of Orissan martial arts. A comparative feature of the martial arts of India and world has been presented. Though many of these skills of the weapons and combative technique are forgotten and many other skills are found obsolete still the present militia class of Orissa preserve this for the sake of mental pleasure as the memory of a brave warrior and valorous race of the bygone days.

S.S. Rath

Acknowledgements

I am highly grateful to my guide Dr. Godavarish Das, Principal; (Retd.) Govt. College of Physical Education, Kalinga Stadium, Bhubaneshwar for his expert guidance and valuable suggestions in caring out the research work successfully.

I am thankful to Late Dr. Jaganath Pattanaik Retd. Professor department of history, Utkal University, Vani Vihar, Bhubaneswar, for his valuable suggestion and encouragement given to the scholar in successfully completing this study.

I express my thanks to the staff members of Directorate of Sports and Youth Services, Librarian of the Utkal University, HKM State Library and Orissa State Archives, Bhubaneswar for the permission to collect data from the library.

I am grateful to Sri Debakar Muduli, Librarian, Govt. College of Physical Education, Sri Manmath Kumar Samal, Librarian, Orissa State Museum for the help rendered by them.

I also express my sincere thanks to Sri Kasinath Nayak, Sri Ramchandra Suar, Sri Kedarnath Das (paika guru) and all the secretaries and paika gurus of the responded akhedas of Orissa for their information and valuable suggestions.

Heartiest thanks are extended to all the members of Jaga Ghar and paikas from the different akheda for their generous help and arranging demonstration programme for the research scholar to get the required information and analysis of techniques without which the work of the thesis would not have been completed.

I am thankful to Sri Srimanta Mishra (O.A.S.) and Mrs. Sumitra Tripathy (Director), Jurassic Fitness Health Club, Bhubaneswar, for their encouragement to complete this work.

I feel it my duty to express my thanks to En. Pravat Mallick Director College of Engineering Bhubaneswar (CEB) and Koustuv

Institute of Self Domain (KISD) for his encouragement to publish this book.

I also express my sincere thanks to Sri Nalini Bichari Mohapatra (Addl. Director) and Sri Sadasiva Dash (G.M. Admn) College of Engineering Bhubaneswar for encouragement to publish this book.

Finally, I express my extreme gratitude to Kalpaz Publications without his sincere help, it would not have been possible for the book to see the light of the day.

S.S. Rath

1
Introduction

Armed combat and fighting have its origins in the earliest development of man's instinct for survival. Because ever since man has thought of protecting himself from the dangers around him, he has tried to find out the devices to make himself stronger and mighter. Man was to secure himself from the dangers caused by animals, natural environment and enemies. Early human beings also contended with invisible enemies in the form of disease and illness. Survival of the fittest was the rule, and dominance was established on the basis of physical superiority. His individual longevity depend on his ability to develop a body physically sufficient to endure the rigors of outdoor life, to carry his burdens to fight his enemies to stalk game, and to make and use tools and weapons. This struggle to subdue another in combat, unarmed or armed, is possibly a legacy handed down to us from our ancestors. Over the centuries, man has formulated scientific principles in an effort to overcome his enemies and their sinister designs. This desire for domination sowed the seeds for martial arts.

The term "Martial Arts", simply means 'art concerned with the waging of war'. Many of the martial arts we know today stem from ancient war skills[1] . Gone are those days when martial arts were given prime importance in the battlefield. With the advance of the modern science, war strategy was changed. Each nation has developed its own technology in the field of defence organisation. Since, warfare has changed considerably in the last hundred years, these once ancient skills have been transferred into artistic disciplines in the modern programme of physical education and sports.

Throughout history, the military emphasis has been closely related to the use of physical education activities[2]. In a society or a state, there have always been the need to develop the physical capacities of soldiers to prepare them to successfully engage themselves in the practice of battles and endure the hardships imposed by war. The concept of physical education certainly is a later concept as compared to the notion of physical fitness and health. Physical education is conducive to build up organic health but it is also responsible for developing the mental and emotional health and some kind of habits which are desirable for the society and peaceful social living. Its contribution is not only limited to the physical fitness, but also it is extended to the spheres like physical efficiency, mental alertness and development of certain qualities like preseverence, team spirit, leadership, discipline, tolerance, etc.

Similarly martial arts training is not just the learning of skilled fighting techniques; there must be disciplined training, a moral philosophy, dedication, a sense of duty and respect. Any martial skill which is not beneficial to both exponent and society is not a martial arts[3]. A thug may use a martial arts technique in a fight but this does not make him a martial artist: had he been taught true martial arts he would not have been a thug. This shows the importance of martial arts in human race.

Physical education today may appear to be far more sophisticated than of early men and women. The objectives, however, are not all that different. Like their pre-historic counterparts, today physical educators are concerned with enhancing physical well-being and improving the ability of individuals to cope physically with everyday life. Thus, the roots of physical education go very deep, and the origins of our profession are, in essence, the origins of the human race[4].

Evidence from the history also indicates that sports and games, dances and festivals, endless play of children have shaped cultural patterns and have become the part and parcel of the history of man, wherever and whenever he has lived. It is seen that the emphasis on sound physical education is no less in bringing up a civilised Greece. The Greek civilization has a great impact on today's systems of physical education. In the Platonic scheme of education, education for the first ten years was predominantly physical. Every school had a gymnasium and a playground. The entire curriculum of education consisted of games and sports and during that period of education the health of children was nicely developed so as to make the medicines unnecessary.

Early in Spartan history there was a rigorous system of State training which was quite developed as well as maintained for centuries. The Spartan citizen devoted themselves exclusively to the military profession. This was possible because the state provided them with land and assigned them serfs to perform the labour on their farms. Other subject peoples carried on the trade and commerce essential for serving their need. All citizens had only one profession, serving the state as a soldier.[5] Spartan education aimed to create obedient and courageous soldiers of such physical perfection that they could stoically endure the pain and discomfort of battle. In the Spartan States, young men were driven by one all consuming desire to be obedient soldiers, capable military leaders, and conscientious citizens. While boys were being drilled as soldiers, girls were being physically conditioned to bear healthy, sturdy children. Their offspring were prenatally dedicated to the state. Young women were not allowed to develop any tender, protective, maternal affection that might make them fear the loss of a son in war. Indeed, women were expected to experience an exhilarated feeling of self-esteem if a son or husband sacrificed his life in the glory of battle. The military excellence was the apogeu of Spartan physical education. Even aesthetic bodily expressions were directed toward military ends. This militant people did not employ the dance primarily to create beauty and grace, but merely as a tool for fashioning an efficient soldier. It was valued because the rhythm caught the military spirit. Plutarch says, "The military dance was an indefinable stimulus, which inflamed courage and gave strength to persevere in the paths of honour and valour".

Both the Spartans and the Athenians were primarily concerned with training the child to assume his civic responsibility, but the Athenians were more liberal. The Athenians wanted youths to develop not only military skills and courage, but also the virtues and capacities needed for the peaceful progress of the nation. Moral training was an important part of the programme. Through physical education, the youngster developed self-discipline, courage, humility, determination, and sportsmanship. There was much more emphasis on the formation of character than on the development of strength and athletic prowess. As one knows, the early education of Athenian youth took place in two kinds of private elementary schools. The palaestra (wrestling school) provided boys with their physical education and the didascaleum (music school) offered courses in literature, music and some arithmetic[6].

Early Roman education stressed moral and military training more than intellectual attainment. While Greeks encouraged the harmonious unfolding of the total personality, the Roman demanded a more definite and practical goal. The Roman curriculum[7] was designed to develop strength of body, courage in battle, agility in arms, and obedience to commands. In contrast with Greek physical education, "The Roman games and exercises were intended only to make men strong and skillful warriors; and it was not for beauty of form or grace of movement, but only for vigor and prowess in battle, that they were honoured by their fellow-citizens".

The home, forum, and army were the educational institution of the early Romans. The Spartan child was educated in military barracks, and the Athenian youngster grew up in the palaestra and gymnasium; the Roman youngster was trained in a well organised home by his parents. The father determined whether the newborn child should survive, and he continued to exert his influence even after the youth was married. The Roman mother, a highly respected and socially active women, assisted her husband in raising their children. The education of a child was seldom entrusted to slaves. As youths, the lads accompanied their fathers on all of daily routines: religious exercises, visits to the Forum (gladiatorial combats place), business negotiations, and exercises at the Campus Martius. The campus Martius and military camps were the physical education schools of Romans. The Campus Martius was a large open area outside the servian wall adjacent to the Tiber River[8].

The early period of the Chou dynasty (1122-249 B.C.) saw physical education granted status similar to that of intellectual and moral development. Physical education was not only as an important component of military preparedness but also as a means of establishing virtue and perpetuating the rituals of tradition. In activity such as archery was combined with many forms of dance and music to provide a total education.[9] Chinese education embraced physical training as well as the intellectual, moral and aesthetic training. From the ranks of the scholars, the most able and virtuous men were selected for national leadership. Even the fitness of an official consisted in his ability to excel in playing a musical instrument, shooting with bow, riding horseback, writing, and arithmetic, while at the same time he was expected to understand the rites and ceremonies of public and private life. In later days, when special examinations were instituted by the government for military man, these candidates were not required to pursue an exhaustive literary training. Laurie states[10], "for the military service a very small knowledge of literature is needed. The special examination consists of physical exercises, the lifting of heavy weights, drawing the long bow, and the drill with the sword".

Many of the games and sports that developed in China were devised for their military usefulness or as a means of diverting the attention of troops from hardship or the boredom of idleness. A primitive type of football, boxing, jiu-jitsu, and "butting", were popular[11]. The Chinese sought to maintain the stability of the state by training each individual to perform his prescribed duties according to the pattern established by tradition. However, the influence of Confucianism Buddhism, beginning about 500 B.C. led to a gradual decline in the importance attributed to physical activity.

Like the Chinese, the Egyptians were one of the first truly civilized societies. Egyptian culture peaked somewhere between 1000 and 1400 B.C., and it was characterized by religious fanaticism and the absolute rule of the Pharaoh. Ancient Egypt was not a particularly militaristic society, and it apparently saw little relationship between physical activity and physical well being. For these reasons, there was relatively little emphasis, placed on physical training or physical education. There was however, involvement in physical activity for the purpose of recreation. The soldier, dancer, wrestler, and acrobat needed to acquire the skills of their professions. The soldiers received instruction and drill in the martial arts from older professional warriors. The warrior class supplemented military exercises with games and sports. The young sons were sent to barrack schools where they underwent rigorous training in handling weapons and exercised to develop speed, strength, and agility. They also practiced wrestling and war dances. Wrestling was a well-developed art; it was utilized by the warriors for conditioning, but also by professionals for entertainment. Children were taught a variety of stunts and games, and activities such as wrestling and swimming were quite popular. Gymnastic games were held to honour one particular God, and through this relationship was established between physical activity and Egyptian religious beliefs.[12]

So far as Eastern world is concerned India happens to be a large region where physical training was given enough importance. The Hindu educational system was based upon the mental, physical, social, spiritual and moral aspects.Ancient Gurukula system was the burning examples to this. In Vedic and Epic periods, the students were learning many types of physical activities like sword fighting, archery, lathi fighting, yoga, Suryanamaskar etc. These types of physical activities were part and parcel in the curriculam of ancient Gurukula system of education.[13] The Kshetrias (Military caste who were mint to protect the territory of the state) were involving themselves in different physical activities to develop physical fitness and motor skills according to their vocational need. Wrestling played an important role in the sports world of Indians. The Indian club, Danda, Baithaks exercises, and the Indian massage system have been credited with contributing to the development of outstanding wrestlers.

The military nobility exercised greater influence in early days than in later times when the Brahmans were firmly entrenched in power. Before 1000 B.C., Brahmans even trained princes in some of the arts of war, especially archery, fencing, and lassoing animals. The men of the military caste were trained for the infantry, cavalry, chariot, and elephant divisions. They learned to use such weapons as spears, battle-axes, and slings. During peacetime, there was a tendency for the army to live in idleness, and to persue sports as a pastime. It was among the military nobility in later centuries that the game of pole originated.

To the Indians, religious exercises such as the *pranayam* and *Suryanamaskar* were part of the daily worship. Yoga a system of religious meditation, incorporated some physical movement. However, the Rajputs (belongs to Kshatrias caste) were devoted to physical training and military arts. Each prince or chief had his own armoury, known as the "Sileh- Khana", which was a proud possession. Their outdoor recreations were meant for hardening the body, improving the mind, moulding the character and developing warlike skills and the spirit of chivalry. A young boy at an early age was made familiar with the sight of blood. He was given a scimitar (a short curved sword) and trained to use it effectively on the heads of small lambs. If he succeeded at his first attempt the occasion served as a matter of great pride to the whole family. The next step in his training was dancing and singing; the former was based on the movements of attack and defence and latter consisted of war songs based on heroic ancestral deeds[14]

So far as the present state of Orissa is concerned which was known as Kalinga, Utkal or Oddradesa in ancient and medieval times, it had a glorious traditions in martial arts and physical education. By the time of Mahabharata, Kalinga, Utkal Odra had entered into Aryan policy as powerful kingdoms. The Mahabharata in Vana parva[15] clearly indicates that the Ganges mouth marked the northern extent of the land of the Kalinga people. By the time of Mahavira and Buddha, the Kalinga-Utkal region on the entire east of India had acquired recognition and fame. The power and greatness of ancient Kalinga is evident from the political relation between Kalinga and Magadha during the Maurya era. When Chandragupta Maurya had almost completed the making of his great empire, the Greek ambassador at his court, Megasthenes,[16] observed in curiosity the existence of an independent territory on the border of the Maurya Empire which he described as the Gangaridum Calingarum Regia and marked its eastern limit on the bank of the Ganges. It was Kalinga the Greek sources contained references to the powerful army of Kalinga because of which "that country has never been conquered by any foreign king" and further that the Kalinga land possessed an elephant force which caused fear in the mind of the nation. The famous Kalinga war between Ashok and the people of Kalinga, the war of Kharavela with Satavahan and Magadhan rulers, the historical expeditions of Narasimhadeva - 1 against the Muslims of Bengal and the far flung conquest of Kapilendradeva etc.; are some of the glaring instances of her great martial achievements.

The Orissa is a modern nomenclature believed to have been vogue from the time of Muslim Suzerainty in this land. This name seems to have been derived from the word "Udra", the name of one class of people living under the permanent identification of militia class in the ancient land from time immemorial.[17] At that time, Orissa was very prosperous and powerful state. Its military power was so great that it retained its sovereignty for a long period from both

Muslims and the British. The glory of the past, though diminished still survives today like the fire in a flint in the martial races of the land. Full of courage and power strength, determination and mental agility they stand even today unrivalled champions of military virtues.

The Mahabharat describes 'Kalingaah Sahasikah', 'Kalingaah Maharathaah', 'Kalingaah Mahachumum'[18]. This identifies that the people of Kalinga were a valorous race, full of vitality, chivalry and the spirit of adventure. The art, architecture, cultural heritage and military systems of Orissa were unique and distinct in nature. The physical training of the foot soldiers was vigorous and systematic in nature." It is quite important to note that in the context of the physical education, the role of "*Paika Akhedas*" of Orissa very much significant. Precisely, *Paika Akhedas* are the typical ancient physical education institutions of Orissa. Physical education was not included in the curriculum of the school or college in early medieval period. There were some private institutions named as "*Paika Akheda*" significantly meant for imparting military training in the semi-urban and rural areas and in some urban areas (specially found in Puri town) called as "*Jagagharas*". These were serving the purpose of health clubs for the development of a good physique. The details discussion about the institution can depict the rich heritage of martial arts that was there in this State, which is one of the important objectives of the work. First of all, it is very much important to see the inseparable interlink between the contribution of *Paika Akheda* and *Jagagharas* for the defence mechanism of the king, the then ruler of the State.

[19]In Puri town, there are a number of such places termed as 'Jagagharas'. They were probably strengthened in late medieval period for protection of Jagannatha temple and its rich treasures from the hands of Muslim Subahdars and other alien attackers. In each Jagaghara, there is a statue of Hanuman (premier disciple of Lord Rama) is installed. The trainees usually commence their course after touching the feet of this God. They then start *danda*, *vaithakas*, wrestling, boxing, bodybuilding, *asanas* etc. *Every jaga* ghara has a main *guru* and a few as his associates who impart training on various traditional physical education to the young entrants. By repeated practice of such exercises the young men build themselves physically stronger to participate in outside competition. The trainees display very high degree of cordiality and companionship among themselves. In course

of their training these boys also learn various techniques of wielding lethal weapons. They were always in readiness to the call of the Gajapati Maharaja for protection of the Jagannatha temple, its deities and the property.

During the later part of ancient and early medieval period, for training of people, to serve under military regiments of Orissan kings, a number of *akhadas* were established in various parts of the kingdom. We have many reference to them in the Mahabharata of Sarala Dasa. Besides, there is reference to the gymnastic performances of the Oriya soldiers in a centre at Barabati fort even in the time of Suryavansi Gajapatis. Almost in all Paika villages in Orissa, we notice such centres even today, where they assemble every day for practice of numerous military exercises. They preserve their vital military weapons at these places and hold annual competitions during the Durga Puja or Dasahara each year.[20]

The "*Paika Akheda*" literally means that the closed place or the clubhouse that transforms a person to a *paika*. It is the institution that creates *paikas* (popularly known as soldiers) for extending their services for the smooth administration of the state by the king and also to fight against the enemies obeying the order of the king. The *paika* learnt all shorts of physical activities and techniques of war from his guru.

Prof Jagannath Pattanaik[21] quoted that, it is very difficulty to say when exactly the *paika* class of Orissa were originated. But it is presumed that it could be established during the period of Ganga dynasty (11th century A.D). It does not mean prior to that no war was held and no military regements were framed by other dynasty. Since the Ganga Monarch were determined to established a great Empire and keeping to this in their mind they thought about to establish a great infantry force and named them as *'Paika'*. In this matter we got evidence from the *'Paika Kheda'* written by Kanhai Champatiray in 1624 A.D. in which he mentioned the velorous war activities of Ganga King Narasingha Deva. So the term *paika* was originated during Ganga period.

The word, Paika seems to have been derived from the Sanskrit word, *padatika* or foot soldier. They were recruited from all classes and castes; but mostly they were belonging to *chasa* or the cultivating caste.[22] Occasionally individuals of the reserved castes such as *Panas, Bauris* and *Kandaras* were also recruited. Even more savage inhabitants of the remote hills, called *Kandhas*, were enrolled.[23] Among them, the record says that many Telugu and Muslim officials were also found. There were also many Muslims among those who took part in the rebellion of 1817 and were sentenced to transportation for life.[24] All these evidences prove that the recruitment into the army was not restricted to any particular caste or class during those days. Physical education, especially military training was open to any communal restriction and though it was possible for anyone who wished to adopt this profession, yet there were few deviations. The Brahmins were not encouraged to enlist themselves as foot soldiers. Besides, the thieves, robbers, cheaters and such other category of persons were debarred from enlisting themselves in the army. Social status and conditions of the family were taken carefully into account in the enrolment of the soldiers. The permission of the head of the family was generally obtained for recruitment into the army. In case there was only one son in the family and in cases of recent marriages, enrollment was not permitted. The elder son of the family was bound to join the military duties of the king and the younger son was supposed to look after the cultivation and family of his house.[25]

For their military services, the paikas were not paid in cash. They were given rent free service lands which they cultivated with there own hands in times of peace and subject to the military and police duties whenever called upon by their chiefs. The Paikas enjoying the lands on hereditary basis.[26] Those non- serving Paikas constituted more or less the standing militia which could be mobilised at a short notice by the chiefs. Only a message was required to be passed on to them and the machinery of mobilisation moved a pace placing at the disposal of the king, the requisite number of man as the occasion demanded.

The various types of physical training that were undertaken during those days, can be well imagined from the process of conducting the war. In a war, a number of types of soldiers and officials of higher ranks were found. This shows that the efficiency of a soldier was taken into account to place him in the rank, suitable for his physical strength and ability.[27] The Paikas were divided into three ranks and were distinguished by the names taken from their occupation or the weapons, which they used. They were called *Paharis, Banuas* and *Dhenkiyas*. The *Paharis* carry a large shield made of woods covered with hides and strengthened with knobs and circles of iron, and the long straight national sword of Orissa, called the Khanda. They are stationed chiefly as guards. The *Banuas*, use the Matchlock principally and have besides a small shield and sword. It was their duty to take the field principally and so on distant expeditions. The *Dhenkiyas* were armed with bows and arrows, and a sword. They were supposed to perform all sorts of duties.

Madalapanji,[28] the temple chronicle of Orissa, mentions three types of infantry soldiers. They were namely, Itikary (lance bearer), Dhanuki (archer) and Phadikares (swordman). The Itikars and Dhanukis were able to fight successfully in the hilly areas and from a distant place, they could repulse enemy attack. The infantry soldiers in Orissa were generally classified into four major divisions under different commanders like Bahinipati, Paikaray (commanders of infantry divisions), Dalabehera (officer commanding detachments) Nayaks, Gadanayaks (garrison commandants) and Bahubalendra (officer-in-charge of non-combatants). There were further sub-divisions of Paika soldiers of Orissa mainly forced the infantry regiments of the latter rulers.

Information is also available regarding the number forming an infantry corps. Twenty-seven Paikas were to form a *'Dala'* or detachment. Seventy Dalas constituted a *Bhiana* compromised of (70 × 27) one thousand eight hundred and ninety Paikas. All these Paikas were placed under one Dalabehera who acted as the commander of the Division. It was followed by one Vaidya or a doctor for five *Bhianas* or one hundred and twentyfive Paikas and on bullock-cart for seven *Bhianas* or one hundred and seventy-five paikas. In each Bhiana, again, there were six cooks and twelve servants in addition to Dagaras (messengers) and Badyakaras or the Musicians. The king issues order to when the battle would be fought. News spread throughout the whole kingdom very quickly. The very fact that an auspicious day has to be found out to take a start was vary much important. The right time was chosen for this purpose, suggests that considerable importance was attached to the military Maneuvers. In the method they adopted for the summoning the army, we have a further proof of the same sentiment.[29]

The Paikas marched to the battle field to the beat of the drum and other Musical instruments like *Bheri, Singha, Turi, Dholki, Changu, Dhipa, Khudua, Jhanja* etc. and the practice of singing songs during the marching of the soldiers was very popular. It not only heightened the importance and grandeur by provided immense inspiration to the pains. Efforts were also made to keep up there spirits. The performance of *Bhopas, Gayas, Bahalias, Kimbirias*, and *Kimbirias* and *Kathias* was a part and parcel of the battle procession.[30] To provide entertainment for the Paikas, dance and feats were performed. Speeches were also delivered with a view to infuse patriotic feelings into their heart and enthusing them to fight against the enemy with courage, vigour and zeal. The king also encouraged his troops with heroic addresses and exhortations. The mainly stirring address of one subordinate Raja during this period to his courtiers, who advised him to make a retreat, is really superb and is worthy of mention in any literature.

The rule, generally observed in this regard, was as follows— "As to open fight, a virtuous king should call his army together and specifying the place and the time of the battle addresses thus:" I am a paid servant like yourself; the country is to be enjoyed together with you", you have to strike the enemy specified by me". His ministry and priests should encourage the army by saying thus: It is declared in the Vedas that the goal which is reached by sacrifice in which the priests have been duly paid for, is the very goal which brave men are destined to attain".[31]

The ideal of courting death in the open field was set before the soldiers. The Paikas regard death in the battlefield to be honour to themselves as they were recruited for the service of the nation.

At this stage the motto of every Paika is found as.

"We do not mind for death; there are many others, it is better to die on the battlefield rather than to accept defeat and be cursed for ever.[32]

The weapons used by the Paikas were numerous. Bows and arrows were frequently used. Other weapons like *khadga, braja, barchha* which were used during the puranic days were in vogue. Besides, various other types of weapons were used by the Paikas in the battlefield. The deadly weapons like Havelivana, the reference to which is found in Sanskrit works were used by them, the paikas were known the use of guns and muskets.[33]

The kings were not dependants on the outsiders so far the supply of arms and ammunitions were concerned. These were manufactured in large scale in the kingdom. Paunsiapatna of Kendrapara, Payak Barabati of Narasinghapur, Kamarpati of Nayagarh, Kalei of Dhenkanal and Marda of Boud were the main centres of manufacturers.[34] The Paika also knew the art of making weapons more deadly and poisonous. The juice of a plant known as *Khadisiju* was mixed with the urine of the horse in order to produce poison. They also could produce cartridges out of the ingredients locally available.

The Paikas were equipped with the weapons like *nail, thunka,* barudakumpa, *jhulikata, sagadinali, olatadhara khanda, khapur, dhal, kanda, katari, bankachuri, katidhal, katimala, rudhi* and *dhanu.*[35]

Position occupied by the armed forces, contingent of horses, elephants etc. in the battle is important inasmuch as upon it depended on the success of war. During the campaigns of this period, elephants usually occupied the front, these were followed by the horses. Last came the foot soldiers. As regards the order in which the troops marched to the field, the Naik or the commander always took the lead. He was followed by the archers, men with shields, swords, muskets, spears and arrows. Behind them there was an officer called Pattanaik. He was in charge of the whole management. In the rear, he was the king in full dress, he was closely followed by men with shields and spears A well decorated cart with vermilion of goddess and the flower offerings invariably followed them to field. Vermillion marks were made on the forehead of the Paikas, then flags were unfurled announcing the commencement of the battle.[36]

Detailed information regarding treatment of the wounded and the sick soldiers were available. If any soldiers received a wound or injury while fighting on the field or fell sick, then he was a regular establishment of physicians. They immediately addressed themselves to the task of healing the wound curing them of the disease. Medicines and medical herbs were instantaneously administered. Those who were in charge of collecting herbs were given the title of *Ugalsingh.*

In case of unconsciousness, the patient was immediately removed from the field. Honey mixed with common salt was administered to him to revive his senses and restore him to health. Vigorous efforts were being made to make him fit enough to get to the battlefield again. In case of bleeding, efforts were being made to check the flow of blood. Sometimes battles were fought at night; so precaution was being taken against drowsiness, methods were devised to ward off thirst and hanger. *Pandurayas* or Physicians were always kept in readiness to deal with matters of health of the soldiers. Thus, was done with a view to keeping them in a state of physical fitness and mental alertness.[37]

Discipline was regarding as an imperative necessary for any success in war and, hence, the Bhoi kings laid great stress on it. There were periodic military exercises for training the soldiers for warfare. The march of the soldiers in attendance upon the king or the Dalbehra served to keep them alert. The appointment of the Paikas was made by the Bhoeemul. After their appointment, they were given badges. They were then placed under the command of discipline in the army. There were also other categories of official for this purpose. The Pattanaik, for example, was employed to enforce discipline in this vital sector of the country's defence. They were engaged to look into all cases of indiscipline and take all possible steps nip it in the bud. Punishment was inflicted in case of a branch of discipline. Those who neglected their duties or violated any order to the higher officials were driven out. Sometimes very severe punishment was inflicted. Branding the permanent pointing of the body or the face in order to mark the culprit out was resorted to punishment, especially when directed against the Paika who had committed treason, assumed more serious and grace character. It ranged from confiscation of property to imprisonment (Harikatha) and even death. The Paikas who turned traitors were even put on gallows (Suli). They were also sent to be impaled alive on a wooden stake thrust upon the belly.[38]

Paikas who were the great warriors used a special kind of dress in the battlefield. This was mainly designed to ensure their safety and security. Uniform wardress was insisted upon. It consisted of a cap and vest made of the skin of tiger or leopard, a sort of chain armour for the body and the thigh and a girdle formed by the tail of some wild animal. Besides by the terror inspired by this unusual habitments, they further brightened the ferocity of their countenances with vermillion, thus exhibiting altogether as savage and fantastic an air as one could well conceive.[39]

Paika Kheda, on the other hand, furnishes us with a list of sixteen military costumes of infantry soldier of the Medieval Orissa. They are *ghantimala, ghagudi, olamala, ganthia, kavacha, kaling, bahuti, hoda, baghapati, vala, rupachandra, katha, rudhimala, chakra, handiapati and jhoba.*[40]

Wars are no longer fought at an individual level; more often than not the enemy dies without ever seeing the man who killed him. Gone are the days when two Paika met face to face upon the battlefield to fight for honour and justice, or warriors armed with spear and sword battled it out steel against steel, when the victor was the man with the highest amount of skill and courage, modern warfare does not allow sports man like conduct or individualism on the battlefield. The glory of death means very little to the modern soldiers.

Nowadays the Orissan martial arts is seen in various parts of Orissa. The physical and martial activities like *Dhal Tarabari, Patta, Banati, Bankachura, Badikhela, Naga phasha, Bhuin ghar bidya* (floor exercises) etc., are demonstrated by the Paika Guru and their disciples in the Bijaya Dasami (Dashara festival). The other festivals like Dolo jatra, Raja Sankaranti, Makarsankaranti, Gamha Purnima etc, are quite important for them. In ancient Orissa the paika Guru could easily beat multiple armed assailants, by using his skill with sword or sphere etc. two thousand years on the modern martial arts master, faced with a similar situation, would come up against modern technology– the firearm. No martial arts system exists that can successfully stop or block a bullet. So then, bearing all this in mind, why does anyone actually learn a martial art? Peter Lewis[41] writely answered it that the same as it was 2000 years ago: to breed a better person, a person who can develop a deeper understanding of the self and of his or her environment, and who can seek what is good in others rather than be perpetually in direct connection. Through the training and philosophies offered by the martial arts that person can build up a greater confidence. This confidence spills over into daily life and he or she is more able to cope with life's day-to-day problems. The trained, physically fit martial artist reacts to adverse situations in a different manner from the average person in the street. The training prepares all students spiritually, emotionally, mentally and psychologically for life's little pitfalls and how best to overcome them.The martial arts are not just composed of fighting techniques; they represent an integrated way of life, an on-going process of individual development, which has not been changed in over 2000 years.

Statement of the problem—The purpose of the study is to critically analise the Orissan martial arts and to evaluate the place of the Orissan martial arts in the ancient Orissan culture. The purpose is also to survey the present statues of the martial arts in different districts of Orissa.

Delimitation—The study is delimited only to the traditional martial arts of Orissa.

The study is confined to the paika, paika guru and akheda of Orissa.

Definition and Explanation of the Term

Art—Perfection of workmanship or execution as an object in itself.

The application of skill is to the subject of taste.

Martial Arts—A martial art is a classical fighting system in which the emphasis is on victory in combat, but which has the secondary motivation of self perfection through training and includes a moral duty to society.

Martial Sports—The martial activity in which exponents compete within a set of rules and in so doing develop a healthy mind, body and spirit.

Critical—Involving or exercising careful judgement or observation.

Fault finding.

Analysis—The resolution of anything complex into its simple elements, the exact determination of its components.

The critical examination of any production, so as to exhibit its elements in simple form.

Paika—The term paika is derived from the Sanskrit word *padatika*, which means foot soldier.

Akheda—A clubhouse or physical training centre where the paikas of Orissa practice all sorts of physical activities and learn the techniques, tactics of martial arts from their paika guru.

The Akheda is the place where a guru imparted training to his disciples in the art of wrestling, swordmanship, archery and horse riding.

Martial way—A Martial way describes a martial skill that has the main motivation of self-developing through training, with a possible secondary consideration of practical use.

Significance of the Study

1. This investigation may help to the physical education teachers and coaches for development of fitness programmed for sports persons. The result of the present research and resultant suggestion and recommendations of the researcher may help to lay the foundation for the formulation of better design and comprehensive programme of physical education.
2. It may also help to conduct state level martial arts competition in planned manner with proper rules and regulations.
3. It will also help to the organic growth and development of the students. It provides fun, joy, and resources for entertainment with means of leisure time recreation.
4. Its usefulness as a defensive skill for the police personnel and as a conditioning activity arousing martial spirit for the defense personnel is also highly commended.
5. The techniques and tactics and the conditioning programme of the floor exercises of the Orissan martial arts are highly commended as it develops the arm eye co-ordination, muscular strength, factors of general motor ability and it contributes to the objectives of physical education on the whole. It has more values of interest for high school boys, youth and the rural population.

References

1. Sports Authority of India, *Indian traditional folk culture and martial arts,* (Cosmo Publication, Delhi, 1988): p. 26.
2. Natalire Marie: *Foundations and Principles of Physical Education* (Ronald Press Company, New York, 1960): p. 15.
3. Michael Finn: *Martial Arts A Complete Illustrated History* (Mackenzie Publishing Ltd, London, 1988): p. 23.
4. Natalare Marie Shepard, *Principles of Physical Education* (Ronald Press Company, New York, 1960): p. 152.
5. Gaston Vuillier, *A History of Dancing From the Earliest Ages to our own Times* (D. Appleton and Co., New York, 1898): p. 17.
6. Deobold B. Van Dalen, and Bruce L. Bennett, *A World History of Physical Education, Second Edition* (Prentice Hall, Inc; New Jersey, 1971): p. 48.
7. A.S. Wilkins, *Roman Antiquities* (D Appleton and Co., New York 1878): p. 58.
8. Deobold B. Van Dalen, and Bruce L. Bennett, *A World History of Physical Education, Second Edition* pp. 70-71.
9. Paul Monroe, *Cyclopedia of Education* (The Macmillan Co., New York, 1919): p. 635.
10. S.S. Laurie, *Historical Survey of Pre-Christian Education* (Longmans, Green and Co. New York, 1900): pp. 130-131.
11. E.N. Gardiner, *Athletics of the Ancient World* (Oxford Clarendon Press, London,1930): p. 15.
12. Deobold B. Van Dalen, and Bruce L. Bennett, *A World History of Physical Education, Second Edition*, p. 11.
13. K. Rajagopalan, *A brief History of Physical Education in India* (Army Publishers, Delhi, 1962): p. 46.
14. Eraj Ahmed Khan *History of Physical Education* (Narendra Bhargavi, Varanasi, 1964): p. 322.
15. N. K. Sahu *Historical Geography* Ed by M.N.Das, *History and Culture of Orissa*, (Vidyapuri,Cuttack,1977): p. 32.
16. M.N.Das *Ancient and Medieval Empires and Kingdoms* p. 87.
17. Sudhansu Mohan Mohapatra, *The Princely States of Orissa in Retrospect*, Edited by M.N. Das, *History and Culture of Orissa*, p. 219.
18. D. J. Paikray, *Oriya Samar Bigyan Kabya "Paika Kheda" Re Ayitihashika Bibarani*, (Oriya) Souvenier, 1993, p. 19.

19. R.P. Mohapatra, *Military History of Orissa*, (Cosmo Publication, New Delhi, 1986): p. 187.
20. *Ibid.*, p. 186.
21. Jagannath Pattanaik, *Odissara Paika Sampradaya Aka Ayitihasika Anusilana*, Oriya, (Prajatantra, Saptahik, July, 19-25, 1992): p. 8.
22. G. Toynbee, A Sketch of the History of Orissa, (*Orissa History Research Journal*, ix. 1992): p.12.
23. S.Rathsarma, *Paika Kheda* (Ed) Bharati Press, puri, *Introduction*, p. viii.
24. S.C. De, *Guide to Orissa Records*, III, p. 35.
25. S.Rathsarma: *Paika kheda* (Ed), *Introduction*, ix.
26. Toynbee: A sketch of the History of Orissa, *Orissa History Research Journal, ix* (1960): p.12.
27. R.D. Banarjee, *History of Orissa* II, Pravati Press, Calcutta, 1931, p. 283
28. R.P. Mohapatra, *Military History of Orissa*, p. 206.
29. P.K.Pattanaik, *A Forgotten Chapter of Orissan History*, (Punthi Pustak, Calcatta, 1979): p. 118.
30. S.Rathsarma: *Paika Kheda* (Ed), p. xiii.
31. Arthasastra, B.R., Y CH iii 367, pp. 425-426, Quoted by S.K. Ayangar, *Social and Political life in Vijayanagar Empire*, (Manisha Publications, Nellor,1972): p. 446.
32. S. Rathsarma, *Paika Kheda* (Ed), p. 14.
33. *Ibid*, p. 13.
34. C.D. Mahapatra, *Utkal Itihasara Eka Agyanta Adhyaya*, Oriya, (Kitab Mahal, Cuttack, 1970): p. 187.
35. S.Rathsarma, *Paika Kheda* (Ed), p. 14.
36. P.K. Pattanaik, *A forgotten Chapter of Orissan History*, p. 119.
37. *Ibid*, p.120.
38. S.Rathasarma, *Paika Kheda*, quoted by P.K. Pattanaik, *A Forgotten Chapter of Orissan History* p. 121.
39. G. Toynbee, "A Sketch of the History Of Orissa", *Orissa History Research Journal*, ix(1960): pp. 12-13.
40. S. Rathsarma, *Paika Kheda* (Ed) p. 14.
41. Peter Lewis, *The Way of Martial Arts*, (Marshall Cavendish Books Ltd, London,1990): p. 12.

2
Review of Related Literature

Das-Gupta[1] rightly mentioned in his studies that the physical education was preparatory to military training and it had common elements in the initial stage of training. Consequently physical and military courses were identical in the beginning but differed in the advances stages of training.

In the study of the martial arts of a region of a country, due emphasis is generally given to its political, cultural military history. It has evidently the relationship with the rise and fall of the royal dynasties, the military glories, literature, art and architecture in a chronological sequence. The modern state Orissa passed under the names of Kalinga, Utkal and Odra Desa, has a glorious history of its own since prehistoric time. In this chapter the military tradition of Orissa from the period of Asoka to British period elaborated. The Martial tradition of Vedic, Epic period and Buddist and Jain literature are also not negelated to depict for the studies the Orissan Martial arts. The history of martial arts of the different countries of the world are explained. The use of arms, martial skills, fort and strongholds and martial arts competitions of Orissa are also elaborated in this chapter.

Physical Training in early India was very much concerned with the development of physique, various sports and athletic exercises, the art of offense and defense; training in military art; games; yogis exercises and physical contests. The military organisation and physical training were of high order.

Vedic Period

From very ancient times the Indian system of Physical Education had a high place in military science. It is not a matter of great surprise for us that the deities in Hindu mythology are all armed. We also find references about fist fighting in Rig Veda. In the Yajur Veda

"Yadhaasidhaaram Karte Avahitaam Apakramet

Evam anrutaat Aatmaanaam Jugpset" i.e.,

A wise man will always guard himself from the dangers of uttering falsehood which will lead him to death, just like the highly skilled swordsman handles the sword in order to save his life. From this we understand that the Aryans were highly skilled in fencing.[2]

The Aryans possessed fine physique and intellect and special prayer to the sun with prostrate bowing (Suryanamskars) was performed more as a religious duty which the individual owed to himself and to society as a more physical exercise or training. It was believed that all energy on this earth, organic or inorganic, is directly or indirectly derived from the sun[3]. It appears that during Vedic period, the military profession was very popular, because the Aryans were engaged in subjugating the non-Aryans and establishing their supremacy in this country. A citizen was expected to defense himself and take part in battles. Military science in fact demanded physical strength, vigour and manual skill. It consisted of hand wrestling, use of bow and arrow, dagger fight, sword fight, hurling the discus and spear or lance, horse riding, chariot driving, hunting, elephant riding and boxing etc., were also needed in battles[4]

During the Vedic period, an important development took place, which has affected the course of physical education in India right down to the present day. This was practice of pranayama, or the holding of breath before each prayer, this was considered beneficial for the lungs and a means of prolonging life, and was develop in to the yoga Asana[5]

Great emphasis was laid in the culture of physique and strength during the Vedic period. In Upanishads[6], physical strength has been said to be greater than academic learning. It is said that a single man with strength shakes hundred men with learning; it is by strength that the earth stands; by strength, the sky; by strength, the heaven; by strength, the mountains; by strength, Deities and men; by strength, the cattle, birds, grasses and trees, beasts down to ants and worms; and by strength does the world stand. Again Upanishads[7] say, "Nor is that self to be gained by one who is destitute of strength or without earnestness or without right meditation".[8] Strength is derived from spirit. Therefore practice of 'Yoga Vyayam' was recommended for the development of spiritual strength, as spirit is the centre of strength in the body. Without physical strength, a youth cannot go into war and pull the string on the bow.

Another feature of Vedic civilisation was training in the use of the lathi, with which a young man expected to defend himself in case of emergency. At a special ceremony, known as 'danda-pradana', the make a youths coming of age he was presented with a lathi, which then accompanied him wherever he went[9].

The Epic Age (C. 1000 - B.C.)

The Epic age is covered the age of Mahabharat and Ramayan: the former deals with the Great War between Kauravas and the Pandavas, the latter with the exploits of the hero, 'Rama'. From these we gather that the period was one of the great conflicts and blood shed, and can deduce that physical training was directed mainly towards military training—archery, Javelin and spear-throwing, fighting with the sword and battle axe.

Ramayan—In this book, a great deal of reference has been made to physical education and recreation. Ram-Ravana battle, hunting, or hiking at the time of Vanavasa, Camping, observance of rules of scouting, love for creatures etc. have been described in great detail. Competitions of physical culture were held in swayamvaras. People used to make through preparations in these contests in which great emphasis was laid on the culture of physique and strength. Viswamitra was a very great teacher who trained Rama and Lakshaman in archery. Parasurama was another teacher of repute.

Rama and his brothers were well versed in the Vedas and physical culture[10]. Rama could ride on elephants and horses and was expert in managing chariots and was ever engaged in the study of archery. The best men engaged in the study of Vedas were also accomplished in the art of physical culture any archery[11].

Ravana's son Indrajit was also skilled in the art of warfare and well versed in the use of all heavenly weapons. There is no one in the three worlds is not aware of his physical and military prowess and skill in arms. Prince Akshaya, another son of Ravana, was also skilled in the art of physical culture and warfare and was highly proficient in aiming and throwing arrows and in hitting the Mark.

Prince Atikaya, another son of Ravana, was also well versed in the use of arms. He was expert in riding on horses and elephants, in use of swords, bows and arrows and in the art of physical culture.[12]

Hanumana, the minister of Sugriva, was well versed in Sama, Dana, Danda, Bheda and physical cultural. He was accomplished in the art warfare, wrestling, boxing and club. In this earth nobody could surpass Hanumana who enlarged his body, expanded his chest and contracted his strength and vigour then fixing his strong arms and feet at the edge of the mountain, he took a long flight (modern long Jump) with a powerful spring of the knees (Modern take off) leading softly in Sundaravana in Lanka[13].

Music played an important part in the warfare of Ramayan. War music was called “Yudha - Gandharva”. Armies used to march to the accompaniment of music both in war and peace. Prof. Dikshitar[14] mentioned that every warrior was distinguished by his own respective conch. When Rama and Lakshman were freed from the grip of Nagaphasa, their soldiers rejoiced by blowing Sankhas and betting Mridanga and Bheri.

Mahabharata—[15]The Mahabharata refers to Kalinga, Odra and Utkala with Rajapuri as its capital. In the *Santi Parva* we come across the description of the *Swayamvara* ceremony at Rajapuri for the daughter of king Kalinga, Chitrangada. Karna, Duryodhan, Sisupal, Jarasandha and others participated in the *Swayamvara* ceremony but Duryodhana forcibly took away the princess from the *swayamvara sabha*. According to another reference in the Mahavarata the king of Kalinga was present in the *swayamvara* ceremony of Draupadi. In the Kurukshetra war Srutayuh, the king of Kalinga fought as the allay of Duryodhana against Bhima with three sons, six-thousand chariots and four thousand elephants. The Kalingans faught in the side of Kauravas and ultimately fell in the hands of the Pandavas. There is another reference that Sahadeva in course of his *digvijaya* confronted the king of Kalinga and defeated him. The king finally accepted the suzerainty of the Pandavas. The *Bana Parva* further elucidates that Judhisthira came to Kalinga and met the sage Lomasa who narrated him the significance of the country and its sacred river Vaitarani. Judhisthira took recourse to perform his *Yajna* in the bank of Vaitarani. According to another reference Sahadeva defeated the

Kalingans at Dantapura which in historic rose to eminence as the seat of administration and religion. The Kalingan army was posted in the neck of *Garuda Vyuha* formed by Drona. "It is also revealed in the Mahabharata that the king of Udra or Odradesa sided with Pandavas in the battle of Kurukshetra even though the king of Kalinga was an active supporter of the Kauravas. Sahadeva defeated Udras alongwith the Kearalas and the Udras came alongwith the Paundras to prosperity in a vast empire and proved beyond doubt its military capability and prowess.

Krishna[16] was a great promoter of physical culture. He advised Arjun on the battle field of Kuruksetra. "He whose food and activity or exercise are properly regulated, whose toil and rest are properly adjusted in all works, and whose sleeping and waking hours are properly determined, to such a one, does the highest benefit come". Krishna also told Arjuna: "Treating alike pleasures and distress, gain and loss, victory and defeat get ready for the fight, then fighting thus, you will not incur sin. This very much resembles with the Modern Olympic Motto. The philosophy of life is expressed in these lines would indicate that in the ancient period physical activity or exercise was highly valued."

The physical and military training of Kaurava and Pandava princes was unique and distinct in nature. Bhisma, the eighth son of Santanu, was an expert in all weapons. He was skilled in all the branches of physical culture and weapons and a mighty bow-man. Drona of mighty arms, endured with high ascetic virtues took all the weapons from Parasuram, the son of the Jamadagni of Bhrugu family. Parasurama, the illustrious grinder of Kshatriya race, communicated to Drona the mysteries of hurling and recalling his weapons. In fact Drona learnt the whole science of arms with its rules and regulations from Parasurama.[17]

Drona taught the Kauravas and the Pandavas, the science of various kinds of military skill which included fighting on horseback and on elephants, in chariots and on the ground. The weapons used were the club, the sword, the lance, the spear, the dart and above all the bow.[18] Two of Drona's pupils become very much accomplished in the use of Mace, namely Duryodhan and Bhima who were jealous of each other. Aswasthama excelled all in the mystery of the science of arms. The two twins, Nakula and Sahadeva excelled everybody in handling sword. Yudhisthir surpassed everybody as a car-warrior and his fame spread all over the earth. But, Arjuna, however, out-classed everyone in every respect of intelligence, resourcefulness and strength. Karna also had this training prom Parsurama and was equal to Arjuna in archery.[19]

In Mahabharata[20], Yudhisthir said to Krishna; When the army is well trained, it does fighting well; untrained soldiers are worthless. Therefore, wise people devote proper attention to their training. Narada asked Yudhisthir among others "Are you giving military training to the princes with the help of military experts? Has your army succeeded in defeating the enemy being trained by the commanders ?"

P.C. Chakravarti[21] significantly mentioned that the principle of bringing all the components of army under one central command was the unique feature in the Mahabharata war. The Udyogaparva of Mahabharata furnishes a graphic picture of Pandav army on the march. "Composed of the four traditional arms (limbs) it moves on as on irregular body amidst the blaze of conch-shells, the beating of drums and frequent war cries. In the army March Bhimasena and several other knights, all in suits of armor. In the second line are the Prabhadrakas and the pancalas. The king is the centre, surrounded by carts and wagons filled with stones and provisions, tents, treasure-chests, arms and Machines. Behind the king proceeds the main army, headed by the knights. The movements of the army causes such a tremendous din that it seemed like the road of the deep sea when the tide is highest on the day of the new Moon.

In regard to the importance of infantry the viewpoint of H.C.Kar[22] is attracted here. "The kings recognised the value of having a standing army where the infantry predominated in number. It was realised that the more numerically strong the army was, the greater was the chance of success. It was intended to frighten the enemy by its size very often they decided the fortunes of battles by sheer numbers. They were also employed in garrison duties like guarding the treasury, arsenal and other stores. They also set up camps and supervised the work of labour force employed in military service. When the enemy besieged the forts and strongholds and started hammering the gates, the chariots, horses and elephants were of no use at that time. It was the foot-men who standing on the walls towers and behind the parapet hurled stones and missiles at the enemy and beat off the besiegers".

Agni Purana[23] gives details about the mystery since under the following heads - the science of archery, the worship of arms, the use of arms on horseback and while ridding elephants and thirty-two kind of military art. The Dhaniveda or the science of archery described as divided into four chapter embodying the account of the training of the five classes of warriors, e.g., the chariot warriors, the elephant-man, cavalry, infantry and wrestlers. The weapons generally used in fighting are described as of five classes viz. weapons thrown or projected with a machine, those thrown with hands, those cast with hands and retained in them after use, those which are permanently retained in the hand, and the hands themselves such as wrestling. The weapons are again divided into two classes, those of straight shape and those of curved shape. Wrestling is the only sort of fight which is possible without any weapon. Instruction in the science of archery drilling and other tactics of warfare is to be imparted by a Brahmana or a Kshatriya instructor. Members of the Sudra caste and mixed Castes could join the army as soldiers. Fighting matches between men of equal strength, power and prowess are to be arranged. A battle fought with bows and arrows should be deemed as most honourable, the one fought with nooses as the second best, but one fought with sword as the worst.

Agni Purana[24], attaches more importance to the use of foot-soldiers in the uneven grounds particularly in forest and hilly regions. "In the defense of forts and strongholds too, foot-soldiers were specially relied upon. The reason is simple. Elephants, charic s and horses could not be used when the enemy was hammering at the gate of a fort.

[25]In the epic military system, music played a very conspicuous role in arousing the spirit of the senapati as well as his soldiers. A number of musical instruments were in use in Mahabharata war and they were collectively known as Viaditram. Bhagavat Gita refers to the following musical instruments used both by Pandavas and Kauravas. "Arousing in him the joy the Kuru elder, the grand size majestic blew his conch, ringing a high blast of lion-roar. There upon Madhu's lord and Pandavas son, standing in a great car yoked with white

spreads, blow each his glorious conch. The high-haired one blew Panchajanya, the wealth winner blew God's gift, the doer of grim deeds, wolf-bowel blew the great conch Pandava".

[26]The Mahabharata furnishes a graphic picture of encampment and the forts including their types. In the Santi Parva, we find six types of forts : (I) Dhana Durga, (ii) Mahi Durga, (iii) Giri Durga, (iv) Manusya Durga, (v) Jala Durga and (vi) Mana Durga. The Vana Prava describes the city of Dwarka, when it was attacked by Salva, the king of Martikavat, was well fortified according to war science with pennons and arches, combatants and carriages etc. "All the entrances and main streets of the city were barricaded with wood work. All troops of dancers and singers were driven out of the city. And all bridges over rivers were destroyed and boats forbidden to ply, and trenches (around the city) were spiked with poles at the bottom. And the land around city for two miles was rendered uneven, and holes and pits were dug thereon, combustibles were scattered below the surface".

B.K. Majumdar[27] quoted the defence of Magadhapur, the capital of Jarasandha, that "Behold, O Partha, the great capital of Magadha standing in all its beauty. Filled with flocks of birds and its stock of water never exhausted; and adorned with fine mansions standing in excellent array; it is free from every kind of calamity, the fire large hills of Vihara, Varaha, Vrisabha, Risigiri and the delightful caityaka, all of high peaks overgrow with tall trees of cool shade, connected with one another, seem to jointly protect the city of Girivraja".

At modern Rajgir there is a wrestling pit known as "Jarasandha ka Akhara" a survival from the ancient times. Bhima, Jarasandha, Krishna and Balaram were remembered as legendary heroes of the wrestling arena.[28]

While describing the Kuru camp Mahabharata writes : "Spreading over an area of five yojanas, it also contained, countless tents and pavilions stored with provisions and arms. As in the opposing camp, so also here, troops were relayed for outpost and patrol duty. But besides tightening men both camps (Kuru and Pandava) included a large and motley huts of non-combatants such as birds, pamegyrists, priests, vendors traders, prostitutes and women of rank"[29].

Buddhist and Jain Literatures

The senses of touch played an important role in physical education. Physical education was mainly concerned with the body-sense or sense of touch. This can be gathered from the physical activities and exercises performed by the king Andhaga-venhi of Dwaraka in his royal gymnasium. The exercises included leaping, limb twisting, wrestling and rubbing (message) of the body by experts. The king Andhaga-Vanhi at the break of the day used to go to his gymnasium where he tired and forespent himself with manyfold exercise of energy, looping, limb twisting stuff of a hundred and a thousand distillations, fragrant oils etc., comforting, gladdening, strengthening, rejoicing all the organs and limbs. On the oiled skin, he was further webbed down like men with tender and dedicate palms as perfect hands and feet, Men with skillful, dexterous, accomplished, clever, wise, possessed of cunning art, Master of modes of anointing, rubbing pleasant to the bones, to the flesh, to the skin and to the hair[30].

Physical training in ancient India reached a high degree of perfection, requiring specialisation in the field. It is mentioned in the Kalpa Sutra how men skilled in the art of Lepakarma of Ointment rubbed and shampooed king Siddhartha of Vaisali, father of Lord Mahavira in the royal gymnasium. Boxing and wrestling reached a perfect stage of development in ancient India which required much skill and technique on the part of the wrestler. Kathasaritsagar[31] tells us how Asokadatta, a young man of a Varanasi having studied sciences, learnt boxing and wrestling and gradually acquired eminence and defeated the famous wrestler who had come from the Deccan.

Specialisation in military and physical sciences was very popular and warriors and rulers received alround training in it with special emphasis on some particular branch of study according to natural bent of mind. Lord Buddha himself in his boyhood received military training along with 500 Sakya Princes in Kanku garden under the careful guidance of Khantadeva, a renewed specialist in military art.[32]

It is learnt from Hemachandra's[33] Trsastisalakapurusacarita, how young Prince Sagar of royal household of Vinita (modern Oudh) made marvelous demonstration of his feats in military exercises before Ajitasvamin, out of a strong desire to learn military science from his teacher. Sagar exhibited his feats in shooting at a target in shooting at a target in water and shooting a clay ball on a wheel with arrows.

He whirled rapidly a lance, a spear and a club giving the appearance of a fiery streak of lightening revolving in the sky. He further showed the science of sword and knife like a dancer showing a dance.

The curriculum of the royal studies, according to Aswaghosa,[34] comprised a number of subjects such as the performances of sacrifices, archery, training of elephants and horses, massage, fording rivers, strategy, rules of battle array, music, dancing the art of playing on the tambourine, the art of playing on the conch, chess and dice etc. Regular military training was imparted to the princes of Sakya dynasty. It was compulsory for them to be proficient in the science of bow and arrow, horse riding and sword fighting. At the time of the marriage of Sidhartha, the father of the Princes Gopa Dandapani, inquired whether Sidhartha was proficient in military training.

Military Science was called *Dhanurveda* according to which an Upanayana ceremony had to be performed by a military student who was given a weapon, while Vedic Mantra was uttered by the preceptor for a Brahmin student, it was a bow; for a Kshatriya, a sword for a Vaisya, a lance for a Sudra, a mace. It was necessary for the military and physical teacher to be proficient in the use of seven weapons - the bow, the discus, the sword, the spear, the mace, the arms and the Kharikara[35].

During the period of Jain influence, women also received training in military science in the art school as they pursued the same curriculum as prescribed for males. It is noticed that the art curriculum included physical and military sciences along with other courses of studies. Evidently the training in military sciences was both popular and through.[36]

According to Buddhist Test Lalita Vistara[37] Physical culture consisted of jumping, leaping, wrestling, dhanirveda, running, dicing, swimming, arrow shooting, elephant riding, charioting, art of bow, horse riding, development of strength and courage, exercise of arms vaulting, diving, boxing, boating, hitting the target with a spear, hitting at vital spot, dancing, music, drama, imitation, massage, magic and yogadarsana.

[38]The athletic art has been described as Vyayamikinam Vidyanam tunanam. It mentions four kinds of fights with *bahu* (arms), *danda* (baton), *Musti* (fists) and *Asthi* (bones). It further mentions the forms

of marksmanship viz. (a) Aksunna Vedhitvam (the art of hitting mark accurately) (b) Marma-vedhitvam (hitting mark of the heart) (c) Sabda-vedhitvam (hitting the mark of the game by its sound). Keay finds that exercises were encouraged in the Buddhist Monasteries, even walking being a favourite exercise.

The Period of Ashok and Kharbela

The Kalinga war was fought in 261 B.C. between Ashok and the Kalinga on the bank of the river Daya, was one of the greatest landmarks in the history of India.It may be significant to note that Chandragupta Maurya could bring under his control the whole of India except Kalinga though it was necessity for the Emperor to crush his near neighbour for an outlet to the sea but he never ventured to invade the powerful Kalinga. The empire-builder after his conquest of northern and western India and victory over the Greeks he thought it risky and hazardous to invade Kalinga.The Greek sources reveal that Kalinga had powerful army and it possessed a vast elephant force which caused terror in the minds of the enemies and the country was never conquered by any foreign king.This cause might have desisted Chandragupta from attack of Kalinga.[39]

Megasthenes refers to the king of Kalinga and its standing army consisting of sixty thousand infantry, one thousand cavalry and seven hundred war elephants. But unfortunately Asoka in his inscriptions did not refer to the name of the king Kalinga though he speaks of the Kalinga war and casualty of the war. It is surprising that when he recorded the names of the contemporary kings of India and foreign countries he remaimed silent about Kalingan king with whom he fought such a relentless war.[40]

The Kalinga war thus had a far-reaching effect, the horrors of the war caused repentance in the mind of the emporer and this was the last war in his life. The war further turned 'Chandasoka to Dharmasoka'. The horror of the war and the remorse touched Asoka as narrated in his thirteenth rock edict. "After that (war) now that the country of Kalinga has been conquered, the Beloved of Gods is devoted to an intense practice of the piety relating to Dharma and longing for Dharma and Circulation of Dharma among people, this is due to having conquered of the country of Kalinga. Verily the slaughter, death, deportation of man which took place in the course of the conquest of an unconquered country are now considered extremely painful and deplorable by the beloved of God........ Therefore, the slaughter, death of deportation of even hundard or thousand part of those people, who were slain or died or were carried away captive at the time of Kalinga, is now considered deplorable by the Beloved of Gods".[41]

According to Greek sources Chandragupta Maurya had possessed an army of 6,00,000 and large cavalry, war chariots and elephants. The large army was expedient to subdue the foreign enemies and the feudatory states of India. Asoka enlarged the size of his army in order to become the master of whole of India. He must have employed his entire army against the independent Kalinga. The rock edict XIII (at Shahbazgrahi, now in Pakistan) record that, one hundred thousand were slained and many times that number died due to the effect of the war.[42] The war was no doubt terrible one fought desparately by the Magadhans and Kalingans. We can well imagine the total number of soldiers engaged in war from both the sides. Unfortunatly, Kalingan lost the war but did not submit before the invader.

The large scale resistance offered by the people of Kalinga to the invasion of Ashoka in 261 B.C. and archaeological evidences indicate that Kalinga was a powerful and well-organised kingdom at the time of the Kalinga war. Orissa had already came under the Jainism and Buddhism were the major religions of Kalinga. The thirteenth Rock Edict of Ashoka mentions about the Brahmana and Sramana inhabitants of Kalinga. Some scholars are of the opinion that Kalinga had became prosperous by her overseas trade and colonial activities in the South East Asian Countries. The discovery of a fort through excavation of Sisupalgarh, two miles away from Bhubaneswar, on the Bhubaneswar-Puri road, proves that some sort of urban culture had developed in Kalinga by third century B.C. the archaeologists have assigned 300 B.C. as the earliest date of Sisupalgarh remains. The Ashokan inscriptions at Dhauli (in the Puri district) and Jaugarh (in the Ganjam district) mention two urban centres. Dhauli inscription mention Tosali and Jaugarh inscription mention Somapa. Most probably Tosali was the capital of Kalinga and became the provincial head-quarter of the Mauryan empire after Ashoka's conquest of Kalinga. Some scholars seek to identify Sisupalgarh with Tosali.[43]

[44]No account of India's ancient history, be it political, social,

economic of military, is complete without a brief reference to the *Arthasastra*, generally ascribed to Chanakya, Prime Minister of Chandragupta Maurya. Whoever may be its author and whatever may be the date of its composition (these are matters of endless controversy), it is a comprehensive work on state-craft, law and military system. It contains some military matters and a good deal of theoretical discussion of methods of warfare, diplomacy and military organisation as a whole. It is unquestionably based on the realities of civil and military administration. The best army should, according to him, confirm to the following qualities.

"Coming down directly from father and grandfather (of the king), ever strong, obedient, happy in keeping their sons and wives well contented not averse to making a long sojourn, ever and everywhere invincible, endowed with the power of endurance, trained in fighting various kinds of battles, skillful in handling various forms of weapons, ready to share in the weal or woe of the king and consequently not falling foul with him, and purely composed of soldiers of Kshatriya caste".

Chandragupta's Army, thoroughly Indian in character organisation and equipments, consisted of four parts : The traditional Chaturangavala-infantry, cavalry, chariots and elephants. According to Meghasthenes the standing Army comprised 600,000 infantry, 30,000 cavalry, 9,000 elephant's and a large number of chariots. On the strength of Kautilya's statement, we may add the fleet and the transport. Magasthenes informs us that the Maurya emperor's huge army was efficiently administered by well organised war office in charge of a commission of thirty divided into six boards, i.e., each board served by five members.[45]

The first board cooperates with the admiral of the fleet and is therefore concerned with naval warfare ships and boats must have been used concerned with naval warfare ships and boats must have been used in battles where was a possibility or river transport or a river attack. The second committee equivalent to the modern commissariat. It supervises the bullock-trains used for transporting equipments, food and other necessities. The remaining four committees are concerned with four branches of the army regularly listed in the Indian sources - infantry, cavalry, the chariots and the elephants.[46]

There were *adhyakshas* (superintendents) for each of the four sections of the army and Kautilya's description of their duties had much in common with Megasthenese's account of the military administration. Stress is laid by Kautilya on the importance of the elephants corps and great attention was devoted to the proper maintenance of elephant forests (nagavana). Kautilya distinguishes different types among the foot soldiers. They were in order of importance, the hereditary troops (Maula) doubtless the same as the fighting class (Kshatriya) whom Meghasthenes placed next to the cultivators in number of importance; hired troops maintained by guilds (Sreni) and corporations (Sanghas) and available to the state at need; and lastly forest tribes who furnished troops to the king in the time of war. The array of the army in the field was an elaborate affair and different formation based on clear distinctions between vanguard, centre, rear, march, attack and defence. The superintendents of the different military army functioned alone or with the assistance of the boards were probably subject to the general control of the Senapati (commander-in-chief) who ranked among the most important officials of the state. Below the Senapati were different grades of officers of the army like *prasasti*, *Nayaka* and *Mukhya*. In the battlefield surgeons with instruments, medicines and bandages and nurses with prepared foods and beverages were in constant attendance behind the lines. The soldiers were encouraged to fight by suitable and timely addresses from the king, his ministers and *purohits* and by rewards and honours for distinction in the field.[47]

A squared of ten under the leadership of officer called Padika formed the smallest unit of the army. For every ten members of the constituents of the army there must be one commander called Padika, ten Padikas under a Senapati, ten Senapati under a Nayaka (leader)[48].

Mahameghavahana Kharavela of the Chedi dynasty raised the status of Kalinga to an Empire and conquered kingdom after kingdom in the north, south and west with his invincible army to an extent unheard in the annals of the past. The Emperor Kharavela left behind his achievements in his lithic record on the rock-cut cave of Hatigumpha at Udayagiri of Bhubaneswar. The recent discovery of a pillar inscription of the Chedis at Gunturpali in Andhra further supplements our knowledge of the rules and achievements of Mahameghavahana Kharavela. We learn from Hatigumpha inscription that Kharavela was the third ruler of the Chedi dynasty. It is significant to note that the founder of this dynasty might have thrown off the Magadgan yoke. The Hatigumpha inscription highlights the childhood of the king, his training in different branches of learning, his administration, achievements, the reconstruction of his capital city and excavation of caves at Udayagiri and Khandagiri hills. His rule through short-lived covering only thirteen years was quite eventful. No monarch of his time could have conquered so many kingdoms in the subcontinent of India within such a short period. The Hatigumpha inscription relates that the monarch in the first year of his reign devoted his attention to the repairs of the gateways and the buildings of his capital Kalinganagar which was damaged by storm. In the second year he organised a vast army consisting of infantry, cavalary, elephant forces and chariots and led an expedition to the south-west against his rival king Satakarni of Satavahana dynasty. Emboldened with the success in the war Kharavela marched further against the Rathikas and Bhojakas. Though these conquests Kharavela held his sway over the major part of the Decan. As a mark of his victory he devoted the third year in the entertainment activities in the capital. The people of his state enjoyed dancing, singing, instrumental music and merry-making and also made preparation for another expedition and defeated Rastrikas and Bhojikas of Berar and Maharastra region. In the fifth year he devoted his attention to the public works. He caused construction of a canal up to his capital and performed a *Rajasuya* sacrifice and remitted several taxes as an insignia of his title *Chakravarti*. The event of the rest two years are hazy. Probably he paid attention to public works and to war preparations. The eighth year is marked for his expedition against Gorathagiri (identified with a fort of same name in the Barbara hill of Gaya district in Bihar). Next he marched against Rajagriha identified with Rajagiri of Nalanda district of Bihar, the earliest capital of Magadhan Empire. After a successful trip in the eight year he erected the magnificent palace of victory (*Mahavijaya Prasad*) in the capital city at a cost of 3800 thousand. The event of tenth year is not clear from the inscription. In the event of eleventh year of his reign Kharavela fought against the confederacy of the Cholas, Pandyas, Sataputras and Keralaputras. Kharavela tactfully won the battle and returned with a large booty. He completed his military achievements by leading an expedition to the north mainly directed against Pataliputra with an intention of bringing back the *Kalinga Jinasana* taken away from Kalinga by

Nanda king. The ruling monarch of Magadha Brihaspati Mitra submitted before his invincible army. He thus won the victory and brought back the honoured *Kalinga Jinasana* thus claiming his military career. Here ended the military and political career of the emperor after successful conquest of the kingdom oin the north, west and south. His *digvijaya* to all directions of the country reveals his statesmanship, political strategy and intense desire for consolidation of an empire. In this respect he can be rightly compared with the empire-builder Chandragupta Maurya.[49]

[50]Martial tradition of the people under Kharavela was maintained by regular exercises of swords-play, bull fight, lion hunting, scaring away of wild elephants and shooting operations. As regards weapons of war of the period we find depiction of bow and arrow, quiver, sword, spear and club in the relief sculptures of Udayagiri and Khandagiri. Shields are found designed in rectangular shape with hooks at one end. It functions as a defensive weapons when attacked by a sword from a short distance. The fighters held it in one of their hands and attack on the other by a sword or spear the opponents sword stroke had to be received on the shield of it was to be returned.

[51]In addition to the weapons of war depicted in the relief sculptures of Udayagiri and Khandagiri hills, the excavation a Sisupalgarh had yield one hundred and ninety seven iron implements, a vast majority of hundred and ninety seven iron implements, a vast majority of which used as weapons of war. They include nails, spikes, staples, ferules, knife blades, borers, lances, spear heads, tanged & daggers, barbed and facted arrow-heads and caltrops. A notable find is that of caltrops, which have been recovered in India for the first time. Caltrop is an iron implement having many spiked branches whichever way it is made lie on the ground, one of its spikes always projecting upwards. It is mainly used in warfare to main and impede the progress of the cavalry or matching elephants. Considerable number of them thrown on the highway would injure their feet. Caltrops occur on the Roman military sites of the early centuries A.D. in western Europe and are therefor of a comparable period. The use of caltrops was revived in the early stages of the first Great War of 1914-18 when cavalry was introduced. Furthermore, similar objects were included in bombs dropped on sites in the middle east during the Second World War of 1935-39 with a view to hindering motor

transport, the idea was thus both old and new one. Kautilya in his *Arthasastra* also mentions similar obstacles being placed adjacently outside the rampart to impede the enemy's progress.

Though we do not get any direct evidence to the military personnel under Kharavela yet the Kirari wooden pillar inscription[52] and the relief sculptures in some of the caves of Udayagiri and Khandagiri caves throw welcome light on the subject. This inscription was recovered in the village Kirari during the course of renovation of a tank. The village Kirari located some ten miles of Chandrapur and is very close to the border of ancient Kalinga and Kosala. It reveals the names of a large number of official dignitaries of the first century A.D., i.e., before the occupation of Kosala and Kalinga region by Gautamiputra Satakarni as indicated by N.K. Sahu[53], the inscription was thus not far removed in time from the Chedi rule in Kalinga and the evidence obtained from it would be more or less applicable to the period of the rule of Kharavela and his successors. The name of the army dignitaries as available from this damaged record are as follows:

Mahasenani	—	Commander-in-Chief.
Senapati	—	Commander of the army.
Nagarrakhin	—	City police.
Pratihar	—	Chamberlain or door-keeper.
Hatharoha	—	Elephant driver.
Asvaroha	—	Horse men.
Padmulika	—	Royal attendant.
Rathika	—	Superintendent of Chariot.
Hathi Vaka	—	Hastipala, perhaps superintendent of Elephants.
Dhavaka	—	Herald, Forerunner.
Janasatayudha Gharika	—	Superintendent of Carriage shed and armoury.

After Kharavela the political stability of the empire gradually declined and it was fragmented into several kingdoms for many centuries, which continued to be ruled by various local ruling dynasties. Most notable of these dynasties are the Mathers and Sailodbhavas of South Orissa, the Bhoumakaras of northern Orissa and the Somavamshies of Western Orissa.Sailodbhavas migrated to their newly established colonies in Indonesia and founded their Sailendra empire which built up a prosperous civilization in those islands. Towards the end of the ninth century the Somavamshi King Janmejay brought the western, eastern and northern regions of Orissa under one administrative umbrella. During this period Orissa's language, culture, religion, arts and architecture gradually took a distinct shape. Orissa experienced its own individuality under the great monarchs of this dynasty. Yayati was the most powerful of all, proclaimed himself as the Lord of Kalinga, Kongada, Utkal and Kosala showing there by his hold over the four traditional division of Orissa, when the whole Orissa ceased to pass under the more famous name of Kalinga. This monarch also fought battles against the kings of Karnata, Lata, Gujan, Anchi, Gauda and Radha and won glorious victories. The Monarchs of this dynasty became most famous in history as great builders of temples, towers and the water tanks, grand monuments like the great Lingaraj temple complex and Vindu Sarovara of Bhubaneswar, Biraja temples and victory pillars at Jajpur and many other places. The enormous size of the monuments as well as the superb artistic decoration on their surface all the brightest testimony to the high degree of architectural as well as sculptures excellence to which the Orissan builders and artists of that period had reached. The grand embankment of the Kathajori river at Cuttack exhibit today the high degree of engineering skill of the builders of the those days.[54]

Warfare in Pre-Historic Orissa

[55]Though Military history begins with the formation of the state in ancient Orissa, we may look at the pre-and proto-historic age to know the nature and motives of war in the earliest period. Pre-historic paintings, weapons of war and fortified settlements found in Orissa speak of the fighting of the primitive tribal over games, mates and sources of food and water. Preservation of land and defence against normadic attacks become added factors of fighting among Neolithic men. During the heliolithic and Iron Age, several regional cultures sprang up in different parts of Orissa as evident from the discovery of a number of copper hoard sites. Printed rock- shelters of Manikmoda and Lekhamoda in Hemgirtahsil of sundargarh district are the earliest

pictorial depictions of warriors and their weapons in Orissa. They denote show regular battle scenes. The human figures executed in monochrome of while and arrange fresh red wielding metallic swords and large dices are plenty in those rock-art heritages. These sketchy pictorial depictions provides useful evidence of the type of weapons in pre-historic Orissa.

Military Traditions of Orissa from 1st Century A.D. to Somavanshi Dynasty

[56]The political condition of Kalinga after Kharavela till the rise of the imperial Guptas is shrouded in mystery. Due to paucity of facts we cannot conclude that Kálinga became politically weak all of a sudden. However, taking the opportunity of decadence of the Chedis in Kalinga the vanquished powers raised their heads. The political powers in the north like Kusanas, and the Satavahanas in the south took recourse to carve out territories from Kalingas frontiers. During the days of political weakness the people of Kalinga being adventures in maritime trade might have busied themselves in this lucrative pursuit. On the basis of availability of a large number of Kusana coins in Orissa some scholars believe that Kalinga was under the dominion of the Kusanas. But we do not have sufficient evidence except the coins to prove the authenticity of the scholar's viewpoint. The brisk circulation of the Kusana coins was perhaps necessary for internal and external trade.

[57]The history of Kalinga in the 1st century A.D. is much obscure and little is known about the political life of the territory till the ascendancy of the Satavahanas, early in the 2nd century A.D. The Satavahanas power under the leadership of Gautamiputra Satakarni was revived in the early part of the second century A.D. Under Satakarni I Deccan rose a very strong military power.

[58]Surrounded as the Satavahanas were by hostile people, they had to maintain considerable forces to retain their supremacy. They are belived to have introduced the system of military governors (strategies), a system apparently borrowed from the Sakas they also appointed the district officers bearing the title of *Senapati*. They were reputed to possess military forces seceed only to that at the command of the king of Prasi, Chandragupta Maurya. The Andhra

territory included thirty walled towns, besides numerous villages and the army consisted of 100,000 infantry, 2000 cavalry and 1000 elephants.

[59]The fall of the Satavahana empire after three hundred years of existence may in all probability be attributed rather to internal aggression and the rise of a number of new promising dynasties in the Upper Deccan and in the far south then to army inherent weakness in its military system. Their political achievements, which are so varied and glorious, may have seen the outcome of their excellent military system. After the decline of Satavahana the Murundas became more powerful in Kalinga and their Political Authority spread over the costal territory from Singhbbhum to Ganjam.

[60]The political history of Kalinga in the second and third century A.D. is rather hazy, though the country was economically very prosperous. On account of her maritime prosperity Ptolemy in the Geography refers to a number of prosperous ports in Kalinga like Palur, Nainagaina, Katikadama, Kanagara, etc. this account leads us to believe that Kalinga was most probably powerful. However, further discovery may fill up the existing gap.

[61]It will not be irrelevant to note that after the downfall of the Kusanas and the Satavahanas, India for about a century was divided into a number of independent states. The internal dissensions and struggle among themselves were the main features of the history of this period. The position of Kalinga during this period was not an exception.

Matharas

[62] Towards the later half of the 4th century A.D., however, a powerful dynasty rose in Orissa to unite a grater part of the land from the river Mahanadi to the river Godavari. It was the dynasty of the Matharas. While the Gupta Monarchs were at the highest of their power in the North the Mathara kings had their independent sway over a large part of Orissa which included the territories through Samudragupta conducted his victorious march. They style themselves as maharaja and even some of them called themselves as Kalingadhipati. A large number copper plate grant of the mathara kings have survived

till now to speak about their various achievements. Umaverman, Sankaravarman, Saktivarman, Anantasaktiverman, Chandtaverman and Pravanjanvarman were some of the most illustrious kings of this dynasty. Their rule covered a period of one hundred and fifty years i.e., from the middle of the 4th century A.D. in the end of the 5th century A.D. they have given to Orissa a sound administrative system almost in the line of the Gupta administrative patterns.

[63]The Mathara rule was a grate landmark in the history and culture of Kalinga. Her history which remained obscure after the fall of Chadi dynasty in the first century A.D. attended grate important with the rise of this new dynasty. It not only launched Kalinga to vigorous political career but also made her cultural life to undergo profound transformations. The king was the supreme head of all branches of administration of the state and he was ruling with the help of a series of officers among whom the military assignments were given to *Mahabaladhikrita* (the General) and *Dandaneta* (the commander of a contingent). Sometimes a single officer is given the charge of both civil and military assignments as in the case of Matruvara who was record keeper, as well as a commander (*Dandanayak*) under king Anantasaktivarman. It is further revealed from the Sakunaka grant issued by Anantasaktivarman that it was executed by two high military officer, the commander-in-chief (*Mahabaladhikrita*) Sivabhojaka and the general (*dandaneta*) vasudatta, both of whom belonged to the cadre of Kumaramatya the employment of military personal for work executing the religious deeds indicates that during the rule of Maharaja Anantasaktivarman, the military had an unusual predominance in the sphere of civil administration.

[64] Kalinga appears to have played an important role in overseas trade of the period depending possibly on her superb maritime activity. The poet Kalidash described the king of Kalinga as Lord of seas. It was during this time that the people of Kalinga established colonies in Burma, Saim, Cambodia and Indonesia, traces of which are found even at present the lower Burma (Pegu region) was called Talaing or Kalinga while Upper Burma (North-west Burma) passed by the name of Ukkala or Utkal. The immigrants from eastern coast of India were called kings not only in Malaya Peninsula but also in Java and the Klings were very likely the most familiar colonists from Kalinga. The Klings of Malaya and Java and the Talaings or Kalingas of Pegu

were subsequently merged with the Mon-Khmer, a Sinu-Tribetan stock, and gave rise to a racial and cultural synthesis in those lands.

Sailodbhavas :

In the southern coastal regions of Kalinga, during the 6th and 7th centuries A.D. a dynasty named the Sailodbhavas ruled over a kingdom which they called Kongada. The name Sailodbhava indicates that the rulers of their territory represented some hilly areas to begin with and scholars have identified, with valid reason, these areas with lands around lake Chilka and Ganjam. The rulers of this dynasty included Sailodbhava, Ranabhita, Sainyabhita, Ayosobhita, Sainyabhita-II, Ayasobhita-II, Mdhavaraja, Dharmaraja, Manabhita and their successors. From the great ports of Palur, Ganjam, Kalinganagar and Charitra, the people of Kalinga were carrying on their trade and commerce from very ancient times with Burma, Malaysia, Siam, Kambodia, Java, Bali, Borneo, Sumatra and other places of the Suvarnadwipa. Taking advantage of the century-old relation between Kalinga and the oversea lands, the Sailodbhavas of Kongada were supposed to have launched upon their colonial adventure in Suvarnadwipa and ultimately succeeded in establishing the great and far-flung Sailendra Empire in the part of further Asia. The Sailodbhava dynasty disappeared from Kongada in 7th century A.D. and the Saildendra Empire of Suvarnadwipa rose into prominence in the 8th century A.D. In the heyday of the empire, the foreign merchants as well as their countrymen called that empire as 'Kalinga' signifying thereby the Kalinga origin of the Sailendra Empire. This empire endured for nearly two centuries.[65]

Charamparaja Ayosobhita-I, another king of this dynasty, acquired royalty on earth by the valour and strength of his own arms and that he was surrounded by a number of feudatories and officers like *Sri Samanta, Mahasamanta, Maharaja, Rajanuka, Rajaputra, Dandanayaka, Kumaramatro, Uparika* and *Ayukta.* This shows that Charamparaja was a sovereign ruler. But the Sailodbhavas under him could not enjoy independent status for long. They came under the sovereignty of Sasanka probably towards the end of his rule or at the beginning of the reign of his son Madhavaraja-II. After the sudden fall of Sasanka, Madhavaraja-II ascertained his independence and took advantage of the situation and marched into the territory of Kalinga. He then assumed the title of *Sakala Kalingadhipati*. But the Gangas could not remain passive to all these happenings. Their king Indravarman-III-probably with the help of the Eastern Chalukyas reoccupied the Kalinga territory some time before 626 A.D. This led Madhavaraja to recognise the political rights of the Gangas. We have earlier discussed the engagements among the three major contending powers of the period and the role of Kongada maintaining a balance with a huge standing army of elephant corps which kept the neighbouring countries in awe.[66]

[67]The Saildbhava charters in their land grants notify several dignitaries of which the Antaranga, *Dandapasika*, *Sandhivigrahika*, *Chatas* and *Bhatas* seem to have been connected with military administration. The *Antaranga* seems to be a kinsman of the ruler or a person to deal with confidential and secret matters of the state. The term *Dandapasika* is one who holds the fetters or noose of punishment, i.e., policeman. The modern village *Chaukidar* is also called *Dandasi* which term is derived from *Dandapasika*. In the *Arthasastra* the law relating to the suppression of crimes is called *Dandapasa*. This officer occurs invariably in almost all the copper plates of the period. Perhaps his main function was to bind down the criminals. *Sandhivigrahika* belonged to the department of peace and war corresponding to modern foreign department which was in charge of a high official or minister. Chatas and Bhatas are mentioned in many copper plates and are taken to be petty police functionaries such as constables. They might also be taken as soldiers. They have often been regarded as irregular soldiers and regular troops respectively. Their duty was probably to maintain peace and order in the state and apprehend criminals.

[68]The relief panels, statues of various Gods and Goddesses and *Dwarapala* figures on the outer walls of the said temple reflect to the type of weapons of warfare in various categories of swords, daggers, battle-axes, spears, tridents, mace, noose, shield, goad, etc. The bas-relief on the northern niche of the viman depicts an interesting hunting scene. A man seated on horse is spearing a lion or fabulous animal, another piercing the body of an elephant, another again defending himself from the attack of a lion or fabulous animal with a shields.

[69] The *Yuktikalpataru* of Bhoja states that Banarasa, Magadha, Nepala, Sourastra and Kalinga were noted centers for the manufacture of swords. Reference to swords is found in the epigraphic records also. An inscription of the Saildbhava king Madhavaraja mentions that he repulsed the armies of all the enemies by the sharp edge of his sword.

[70]The sailodbhava records mention that forts formed an important part in the military system of Kongada in the 7th century A.D. Alanghapura was a fort. It can be identified with Donghara near Khalikota. Bankada, the capital of the Sailodbhavas, was a hill fort.

Bhauma-Karas

[71]After the Matharas and the Sailodbhavas, the next significant chapter of the political history of ancient Orissa began during the rule of the Bhauma-Kara and Somavamsi dynasties. The later Bhaumakaras and the early Somavamsis were contemporaries and at one stage, the former were ruling over the Utkal portion of Orissa and the latter over the Kosala region. In course of time the Bhauma-Kara rule yielded place to the rule of the Somavamsis and the land mass of Orissa came under the rule of one powerful dynasty. The time of these two dynasties running over a period of nearly four centuries, i.e., from 8th to 11th centuries, saw a formative period in the life and culture of the Orissan people. Geographical demarcations and territorial centres, religious traits and linguistic developments, all tended to bring about a clear and distinct picture of a compact socio-political unit. In the evolution of Orissa, the Bhauma-Kara-Somavamsi period is indeed a remarkable epoch.

[72]The most notable rulers of the Bhauma-Kara dynasty were Subhakaradeva, Santikaradeva, Subhakaradeva-II Santikaradeva-II and finally Dandi Mahadevi, a powerful woman ruler. It was king Subhakaradeva-I who wrote a religious text in his own hand and sent it with a letter to his contemporary Chinese Emperor Te-Tsong in the last decade of the 8th century.

[73]In the Bhauma dynasty we find as many as six female members who ruled over Orissa as full-fledged sovereigns with all sovereign titles. This is perhaps the only example in the Hindu history of India in which we find the women occupying the throne as successors of

their late husbands or fathers. Rudramba of the Kakatiya dynasty and the Kashmiri queen Didda are perhaps the only two other examples of the Hindu history in which female members ruled after their father and husband respectively. It seems to us that the Bhaumas, being a non-Aryan tribe, had a custom of allowing their female members to succeed the late husbands or fathers by virtue of their own rights.

[74]The new kingdom of the Bhaumas started its existence since 736 A.D., which was the initial year of the Bhaumaera recorded in their inscriptions and fixed their capital at Guhadeva pataka or Guhesvara pataka mentioned in all their copper plate grants. The Bhauma-Kara kingdom in its palmy days roughly included the territories now comprising the Midnapur district in the north, Mayurbhanja, Keonjhar, Dhenkanal and Baud-Phulbani districts in the west, Ganjam district in the south and the districts of Puri, Cuttack, Balasore bounded by the Bay of Bengal in the east. Some time, as during the time of Sivakaradeva-I Unmatasimha, the kingdom embraced wider areas but the acquisition of such areas was temporary for the successor of Sivakaradeva-I failed to retain them. The Bhauma-Kara kingdom in fact was almost of the same extent as the major portion of modern Orissa with the exception of the Midnapur district which is now in West Bengal. The upper Mahanadi valley comprising the modern Sambalpur. Sonepur tract formed a separate state known as Kosala and was ruled by the Somavamsis.

[75]It was divided into two large administrative units, viz., *Uttaras* (Northern) and *Dakhin* (Southern) Toshala, which seem to have situated respectively to the north and south of Toshala (modern Dhauli near Bhubaneswar in the Puri district), a city of great antiquity and renown. The extent of these two divisions varied from time to time in accordance with the extent of the kingdom of a particular dynasty.

[76]The reference to the Bhauma army of about 300,000 soldiers in the Hudud-al-Alam though seems to be highly exaggerated in view of the fact that the Bhaumas controlled a small principality in comparison to Harshavardhana, the system of obtaining feudal militia was probably mustered during times of war. We find mention of such systems in the *Aihole* inscription relating to Harshavardhana. Similarly the Rastrakuta king Govinda-III and Chalukyas of Vengi

collected forces and tributes from their vassals. Under these circumstances we can safely presume that feudatory chiefs supported the cause of their Bhauma overlords with armies at the time of war and paid tributes at the time of peace. The feudatories used to attend the courts of the Bhauma kings on ceremonial occasions and in time of internal crisis.

The military system under the Bhauma-Karas appears to have very strong and efficient or else the small principality founded by them would not have developed into a vast kingdom. The military strength of the Bhauma-Karas is convincingly certified by the accounts of Ibn Khudabhbin which clearly mentions that the Dahum (the Bhuama ruler) "does not consider anyone superior to himself" and "is said to have an army of 300,000 men. It is further testified by the Dhenkanal plate of Tribhuvana Mahadevi-I which states that the rulers of the dynasty possessed a strong army.[77]

The monarch was as usual the head of the administration and exercised unfettered powers. From the Talcher plates of Subhakaradeva-IV it is learnt that during the rule of Tribhuvana Mahadevi-I the country advanced in three branches (of administration)- the foes were extirpated, the glory spread abroad and there was harmony among the people. To fulfil these objectives the king depended on three regal powers of the state. They were the sovereignty or the majesty of the king (*Prabhusakti*), the wise counsel (*Mantrasakti*) and the energy, power and strength (*Utsahasakti*). These three powers correspond to the three major limbs of Government, the sovereignty, the officers and the army which were not only essential but also indispensable and irresistible powers. We notice in the Talcher plate of Sivakaradeva-III that Tribhuvana Mahadevi-I made her three energies shine perpetually.[78]

[79]The king was the supreme commander of the armed forces. He not only led the army but also fought in the battlefield himself. This is brought out by the Talcher plate of Sivakaradeva-III which states that Sivakaradeva Unmatasimha "alone in a battle formidable with vast numbers of warriors poured forth sharp arrows from his bow drawn up to his ears and took away in victory the daughter of the king of Radha like the latter's kingly fortune".[80] The title of Senapati or chief of the army is not traceable in the Bhauma records. It is just possible that the rulers of this dynasty were in the command of the army. Subhakaradeva-I of this dynasty led the Bhauma army against

Kalinga.

[81]The elephants assumed greater importance as a beast for military purposes than the horse in the early medieval period. The various small kingdoms that rose to prominence on the ruins of the Gupta empire attempted to trace out effective methods of warfare in their bid for supremacy. The numerous smaller kings probably took to fortifying their kingdoms which could be overpowered only by storming the fortresses for which elephants would be unusually suitable rather than the horses on whom the Guptas have given maximum emphasis.[82] Bana's metaphorical description of Harsha's favourite elephant as "a moving hill fort with its high frontal globes as so many towers confirms the above supposition.[83] The Aihole inscription of Pulkesin, too, refers to Harsha's mighty elephants.

[84]The Chinese pilgrim giving a general observation of Indian war elephants tells us that the destructive power of the elephants was increased by covering them with a strong armour and attaching sharp spurs to their tusks. [85]Bana refers to the various uses of elephants in the battlefield. The elephants apparently were trained to create havoc in the adversary's camp by ramming, crushing soldiers in their trunks and calculatingly going a mock. All these prove that elephant crops became an important factor in the army right from the seventh century A.D.

[86]In addition to the standing army the feudatories were expected to rally around their suzerain with their armies during the time of war. Probably there was no conscription and the appropriate number of men were only invited to join the army by promise of reward or a certain salary. After the expedition some of the troops might have been disbaded.

In this connection it is striking to note that "greatly eminent maharajas such as Unmatakesari, Gayad and others possessed famous army"[87] and that Bhauma kings "extorted enemies' fortunes with the power of their bright swords and trampled the proudly heaved heads of the kings" with the able assistance of their mighty army.[88]

In addition to the military designations like Antaranga, Sandhivigrahika, Dandapasika, Chatas and Bhatas under the Sailodbhava dynasty we find a few more under the Bhauma-Karas.

They are Sthanantarika, Sandhyadhikarana and Kutyakalasa. The terms like Mahasamanta, Samanta and Ranaka have already been referred to in connection with the feudatories. The term Sthanantarika was probably the officer incharge of the criminal department under the Bhaumas.[89] D.C Sircar on the other hand suggestes that he was probably a spy.[90] It is difficult to say anything definitely but he seems to be connected with certain secret departments. The title Sandhyadhikarana meant the Commander of the cavalry which indicates to the fact that cavalry was a part of the Bhauma army also.[91] The mention of this designation is not available in the administrative hierarchy of other dynasties of Orissa. The word Kutokola or Kutyakolasa is derived from Kuta which denotes fort or mountain peak. In fact forts are generally situated on the mountain peaks for military strategy. The existence of mountain peaks is not an improbability in the Bhauma kingdom which consisted mostly the mountain tracts of Orissa. This presupposes that the Bhaumas must have maintained a large number of forts situated in the forest tracts. Kutokolasa, therefore, may be interpreted as officers incharge of the garrison stationed at such forts. These officers, in the Bhauma records, have been given the status of district officers. They probably remained incharge of the provision, dress, arms and discipline of the troops stationed in the forts. Such troops were invariably engaged against foreign aggressions, internal disturbances and in the matter of maintenance of law and order within the kingdom. The term Kutyakolasa mentioned in the Santiragram grant of Dandi Mahadevi is identical with Kutokola in other records.[92]

War weapons like double-edged long swords, short daggers, bows, arrows, quivers, rectangular and circular shields, battle-axes, trident, spears, noose, clubs, goad, thunderbolt, disc, etc., are profusely represented in the sculptures of the period. The figures of Ganesa, Kartikeya, Mahisasurmardini, Durga, Dvarapalas, etc., are all provided with such weapons in their hands. The two Dvarapala figures at the base of the door-jambs of the Ratangiri Mahavihara are shown with long double-edged swords either held in their hands or fixed to their hip belts Sometimes short daggers, too, which we may call Kataris, are seen to have been affixed to the band of cloth or girdle around the waist. The Kris variety of daggers to which we have made earlier reference in the Sailodbhava period have also continued during this period. Bows are generally held in the left hand and arrows in the right, quivers filled with feather-tailed arrows are noticed fixed to the right shoulder. Spears and battle-axes fitted to long metal or wooden shafts appear to be very commonly used by the figures depicted on the outer walls of the temples or stray figures of Durga, Ganesa, Parvati and Kartikeya. The shields were either held in hands or tightly attached to the forearms. The Somavamsi king *Janamejaya* killed the brother of his son-in-law with a sharp-edged kunta (long spear) in a battle and thus paved the way for his daughter to assume the authority.[93]

Somavamsis

[94]The Somavamsis, originally known as the *Panduvamsis,* were a powerful ruling dynasty in medieval Orissa. They commenced their rule towards the end of the 7th century A.D. in a small kingdom in the western part of South Kosala and subsequently expanded their power to the east and in course of time became the undisputed master of almost the whole of modern Orissa. The dynasty became more effective in raising Orissa to its definite individuality. From the last years of the 9th century A.D this dynasty came forward to play its spectacular political and cultural role and continued to represent its vitality till the later part of the 11th century. *Janamejaya Mahabhavagupta-I, Yayati Mahasivagupta-I, Bhimaratha mahabhavagupta-II, Dharmaratha Mahasivagupta-II, Nahusa Mahabhavagupta-II, Yayati-II, Udyotakesari Mahabhavagupta-IV* and *Janamejaya-II* were some of the illustrious monarchs of the Somavamsi dynasty. The dynasty ruled for more than two centuries. With the title "*Keshari*" used by some kings of this dynasty the traditions of Orissa remain eloquent about the achievements of these rulers by describing them as *Kesharis. Yayati-I* famous as *Yayati Keshari,* is said to have performed an *Asvamedha* sacrifice at Jajpur, and to have brought ten thousand Brahmins from Kanauja for settlement in that holy place. Historically he is the monarch who united the two identifiable parts of the then Orissa, namely, Utkal and Kosala, and consolidated the two areas in one homogeneous territory laying thereby the foundation of a solid powerful state.

[95]The records of the Somavamsi dynasty reveal that the king

was at the head of the military organisation being the supreme commander of the armed forcers. He also actually fought in the battlefields. This fact is evident from the description of Somavamsi kings found in their records. We have made reference to the heroic activities of *Yayati-I* in his conflicts with the *Kalachuri* king *Yuvaraja-I*, The Banapur charter reveals that *Indraratha* had defeated *Abhimanyu*, who was the governor of *Odra*, and assumed independence after the death of *Dharmaratha*, by the strength of his own arms and with the assistance of a small infantry. Inscriptions of *Yayati*-II and *Udyota Kesari* are replete with numerous such references. In the Brahmesvar temple inscription it is mentioned that *Udyota Kesari* as a young prince was associated with his father's military activities. This presupposes that *Yuvarajas* (princes) of royal blood were training on military operations and were actually engaged in wars to build themselves up as successful rulers in future.

[96]We get scanty reference to military designations in the Somavamsi inscriptions and *Madalapanji*, the temple chronicle of Lord Jagannatha. *Sandhivigrahins* are generally appointed to advise the kings on matters of war and peace. This designation is found mention in the records of several earlier ruling dynasties. During the Somavamsi rule we get the names of *Malladatta*, *Dharadatta, Sadharana, Singhadatta, Kumbhandipala, Chichatesvara, Rudradatta* and *Krishnadeva* appointed as *Sandhivigrahin* under different kings of this dynasty. Some of them were also represented as Ranaka in the copper plate charters of the period. Up to the reign of *Udyota Kesari* the members of the Datta family appear to have continued in a hereditary manner as the *Sandhivigrahin* of the ruling chiefs. But during the time of Karnadeva we find Krishnadeva superseded these members of the Datta family and was appointed *Sandhivigrahin*. Much of the independence and integrity of the empire depends on the personal velour and wisdom of these officers. The Ratnagiri charter is in high praise of the *Sandhivigrahin* Krishnadeva, of the time of Karnadeva. The *prasasti* seem to praise the minister that king Karna was made the lord of the earth in the real sense by the various kings killed by this minister, Krishnadeva, and that the earth, including the territories of those rulers, came into the possession of a better master.

[97]It is evident from the Somavamsi records that members of the army were generally paid in return of their services. The regular

troops were probably paid in metallic currency and rent-free land holdings. On the other hand the irregular troops who were called upon to participate in military activities enjoyed rent-free land holdings. Besides a tax called *Padatijivya* was levied upon the people for the maintenance of the army. This tax has been interpreted as a subsistence collected from the inhabitants for the infantry troops that happened to pass through the countryside.

[98]From the recently discovered Deogaon copper plate grant of Janamejaya-I we come across the word *Chaturanga* indicating to the traditional four-fold division of the army, i.e., infantry, cavalry, elephant forces and chariots. But it is an established fact that chariot as a part of the armed contingent has long been disappeared. We do not get any other direct reference in literature or representation in sculptures as regards to the chariots in the Somavamsi army. It seems therefore reasonable to divide army organisation of the period into infantry, cavalry and elephant corps. The Brahmesver temple inscription reveals that Udyota Kesari defeated the whole forces of his enemies of Dahala, Chola and Gauda as it were in child's play with the help of well-armed warriors and elephants and made the earth (tortoise) sink with the weight of the swift marches of his army, *aksauhini* in number, and was victorious and made a large number of kings bow down at his feet. From the above description it is evident that infantry soldiers and elephants played the vital part in Somavamsi military expeditions. *Aksauhini* which refers to his complete army probably consisted of 21,870 *pattis* as per traditional theories. A *patti* was the basic unit of the Indian army which was a mixed platoon consisting of one elephant, one chariot, three horses and five foot soldiers. Since chariot has been neglected it is reasonable to believe that one more elephant was added to the unit in its place.

[99]A cursory glance to the sculptural representation in Somavamsi monuments like Lingaraja and Brahmesvara and the loose figures of various divinities give us a idea regarding the prevailing type of war weapons, costume of the infantry soldiers, equipment of the cavalry and elephant forces as well as the marching order of the armed contingent. The long drawn panels on the face of the *pidha* tiers of the jagamohana of the Lingaraja temple and the inner projections of the *jagamohana* roof of the Brahmesvar temple at Bhubaneswar reveal

the marching order of the Somavamsi army. They are invariably led by the elephants followed by the cavalry force and the infantry soldiers. The royal figures or the Commander-in-Chief generally mounted over the leading elephants with series of retinues and umbrella bearers. The elephants were decorated with thick cushions, tusk guards, and chain armours look very ferocious in nature. The marching of the cavalry is rhythmic. They are all equipped with military accessories like saddles and bridles and mounted by soldiers with sword, shield or long spears in hands. The infantry soldiers in the rear are armed with long swords, spears and protective shields. Their physical strength has been amply demonstrated in the sculptures.

[100]The inscriptions of the period made numerous references to the sword and spears held in the hands of the ruling chiefs. They, in addition to several other weapons, are elaborately displayed in the hands of the Gods, Goddesses and Dvarapala figures. They include short and long swords invariably double-edged and within or without scabbard. When spear is held in one had of the soldier the swords appear to be resting on the waist belt. Shields are invariably made in rectangular and circular designs with spikes and knobs fitted in front. Breast plates, body armour and protective boots for legs are very often met with. Among other notable weapons we trace battle-axes, clubs (*gada*), hammer (*mudgara*), noose, disc (*chakra*), bow, arrow, quiver filled with arrows, daggers, tridents, goad, gauntlets, etc.

[101]In this connection it will not be out of place to discuss the word Bhujavala, apparently a military designation which survives even today in Orissa. Scholars associate this title with the Telugu Choda Somesvar-III who ruled in Sonepur area towards the final stage of Somavamsi rule. "Like Keshari and *Gajapati*, *Bhujavala* was a popular title or name by which all the Telugu Choda rulers of Sonepur were known. It means the ruler who depends on the strength of his own arms. The virudas of the Telugu Choda rulers found in their copper plate records begin as ari-durdhara-vara-bhuj-asibhasura, etc. They therefore claimed that their arms were so strong that they could wield such swords as could be carried with difficulty by their enemies. This claim would have given them the popular name Bhujavala. Bhujavala as a title or surname still survives in Orissa. A chieftain bearing the title Bhujavala rose into revolt during the Bhuyan rebellion in Keonjhar during the rule of Dhanurjaya Banta Deo."

[102]Thus the rule of the Somavamsi dynasty which survived more than two centuries in Orissa gives us immense materials to understand its prowess based upon sound military organisation and dynamic leadership. But nevertheless the Oriya people who formed the core of the fighting forces of the Somavamsi army should not be forgotten. It was the boundless spirit and fighting ability of the Oriya race that kept the Somavamsi banner flutter for such a long period.

Ganga Dynasty

[103]With the decline of the Somavansi dynasty and disintegration of their kingdom, the Gangas came forward to avail of the opportunity and to create for themselves a big empire. It was Anantavarman ChodaGangadeva of this dynasty who united the whole of Kalinga within its traditional boundary between river Ganges and Godavari, built a powerful empire, which lasted under state of India against continuous Muslim onslaughts from different corners. From Anantavarman ChodaGangadeva to Bhanudeva-IV, with whom ended the Ganga dynasty, there ruled a series of kings, including Anantabhimadeva-II, Anangabhimadeva-III and Narasimhadeva-I who were exceptionally brilliant like the founder of the empire. The Hindu kingdom of Orissa in those days had to come face to face with Muslim powers of the adjacent lands and a prolonged conflict between the rival forces became inevitable. The Ganga Monarchs rose equal to the task and kept the territorial bounds of their domain vigorously defended and well protected.

Chodaganga had his ancestral capital at Mukhalingam but after the occupation of Orissa, he transferred the capital to Cuttack which was more centrally located in his vast kingdom. ChodaGanga built a number of forts in Orissa of which Jajpur, Amaravati (near Chatia), Chaudwar, Cuttack, Sarangagarh (near Baranga) became most famous. The Kenduli copper plate[104] revals that he was the master of the white umbrellas of enemy kings. The Kendupatna and Punjabi Matha copper plates reveal that ChodaGanga's army consisted of a huge infantry and a large number of elephants. Conquering Utkal he had taken away thousands of elephants, ten thousand horses and vast amount of wealth. ChodaGanga had an elephant force numbering 99,000 as it is known from the Rananki stone charter. From the

Ratnadeva title of Chodaganga it is presumed that he had a great cavalry force in his army.

Chodagangadeva was proficient in sword fighting and displayed his efficiency in shooting arrows from a long distance. He supressed many rebellious chiefs who ultimately owed their allegiance to him. The Chateswar inscription informs as king Chodaganga whose sword a veritable hermit on the sacred banks of the river of rut of the (enemy) elephants flying into a frenzied range, helped the hostile princes attain the blessings of salvations. The Kendupatna copper plate glant while describing his fighting ability maintains. In duels, before the blood flowing from the wounds inflicted upon his body with the weapon in the antagonists hands reached the grounds, kings (ChodaGanga) with the sword held in his hand cut them to pieces and made lie prostrate upon the ground". His waving of the sword in hand in the battlefield appears like flashes of flighting and clasp of the *arach* arm roaring like thunder for which no hero could venture to conquer him.[105]

[106]Chodaganga was succeeded to the Ganga throne by this four sons one after another during the period from 1147 AD to 1198 AD. The four sons of ChodaGanga though of attributed with any remarkable military achievement yet they successfully retained the empire. A series of ruler who among them Narasimhadeva-I was valant and regarded as great refer in this dynasty.Narasimhadeva-I, otherwise known as Langula Narasimhadeva in Orissa traditions, ascended the throne after the demise of his father Anangabhumadeva-III. He was by far the greatest ruler of the imperial Ganga time and his name used to strike terror into the hearts of the Muslim Governor of the Bengal. During that period the Muslims had conquered the north and south Bengal and had firmly established themselves there. The Muslims with their base in Bengal wanted to conquer Orissa and made several attempts during the reign of Anangabhima-III. Narasimhadeva-I faced this new political situation and challenge. He became determined to attack the Muslims of Bengal without waiting for their attack on him. Towards the end of 1234 A.D. Narasimhadeva appeared at the head of army on the frontiers of the Muslim Bengal. The Kandupatna copper plate of Narasimha-II describe the horrors of the wars on the following words. "The white river Ganga, blackened

for a great distance by the colyrium washed away by the tears from the eyes of the weeping Yavanis of Radha and Varendra and rendered waveless, as it by this astonishing achievement was now transferred by that Monarch (Narasimhadeva-I) into the black watered Yamuna".

[107]Narasimhadeva-I, who stands as the most brilliant ability, has been aptly described in the Kendupatna copper plate grants "The king surpassed all in his strength of arms and crushing his enemies all over earth enjoyed the unsurpassed pleasure of his kingdom for thirty three years". His achievements in the field of art and architecture were as brilliant as his achievements in the fields of politics and wars. He was the builder of the world famous Sun Temple of Konark. Many war activities were reflected in the temple of king Narasimhadeva-I. The two huge war horse of stone are still to be seen at Konark with their dismounted riders, most likely the war memorials which Narasimhadeva created after his victories in Bengal. From an inscription of the Lingaraj temple it appears that he also defeated the great Kakatiya king Ganapati of the Andhra country. Thus he was victorious in his wars both in north and south. His successes in wars and art and architecture were equally great and therefore his reign is considered to be the golden period of Orissan history.

[108]Kings under the Ganga were generally at the apex of administration and the command of the army. They led the army to the battle-field and as evident from the inscriptions and account of Muslim travellers were quite proficient in mounting horses, riding over war elephants, wielding sharp swords, spears and well versed in shooting arrows from long distances. During the period of crown prince, they also accompanied the kings in all leading war operations. The Gangas extended the boundary of Orissa from the river Gangas in the north to the Godavari in the south and the Bay of Bengal in the east to the territories wrested from the Kalachiris in the west.

In the Ganga inscription Senapati (Commander of the army) and Mahasenapati (Commander in chief of the interior army) also functioned as the defence minister. He always enjoyed the confidence of the king in the battlefield.[109]

[110]Kalinga Pariksha or Kalinga Dandapata Pariksha was a high office, the incumbents of which were known for their administrative

ability, high character and military achievements. Generally persons from high families, princes of feudatory families like the Chalukyas and military generals of high rank appear to have been appointed for the generals of high rank appear to have been appointed for the post. Among the Kalinga Parikshas, we find persons bearing the honorific titles of Patra, Mahapatra and Padiraya; persons bearing titles indicative of their social status such as Jiyana or Jena (a member of a noble family) and persons bearing titles indicative of their military rank or valor such as Senapati, Mahasenapati and Sahasamalla and persons with titles indicative their official status such as Sandhivigrahi, which may refer to the substantive post held by them".

The Ganga charters maintain three types of Sandhivigrahikas who are generally considered as ministers of peace and war. They are Mahasandhivigrahi and Sri Samanta Sandhivigrahi. Sri Samanta Sandhivigrahi is normally associated with office of the peace and war of Yuvaraja who bore the title of Sri Mahasamanta. Mahasandhivigrahi or the Brhat Sandhivigrahi was the minister who was in overall charge of the department of peace and war or in other words external affairs, under whose guidance or control worked the Sandhivigrahis. The ministerial status of the office of Sandhivigrahi is indicated by the epithet Mahapatra which usually accompanies it.[111]

The Chatas and Bhatas were two classes of the soldiers in the army. The Chatas constituted the regular standing army while the Bhatas were irregular forces and recruited only in times of emergency. The chief of the police was called Mahadandapani whose position was like that of the present Inspector-General of Police. Military officials like Mahapasayati, Pasayati, Dalapati and Nayak in addition, are available from Ganga records.[112]

Under the Ganga monarchs, there was a supreme commander of all the armed forces (Sakalabalapati) under whose authority should have served a number of commanders in chief, cavalry officers and officers of the elephant corps. The Srikruman inscription dated S.1157 mention one Maha Banavarman as Sakalabalapati of the supreme commander and one Sri Karna Mahanatha Senapati as a Senadhyaksavara or commander-in-chief. The inscriptions of the Ganga period further provide references to a number of military designations like Senani, Senapati, Senadhyakasa, Senadhyaksavara, Chamunatha or Chamupati, Dalapati, Vahinipati, etc. thus giving an idea to the division of Ganga army into sena, chamu, vahini, dala, etc., under the command of Senapati, Chamupati, Vahinipati and Dalapati. It is just possible to infer that the Ganga's followed the traditional practice of recruiting soldiers from the following sources, i.e., hereditary army (Maula), mercenary army (Bhrtaka), guide army (Sreni), the army of an ally (mitra), the army of an enemy (Amitra) and the forest tribes (Atavi).[113]

Some military scenes of Konark depict the soldiers, vigorously engaged in actual fighting. One panel is shown as foot soldiers fighting with sword and shields. The same frieze also acquaints us with the mode of fighting with an angry elephant by the help of long spears. One panel in the verandah of the platform represents a defeated party, paying homage to the monarch. In other scene a vanquished king offers submission to the conqueror, who proudly waves his sword. In the adjacent panel an empty palanquin, umbrellas and rider less horses are depicted. Evidently that belonged to the defeated king. In one of the panels in the interior of the Jagamohana of Chhayadevi temple, a seated king being approached by defeated soldiers.[114]

Of the six animal sculptures, the two of the warhorse, because of their superb execution and special significance, deserve our painted attention. In spite of years of neglect, wear and tear caused by the actions of the elements to which they have remained exposed in the open, Havall's[115] classic eulogy of them still holds good.

"Had it by chance been labeled 'Roman' or 'Greek', this magnificent work of art would now be the pride of some great metropolitan museum in Europe and America. Here Indian sculptor have shown that they can express with as much fire and passion as the greatest European art the pride of victory and the glory of triumphant warfare: for not even the Homeric grandeur of the Elgin marbles surpasses the magnificent movement and modeling of the Indian Achilles, and the superbly monumental war-horse in its massive strength and vigour is not unworthy of comparison with verochhio's famous master - piece in Venice".

[116]In medical warfare cavalry occupied a very important place as swift and lighting charges on enemy forces were possible only with the help of the cavalry forces. The inscriptions of the Gangas

reveal the importance placed on the organisation of the cavalry forces. ChodaGangadeva said to have maintained an excelled Cavalry. While discussing the war horses preserved in the premises of the Konark a temple R.L. Mitra[117] considers "He is very richly caparisoned with bosses and bands round the face, heavy chain armour on the neck, tasseled necklaces, jeweled bracelets on all four legs and a tasseled breast band which keeps the saddle in position. The saddle resembles the medieval ones of western chivalry, with a high pommel and well-marked cantle of a sumptuous saddle cloth. The stirrup irons are round, like those of our own cavalry. A scabbard for a short Roman sword hangs down on the left, a quiver filled with feathered arrows on the right while a groom adorned with necklaces and breast jewels runs at the horse's head, holding the bridle. The fierce war stallion has stamped down two of the enemy not kicking or prancing but fairly trampling them to the earth".

We notice glimpses to the war weapons like sword, dagger, shield, bow, arrow, mace, spear, battle-axe, etc., very prominently displayed in temple sculptures. The sword both double edged and single edged are often represented with pointed tips, rounded tips shaped like lotus petals. Battle-axes, body armour, boots, breast plates, head gears, noose, flags, trumpets, palanquins are some of the war accessories and military equipments that are profusely represented in the temple sculptures of the periods. Mace or club has very rarely been depicted in war sequence but they are held usually in hands of several gods and goddesses of the period.[118]

[119]The dagger or the short sword, being a handy weapon, was used by both soldiers and civilians. Shields as a defensive armour in circular shape and rectangular design are usually held in the hands of infantry soldiers. When not in use they are attached to the waist belt or fixed behind the shoulder. At times the rectangular shields are shown curved at both ends. They are fitted with knobs and occasionally with pointed hooks to pierce the enemy's body. Their outer surfaces seem to be fashioned with numerous decorative designs. R.L. Mitra[120] gives a vivid description of the shied of the warrior of Konark temple in the following words. "It in nearly two and a half feet in diameter, bound round the edge with a metal rim and decorated with an outer band formed of circular plates of metal bearing impressions

in relief of man, horses, elephants, deer, fishes, birds, tortoise, lizards and floral scrolls and having a scalloped inner edge. The medallion of a chaste design covers the centres and to it is attached a thick bushy yak tail chauri, a second chauri of the same kind, but with a differently formed handle, hangs from the top. For distinctive badges it has two well formed Lizards".

The series of rulers who occupied the Ganga throne after Narasimha I have not shown any marked display of their military prowess. Of the seven rulers who came after Narasimhadeva I, three bore the name of Narasinha and four Bhanudeva. It is under Vanudeva-IV the Ganga empire passed to the hands of the Suryavashi Gajapatis who again revived the lost glory and authority of Orissa and maintained it till 1568 A.D[121].

Suryavansi Dynasty

The imperial Ganga rule came to an end when a new dynasty named Suryavamsi dynasry came to the throne. This new dynasty gave Kalinga three illustrious emperors - Kapilendra, Purusottama and Prataparudra. They ruled for a period lasting little over one hundred years. However, Kapilendradeva was superb ruler among them. A born leader of man, he justified his accession by a remarkable reign of thirty years, a regin that was one of the most successful regions of the Kalinga history. In a very dark hour of Kalinga history when the independence of Kalinga was ruthlessly challenged from the powerful quaters of the Bengal sultan at Bahamani kingdom and Vijayanagar empire. Kapilendra not only succeeded in giving a bare protection to this empire from outside aggression but also carried on successful campaign into the lands of the aggressors and annexed extensive territories from the kingdoms of Bengal, Bahamani and Vijayanagar to the empire of Kalinga. "In the long annals of her listing no emperor of kalinga territory as Kapilrndra. He appeared like a meteor in the political firmament of Kalinga when dark clouds of foreign invasions were first gathering on her horizon and during that meteoric career he brought laurels to the glory of the motherland and caused a bright chapter to be added to her history.[122]

[123]The kings under the Gajapati dynasty enjoyed the supreme power of the state. From the reign of Kapilendra, the Suryavamsi

kings assumed high sounding titles such as *Maharajadhiraja, Gajapati, Gaudeswara Navakoti, Karnata, Kalavargeswara*, etc. The Suryavamsi records enable us to form a clear picture of their military organisations. Godavara Mishra, a celebrated minister of the time of Prataprudra, prepared very valuable treatise on military science entitled *Harihara Chaturanga*. It contains various rules and regulations for the Government in time of war and peace, besides furnishing relevant matter on welfare, array of troops, division of the army into four-fold divisions, military training, etc.

Sarala Dasa's[124] Mahabharata gives us an idea about the different divisions of the Gajapati army on March. The first division was known as the *Hantakaru Dala*, i.e., the pioneer force clearing jungles and making roads. The second was known as the *Aguani Thata*, i.e., the advance units; the third was *pradhana vala*, i.e., the main army and the fourth division was *pachhiani thata*, i.e., the rear guards. The king and big military officers were furnished with the bodyguards who were known as *Angavalas* and the detachments which were placed in charge of the captured forts and conquered territories were known as *paridandas*'.

Besides[125]participating in military expeditions, the infantry soldiers guarded the forts having strategic importance. The garrison at Udayagiri according to Nuniz consisted of 10,000 foot soldiers. Duarate Barbosa agrees with Nuniz. 'The people of Orissa', he writes, "are very good fighting men". The king of Orissa " has a mighty army of foot soldiers". According to Nuniz, the Raja of Orissa had 5,00,000 foot soldiers.

[126]The Rayavachakam makes references to the garidis or the gymnasiums of the Gajapati in his capital, and the kind of physical exercises with men of the infantry and cavalry underwent to keep themselves fit. It says that the gymnastic feats of all soldiers of the Gajapati was unparalleled anywhere else. These feats of physical strength and endurance consisted of heavy weightlifting. The training items mentioned are lifting of weight iron bars and balls, the hanging from a beam with a bag filled with stones and weighting paddes, held between the legs. It is said that this weightlifting was practised in order that on the battlefield, when it become necessary, the soldiers might carry away the enemy together with his horse. With a weighty sword called Rummi Martyakhandam, these soldiers would easily

break walls 100 yards (?) in width and would split the trunks of huge tamarind trees, as if they were the trunks of plantains. They break into pieces huge crowbars. They would twist several iron rods into a single thread which the blacksmith could separate after great efforts in their smithies.

[127]About the size of the Gajapati army different sources give us different accounts which may not represents the actual number of man and animals employed in it. The Muslim sources have sometimes exaggerated or sometimes belittled its number. In the Bruhan-in-Mansir it is stated that Kapilendra possessed elephants numbering two hundred thousand, which in obviously an exaggeration. Nizam-Uddin tells us that Purusottamadeva had encamped on the bank of Godavari with 7,00,000 foot soldiers. Azizullah writes that Kapilendra attacked Bidar with only ten thousand foot, which appears to be an absurdly small number. The figures given by the Portuguese writer Nuniz appears to be more reliable. He states that the king of Orissa opposed Krisnadeva Raya with an army of thirteen hundred elephants and twenty thousand horses. The people of Otisa" writes Nuniz "are very good fighting men". The king of *Otisa* " has a mighty army of foot soldiers".

[128]In one section of Rayvachakam an account of feats of strength exhibited in the Gymnasia of the capital of the Gajapati has been given. This account was given to the Viyayanagar emperor Krushnadeva Raya by his spices, who had been employed by him for ascertaining the military strength of the Gajapati Prataprudradeva. Some Southern scholars have considered the account to be an exaggerated one. Even granting that it is an exaggerated one, we have to respect the basic truth that the Oriyas of the time possessed great physical strength and were capable of showing wonderful physical feats. We veproduce below a summary of this account as given in further sources of Vijaynagar History Vol. III, PP. III.

"We entered the city, and saw the palace of the Gajapati, the Mansions of the sixteen patras, the Gymnasia and the people who take exercise theirin. Even the gods and demons are not capable of exhibiting such skill in physical exercises as they show. Your Majesty might have observed the skill in physical exercises shown by the great wrestlers of other countries; but the style of the people at the capital of the Gajapati is totally different. They alone are capable of lifting up such heavy dumb-bells. They lift them up, what is more, they life them up cross-wise . They raise a sack weighing 10 paddes to the height of the uplifted arm of a standing man and throw it upon their own bodies moreover, they catch the sack between their thighs, and suspend themselves in the air taking hold of the cross-beam (of the gymnasium). The reason for taking this exercise is thus : while engaged in battle, the troopers are accustomed to carry away their opponents bodily imprisioning them between one of their arms and the bodily imprisoning them between one of their arms and the body; if, however, the opponents fight without losing their hold on their steeds, they abandon their attempt, considering the opponent to be unmanageble. The riders on the armoured horses are not afraid of any wound which they might receive. They attempt to carry away under their arm such riders. The soldiers practise this exercise in order toremain firm corurageously(in their seats) on such occasions. They competely demolish walls of hundred feet with a rummi mattakhndam, Which is heavy enough to be carried by a man on his head. They also cut with that sword strong tamarind pillars as easily as they cut the pitch of the plantain trees.Two Crow-bars together on the ground they cut them to pieces with their sword. They bring a basketful of cymbal-discs, and twist four or five of them togrther. As the blacksmiths are not able to separate them, they place them on the anvil, and datch them (with the aid of hammer), and being them again in good condition for the next days use. Moreover, they break iron clubs at any given point.The wrestlers of the country who there return with a feeling that it is not possible for them to cope with their methods of taking exercise. The wealth and strength of that place cannot be seen any where else".

The entire population of Orissa involved in the military system of the Gajapati rulers. "During the region of Kapilendradeva, this total militarism reached its peak and was based on a stren dispcipline, an unquestioning obedience to the king and above all on the single minded devotion to lord Jagannatha who was conceived to be the only source of all powers and all inspirations".[129]

During the reign of Prataprudradeva (1497 A.D. - 1541 A.D.), the third ruler of the said dynasty, the process of disintegration started. The disintegration can be attributed to both external as well as internal. Externally, Prataprudradeva found himself faced with formidable enemies in three quarters. Internally, he could not get the whole-hearted support and co-operation from his officials. According to some historians during this critical period the wave of Neo-Vaishnavite religious movement, the prophet of which was chaitanya of Bengal chilled the sprit of the people and demoralized the whole government machinary ."The Chiatanya movement", Prof. Mukherjee holds "can be hardly blamed for this sad decline in military sprit of the prople".[130]

Bhoi Dynasty

The seven limbs of the body politic were i.e. the king, ministers, territory; fort of the state army was regarded by the Bhoi kings as the most important one. The Bhoi kings of Khurda had a large standing army. The extent of the kingdom, large as it was, necessitated the maintenance of a highly organised and well-equipped military force and the Bhoi kings devoted much of their time to the development of Akhada and strengthen the military organisation in the kingdom.[131]

[132]King was at the apex of military administration. He was in fact the Commander-in-Chief of the army. The kings of the Bhoi dynasty used the epithet "Gajapati" or lord of the elephants. His primary responsibility seems to be the safeguard of the country from external aggression. He usually led all wars to the battlefield. During the absence of the king the *Yuvaraja* normally stayed in the capital. There are instances when they also marched to the battlefield along with their fathers. The *Yuvaraja* became king after the conventional coronation ceremony. This coronation ceremony was not exclusively confined to the capital. We find reference to the coronation ceremony of Raja Divyasimha-deva-I in the palace at *Rathipurgarh* instead of at Khurda. In addition to the safeguard of the country form external aggression the Rajas of Khurda also considered it their sacred duty to preserve the sanctity of the Jagannatha temple and its rich treasures. They very often fought the wars in the name of Lord Jagannatha and the ruling chiefs of various feudatory states acknowledged them as the saviors of the dignity and status of not only the motherland but also their great national deity and temple of Lord Jagannatha.

[133]*Rajagurus* of *Vatsa* and *Kausika* *gotras* functioned as the prime ministers of the king. They were the principal advisers of the king in matters of all external policies and internal administration including religious affairs. They hold this responsible post almost hereditarily, except, however, in cases of incompetency and incapability. Besides looking after the internal management they accompanied the king into the battlefield. Ramachandradeva-I resisted the advance of the Nizam's forces with his Mughal commander, Murad Khan, and

his trusted *Rajaguru Paramalakshmi*. Similarly *Bardhan* Rajaguru who accompanied Ramachandradeva-I to the battlefield was killed.

[134]The Bhoi kings used to confer titles on chiefs various places from time to time. This was either in appreciation of their loyalty or devotion or for their meritorious service rendered in war. " Even in the fallen condition of Rajahs of Koordah", Ewer wrote, "they continued to exercise regal privilege of conferring titles on the inhabitants of the *Mouglebundee* and the *Gurjhat* countries which was never objected to by the Mahrattas". I am informed, indeed, "He further remarked, "that no title granted by the Maratha Government was considered to confer any distinction in Orissa, until confirmed by the Rajahs of Koordah". Even Raja Mukunda Deva II while living as pensioner on the bounty of the British Government frequently conferred titles on the natives of Cuttack.

[135]Various titles were conferred upon the chiefs who were directly under the Raja.

	Chiefs	***Titles***
1.	GangaPada	Bariganjan
2.	Baunsagarh	Fatesingh
3.	Kamaguru	Jhapatsingh
4.	Barunai Jagannatha, Cuttack	Dalei
5.	Siko	Bahuvalendra
6.	Bangaroba	Uttarkabata
7.	Rathipur	Ranasingha
8.	Ghatikiagarh	Champatiray
9.	Ranpur	Dakhinkabata
10.	Namagaria	Ranavada
11.	Nandapur	Baliarsingha
12.	Andharua	Gadavada
13.	Kasanda	Dalbehera
14.	Baghamari	Mansingh
15.	Bolgarh	Raisingh
16.	Kusupalla	Balabantaray
17.	Girima	Chamupati
18.	Kuria	Mattagajsingh
19.	Konkal	Pattanaik
20.	Rodanga	Bakshi Bidyadhar
		Bhramaravara Ray
21.	Garamanitri	Paikray
22.	Dhauligarh	Sangramsingh

[136]The titles used by some of the rulers and Zamindars who were once under the suzerainty of the Bhoi kings of Khurda are available.

	Rulers	Titles
1.	Badamba	Virabar Mangaraj Mohapatra
2.	Dhenkanal	Mahendra Bahadur
3.	Hindol	Mardaraj Jagadeva
4.	Khandapara	Mardaraj Bhramaravara Ray
5.	Narasinghpur	Manisingh, Harichandan, Mahapatra
6.	Nayagarh	Mandhata
7.	Ranpur	Vajradhara, Narendra, Mahapatra
8.	Talcher	Viravara, Harichandan, Mahapatra
9.	Tigiria	Viravara Chamupatisingh Mahapatra
10.	Nilagiri	Mardaraj Harichandan

	Zamindars	Titles
1.	Madhupur	Vieavara Dhira Narendra
2.	Sukinda	Harichandan, Mahapatra
3.	Chadra	Narendra
4.	Dompara	Bhramaravara Ray
5.	Parikud (Banpur)	Manisingh, Harichandanm, Mardaraj, Bhramaravara Ray
6.	Banki	Bhramarvara, Scrichandan
7.	Tarala	Harichandan
8.	Surangi	Harichandan, Jagadeva
9.	Tikkali	Harichandan, Jagadeva
10.	Khallikota	Mardaraja
11.	Pachikota	Narendra Mohapatra
12.	Balarampur	Dhira, Viravara,Harichandan
13.	Chausasthipur	Viravara, Chhotara,Bhuyan,Mahapatra

The author scholar also visited many paika villages of Orissa like Badapari, Kuhudi Gada etc, where he found titles like Bhramaravara Ray and Mansingh respectively.

Dalbeheras were the hereditary military chiefs of the kingdom. They were head of the military contingents and in charge of the garhs of fortresses of brick, stone or mud. They enjoyed certain jagirs under very nominal quit rent called Tanki for their maintenance. They are bound by agreements with the king to perform military services. They supplied paikas in war and certain proportions of grain and cloth for the kings wardobe and household expenditure. The dalaee was inferior in rank to the dalbehera. He usually resided in the garh or mud hovel surrounded by a stockade, a fence of bamboos, and a mud wall or often by no enclosure at all. He commanded the devices of a number of *Paikas*[7]. The Dalaee was ready at all times to obey the order of the paika and performe other services like swetting his retinue on occasions of state, keeping guard of his palace defending a pass or attacking the possession of a neighbour.[137]

[138]The *Dalaaee* was inferior in rank to the *Delbehera.* He usually resided in the *garh* or mud hovel surrounded by a stockade, a fence of bamboos, a mud wall or often by no enclosure at all. He commanded the services of a number of the Paiks. The *Dalaee* was ready at all times to obey the order of the *Raja* and perform other services like swelling his retinue on occasions of state, keeping guard at his palace defending a pass or attacking the possession of a neighbor. Besides they had the power to apprehend and punish criminals and maintain peace in their respective areas. They enjoyed also rent-fee *Jagir* in lieu of the their services. They were held responsible for the collection of rents and for the entire management of their *Mahalas*. The *Naiks* of Banapur area had to perform similar duties in subordination to the *Bisoye*e as the *Dalaee* to the *Dalbehera*.

[139]*Pradhans* of villages acted as headmen of their villages and looked after collection of revenue and maintenance of law and order.The Gajapati army under the Bhoi rulers of Khurda was divided into infantry, cavalry and elephant forces. Next to the king, the *Bakshi* was in charge of the operation of army in the battlefield. The *Garjat Rajas* regarded the *Bakshi* as second to the representative of the ancient royal family of Orissa. The *Bakshis* were generally of royal blood and enjoyed the other epithet *Vidyadhara*. Bakshi Jagabandhu was matrimonially related with the king of *Shergarh* in *Ghumsara* border and *Baramba* in Orissa. He was the fountain-head of duty, courage and velour. The success of failure in war depended upon the strategy employed by him.

Raja Mahindra Bahadur, has gone down in the pages of history of the outstanding achievements of war, for the soldiers were also bestowed with highest military awards like Kalika Prasad, Mulk Maidan, Chandi Prasad, Balabhadra Prasad, Krishna Prasad Jaiwal, Jamber,

Nishapati, Ghana Garjan, Satru Mardan, Chaupahal, Mahabal, Madan Mohan, Durga Bandi.[140]

It is said that the Gajapati Raja of khurda conferred upon him the title of Mahendra Bahadur which is borne by the chiefs of Dhenkanal as hereditary right the army of Dhenkanal. During the rule of the Raja consisted of 10, 000 paiks, 1800 Telgu and 500 Nagas. The Raja was himself fund of wrestling and had recruited 13 wrestlers from outside Orissa to impact his soldiers training in gymnastics every day.[141]

[142]*Paiks* formed the main contingent of infantry militia of the Bhoi Gajapati and other rulers of *garjat* states of Orissa during the period. The military powers of these rulers entirely depended on the unflinching courage and loyalty of this formidable class of people. During peace time, the *Paiks* turned cultivators and their hereditary *Jagir* lands. When the bugles blew for battle they left the plough, donned tiger-skin dresses and chain armour and marched to meet the enemy. A. Sterling writes: "The Paiks or landed militia combine with the most profound barbarism and the blindest devotion to the will the their chiefs, a ferocity and unquietness of disposition which have ever rendered them an important and formidable class of population of the province. They are paid by service lands which they cultivate with their own hands in time of peace, subject to the performance of certain military and police duties whenever called on by their chiefs."

As regards strength of the militia Abul Fazl estimates the number of *Paiks* or *Zamindari* militia liable to the required for the service of the state according to the condition of the tenure of the *Zamindaris*, to be about 155,000 for the district of Cuttack and Midnapur. This he, however, thought formed but a small part of the entire force maintained by these chiefs. The *Paiks* of *Kujanga* were estimated in 1817 to be about 2,000 to 3,000 and those of *Kanika* nearly the same. During the period of the Bhoi kings of Khurda the number of Paiks was from 10,000 to 12,000[143]. The *Raja* of Dhenkanal fought with the Marathas with an army of 10,000 *Paiks*, 1.800 *Telugus* and 500 *Nagas*. [144]

The military organisation during the Bhoi period was efficient. That was ably managed may be evidence from the extent of territory held by them. The British authorities were so much impressed by the superior force of the paiks that they did not hesitate to record their appreciation about it. "However wild and motley their appearance and composition," Stirling wrote, "they certainly did not fight badly, when encouraged atleast by the proximity of their Jungles, since we find them constantly sustaining the most bloody battle with the mughals, and it may be doubled whether they were not superior to any infantry which the Berar marathas even brought into the field during their Government of the province".[145]

The Bhoi kings of Khurda as well as the feudatory chiefs of Orissa maintained their own cavalry corps to take up measures against the fighting Mughal army and depredations of the Maratha force. Though Orissa was not very famous for good breed of horses, they must have been obtained from distant lands. We have consistent references to the division of Orissa army into cavalry force since the days of the *Gangas* and the imperial *Gajapatis*. Large number of panels in the temples of Orissa represent cavalry as one of the main contingent of the Orissan army. The horses are well caparisoned and the soldiers on them equipped with long spears, swords and shields. At times they march to the battlefield with the national banner. The Sanskrit and Oriya military treatises of Orissa referred to earlier are replete with accounts of the cavalry force. Names of eight prominent horses of the Bhoi kings are available to us from records. They are *(a) Rajahans, (b) Jayamangal, (c) Adilakshmi, (d) Bhudevi (e) Bijayalakshmi, (f) Jagamohini (g) Panchakalyani (h) Ucharisraba.*[146]

The predecessors of the Bhoi rulers of Orissa were mainly depending on the elephants for waging successful wars in distant lands and defending their kingdom from the onslaughts of the Muslims. Orissa was noted for best breeds of elephants from time immemorial. The rulers of the *Ganga* and *Suryavamsi Gajapatis* were in the habit of using the royal epithet "Gajapati". The Bhoi rulers of Khurda too continued to use the name epithet but number of elephants in their army reduced to a very lower extent. The small kingdom of Khurda maintained as many as 360 elephants of which 34 bore distinct names.[147] They are: -

1. Sundaragaja	2. Senapati
3. Raja	4. Narasingha

5. Gopalmurty
6. Balaramamurty
7. Govindamani
8. Mrutunjaya
9. Prataprau
10. Abobal
11. Bedardei
12. Udayadri
13. Seshabala
14. Chakrapani
15. Srinatha
16. Anantamani
17. Bikramanka
18. Karamrau
19. Jayabanta
20. Birat
21. Harikrishna
22. Nilakantha
23. Prakashrau
24. Kumaraswami
25. Garudadri
26. Arunachala
27. Paramjyoti
28. Gadadbara
29. Damodara
30. Birabara
31. Bhima
32. Barahamurti
33. Gajadhipati
34. Parambrahma

[148]Pals, a contemporary British traveler, gives a graphic account of the maintenance of elephant corps as well as their equipments: "The elephants in the same way are covered with caparison of velvet and gold with fringes and rich clothes of many colours and with bells so that the earth resounds, and on their heads are painted faces of giants and other kinds of great beasts. On the back of each one of them are three or four men, dressed in their quilted tunics and armed with shields and javelins and they are arrayed as if for foray.

[149]The local rulers on several occasions arranged *Kheda* operations for acquiring elephants. The Rajas of Dhenkanal, Angul, Jeypore and many others close to the deep forests continued to capture elephants till a very late period. The fighting over chariots was long discontinued. But there is a reference to chariots in the army of the Bhoi kings under Purusottamadeva who marched to Puri to meet the challenge of one Kesodas Maru. The mention of these chariots need not be taken into consideration as war chariots. Since

it was the time of car festival at Puri, the Raja conveniently utilised the *Rathas* of Jagannatha, Balabhadra and Subhadra, which were available on the *Badadanda*. The soldiers of Kesodas Maru burnt these chariots by setting fire to oil and ghee-soaked clothes attached to bamboo sticks. These were thrown to the chariots and the chariots along with a number of the Raja's soldiers were severely burnt. There is no other reference to chariots as war machinery during the period under review.

There is no doubt about the existance of a naval force during the Bhoi period. Of course, we have not come across any naval war being fought in the sea during this period. Scarcely any historian of the period has made any mention of sea fighting. Even then, it is safe to assure that navy was not unknown to the Bhoi rulers. There is mention of Bari Durga or Fort in water along with other forts. There is also mention of vessels used for war purpose such as Lanjua, Khaijanga, Ganga Prasad, Nandia, Khudapa, Chaturi etc. In view of these facts there is one doubt that there existed naval organisation, although in its rudimentory form only, which was quite natural in those times. The main weapons used in a naval war were, of course the bow and arrow. The soldiers also knew the use of javlin and catapult. Fire arms appear to have been used to destroy war vessels of the enemy.[150]

The ships used by Sadhavas were three storeyed, each storey of which was utilised for special purposes. The names of the storeys (1) Sarbamandira (ground storey) meant for carrying treasury, horses and for the aristocratic female travellers, (2) Madhya Mandir (Middle storey) meant for the princess and the special political guests in reany season and (3) important of the storeys is Agra Mandira (Top storey). The top storeys was used for the soilders, war weapons and the king in summer and winter seasons. It may be calculated on the basis of the above references that Kalinga in the Eastern sea-board was famous for its sea born trade, colonisation in far-off cuntries and for spread of culture[151]

[152]The title of *Mangaraja* or steersman seems to have been associated with naval crafts. But it is a fact that the Raja of Kanika maintained a good naval fleet, which challenged the authority of the Maratha and the succeeding British power in Orissa. The following

extract from Hamilton's Hindusthan (published-1820) is highly interesting, throwing a flood of light on the now-forgotten maritime glories of the historic *Oriyas* and reminding readers of the invasion of England by the Spanish Armada.

"Prior to the acquisition of Cuttack by the British, the Raja of Kanika had baffled the Maratha generals in all their attempts to subdue him. The Marathas had been accustomed to embark troops and artillery on large unwieldy flat-bottomed boats unmanageable in large streams or near the sea in consequence of which their ill-constructed fleets always fell a prey to the Rajas light-armed vessels which were long, narrow with barricades to cover the man, some of them having 100 paddles or oars. When these squadrons met, the Oriya boats moved quickly round the heavy Maratha armada and picked off the man with their matchlocks, until the remainder were compelled to surrender ... On this account, the Kanika Chief and his country were viewed with vast horror by the Marathas.... To the British Government also its subjection presented a task of real difficulty.... The Oriyas were expert in stockading both their country and streams." .

In oriya literature specific information about ship building, maritime trade of Oriya sadhaba and paikas were available. These leteratures were 'Parimala Kabya'of poet Narasihna (1530 B.C.) 'Prashaba Sindhu' of Dinakrushna (1650 B.C.) 'Labanya Bati' of Kabi Samarat Upendra Bhanja (1685 B.C.) 'Gangavanshanu Charita Champu' of Basudev Rath.[153]

[154]Standard bearers either on foot or on horse back were given special status. They carry the national flags containing national emblem to the battlefield in great pomp and ceremony. The lowering of the flag in the battlefield signifies to the loss of the war. Similarly the on the occasions of victory flags raised high over the actual site of battle and the soldiers vie round it in great sprit. We find several traces of these flags carried by infantry men and cavalry forces in stone sculptures of the early period. Standard bearers are generally surrounded by musicians playing on cymbals and trumpets. Kings too, march to the battlefield in great pomp and rejoicings. Flags carried to the battlefield were generally represented with state emblems. The feudatory rulers of Orissa were each identified with separate emblem of its own. These emblems were not only represented in the flags but also figured in the front apartments of their fortified palaces

and in all important state documents. Below are given names of some such emblems.

Athagarh —	Radha Krishna
Athamallick—	Kadamba Flower
Bamra—	Conch (Samkha)
Baramba—	Dog metamorphosed in a lion (Heraldic Monster)
Bonai—	Peacock
Daspalla—	do
Keonjhar—	do
Boud and mayurbhanja—	do
Dhankanal—	Fish
Gangapur—	The deity of jagadal
Hindol—	Dagger
Kalahandi and Nayagarh—	Tigers head
Narasinghpur—	Scorpion
Nilgiri—	Karalla flower
Patna—	Charka
Rairkhol—	Conch-shell and lotus
Ranpur—	Sword
Sonepur—	Chakra
Talcher—	Tiger
Tigiria—	Five weapon

Muslim, Maratha and British Period

The Muslim rule in Orissa lasted from 1568 AD to 1751 AD yet the whole of Orissa was hardly brought under complete Muslim subjugation from 1568 AD to 1575 AD the Afghans were in possession of Cuttack and they settled on the border distinct to the north of river Mahanadi. Under Akbar the Mughals established their authority only on the northern portion of Orissa while the central portion was ruled by the native princes who enjoyed semi-independent status. Some of them only were given the title *Manasabadars* with rank in the Mughal peerage. The rest were regarded as *Zamindars.* From Golkonda in the south the Qutb Shahis held sway over the southern extremity of the province as far northwards as the lake Chilka.[155]

For administrative convenience the Mughal territory of Orissa was divided into five Sarkars viz.-Jaleswar Bhadrak, Katak, Kalinga Dandapata and Rajahmundri. Though Orissa was detached from Bengal during the period of Jehangir, yet it was entrusted to the Viceroy of the adjoining province of Bengal.The head of the province under the Mughals was known as Subahdar. He was later on called Nazim. The Subahdar was the vice-regent of the sovereign and was responsible for the executive, defence, criminal justice and general supervision[156].

The Gagapati Raja of Khurda was the most important Jamindar of Orissa who commanded two hundred forts and thirty-one feudatory chiefs. The Raja of Khurda was in the rank of a commander of 3,500. His own estate was crowded with seventy-one qilas and the feudatory chiefs of the hilly tracts under him had one hundred twenty-nine others. The two sons of Mukundadeva were assigned respectively with the title of Raja and the rank of two hundred, patta, sarangarh, and Alu with Derabissi. The Zamindars of Keonjhar, Mayurbhanja, Bishenpur, Futtihabad, Maraingarh, Karamangarh and Nag of Baghbhum remained outside the control of the Raja of Khurda. These ruling chiefs invariably kept contact with the imperial authority and very often disobeyed the order of the subahdars in regard to the payment of tributes. They always intended to be ruled by imperial farmans and rebelled against the Subadars in time of undue interferences with their authority or encroachment in their rights.[157]

[158]The rest were regarded as Zamindars. From Golkonda in the south the Qutb Shahis held sway over the southern extremity of the province as far northwards as the lake Chilka. During the reign of Shahjehan, the power of the Golkonda rulers was broken by the

Mughals and Qutb Shah became a loyal feudatory chief of the Mughal Emperor paying him an annual tribute. The western tract of Orissa including Samablpur region never came into the Muslim Fold.

[159]Under the *Subahdar* or the *Nazim* the *Faujdar* held the first place as a subordinate and assistant. According to the *Ain-I-Akbari* he was to guard the countryside and put down robberies and small rebellions with the help of local militia kept well equipped and in good trim under him. He was also to help in collection of tributes so he was both the local military and police officer incharge of territorial military division called *Faujdari. Faujda*r as Police Officers maintained law and order in his jurisdictions, arrested all disturbers of peace and committed them to *Faujdari Adalats* for trial.

[160]*Kotwal* was next to the *Faujda*r in rank. He was essentially concerned with cities and was the chief of the city police under the *Faujdar*. It was the duty of the *Kotwal* to punish all such criminals and misdemeanours as were too insignificant to be admitted before the more solemn Tribunal of *Durbar*. For the police administration of the rural areas the *Faujdari* was divided into two parts, i.e., the areas under direct administration of the *Faujdar* and the area under the charge of the Zamindars. Faujdar had police outposts or Thanas in different parts, each under a *Thandadar* who carried out their police duties with the help of armed men under him. For the exercise of the powers vested in him, the *Zaminda*r had to maintain a number of people under him. The servants of *Zamindar* may be broadly classified under the following four heads :

(a) Village staff including Village Watchmen.

(b) Frontier Police of a military character for resisting external aggression.

(c) Regular Police for external disorder.

(d) Personal guards or *Barkhandazes*.

[161]Since the *Zamindar* was to assist the *Faujdar* of his area with all his resources in apprehension of robbers and maintaining law and order, a part of his servants were to be kept at the disposal of the *Faujdar*. The *Subahdars* for the governance of the occupied portions of Orissa were stationed at the Barabati fort of Cuttack in the earlier stages. Subsequently they built the Lalbag place close to

the river *Kathjori* for it is the abomination of the Mughals to rest or sleep under the roof of a house that another man had built for his own honour. It is a building laid out in a number of courts in the Morisco taste.

[162]Pipli located midway between Cuttack and Puri also became a secondary seat of the Mughal authorities in Orissa in order to check the movements of the Raja of Khurda. For the present we find vast ruins of a mosque, several tombs and a residential building. A tower about 50 ft. high, 8ft. to 10 ft. diameter, half of which is covered in earth and rubbish and the other half with a stone staircase sort of thing leading from the bottom to the top is also noticed at this place.

[163]From the location of villages still inhabited by the Muslims in the Puri district it is evident that military experts of Mughal Orissa had made vast preparation to guard against this dangerous route. With Pipli as vertex, one line of defence extended to the south right up to Malud, a *pargana* near the entrance to Chilka Lake while the other line of defence extended to the east right up to the sea on the Kakatapur side. On the line extending from Pipli to Malud there are still existing a number of villages predominantly inhabited by Muslims –one of these villages is Ahmedpur about 10 miles south of Pipli. At Ahmedpur there are ruins of an ancient fort. On the line from Pipli to Kakatpur is located Nepaniagarh now known as Shujagarh after the name of Shujauddin Mahammed Khan. Here also is noticed the ruins of another fort.

[164]The Mughal Subahdars stationed at Cuttack had several engagements with the Rajas of Khurda. On many occasions they overpowered the Rajas of Khurda under very humiliating conditions. Some of the Subahdars also maintained cordial relations. The rich property of the Jagannatha temple has become the subject matter of loot and plunder of the greedy and ruthless Subahdars. To prevent their attack on the Jagannatha temple the Raja hade to safeguard the deities and property with great difficulties with the assistance of the neighbouring feudatory chiefs. During the period of Maratha depredations, the Rajas of Khurda played vital roles in supporting the course of either powers in the exigencies of situations.

[165]As regards the character and organization of the Mughal army it can be said that it was Turkish in its origin and retained the

Turkish character and words to the end. The army was divided into distinct groups, each under its separate commander, holding its allotted place in a duly graded series of ranks from a company to an army division. When led by a strong and able sovereign personally present in the field this habit of discipline and cooperation with other parts gave the imperial army an inestimable advantage when compared with the hoards of clan levies of the Hindus each little platoon of it could silently take up its position in the line and it could be shifted to a new place in the field with any change in the tide of combat smoothly and promptly like the pawns on a chessboard.

[166]The battle formation of the Turks brought to India by the dynasty of Babur was scientific, clear cut and effective till in later days luxury and excessive numbers ruined the entire machine. There was, first, a strong vanguard of specially selected brave and well-equipped troops with artillery, before whom spread a loose screen of skirmishers (horse-archers) with out fire-arms, advancing and falling back, without disordering the vanguard but skirting its flanks to the rear, if driven hard. Behind the vanguard came the main army- Left wing, Centre (the strongest in number of men and officers and inspired by the supreme commanders presence) and Right wing. And finally stood the rearguard or more correctly Reserve (which was distinct from the baggage-guard). This simple arrangement was later on further improved by adding detached flank corps to each wing and the center, when the total rose to unmanageable numbers.

[167]The Mughals have rightly been credited with several innovations in the Indian mode of fighting. Following the Central Asian nomads, the Mughals relied more upon their stirruped cavalry than on the war elephants. This created a revolution in the military strategies. The horses were, no doubt, employed by the Indians in the battle but in the absence of stirrups the warriors found it most difficult to manage them in the course of fighting. It was mainly useful for drawing a chariot in war, transporting the warrior or fighting small battles. With the use of stirrups the situation completely changed and the rider could now with his feet firmly in the stirrup stand up and shoot arrows, hurl lances or fire matchlocks. It was the mastery of the horse facilitated by the use of the stirrup that enabled the Turks of Central Asia in the 12th century to conquer India. The heroism of the individual Rajput warriors and the training of war-elephants

were of no avail before the rapid manoeuvres and impetuous changes of the Turkish horseman. With the Mughals a new factor, i.e., artillery, entered the scene. Though the mechanical artillery and gunpowder were known to Indians but it was Babur who effectively used the cannons in the battles of Panipat and Khanwa. Later on a full-fledged *Topkhana* was established. Navy also received new impetus under the Mughals. Efforts were also made to maintain orderliness and cohesion. Rules were prescribed for entering the services, regular drills, marches, camps, etc. The chariots and outdated Indian weapons were abandoned and only those were retained which could fit in with either the then warfare or for the pomp and show of the court.

[168]During Muslim rule, all most all the *Jaga-ghars* of Puri town and the most important role. The *Pandas* and *Pratihari* and other Sevayatas of Jagannath temple regularly practiced the sword, lathi, patta, and other weapon art to protect Lord Jagannath Temple from foreign invaders. The *Sahi Nayak* of each *jaga-gharas* were incharge of their physical training and discipline. A paika sahi was established at the entrance gate of Puri town. Gradually *akhada*s and *Jaga ghars* were established by the Kings of the Ganga Dynasty.

Weapons of the Mughal army generally consisted of sword, shield, bow, arrow, mace, battle-axe, spear, dagger, knife, matchlock and flint guns, light guns and heavy guns. The swords of the Muslim period were both straight and curved and also single edged, double-edged or both. Dhup, a variety of sword was about 4 to 5 feet long, double-edged, straight sword copied from the Deccan Sultans. *Tegha* was a curved sword. *Gaddara* was another type of sword, which was shaped like tegha but abruptly became more board and curved towards the point. Sword blades were made of iron mixed with other metal and there was so much of elasticity that it could be bent like the stave of a bow.The hilts of the swords were fashioned with costly stones (very often colored) and metals with engravings of floral devices and animal figures. The blades too had decorative devices and inscribed letters. The scabbards were made of with wood and covered with velvet. Those covered with lether were painted and vanished. Metal sheaths were generally engraved. The scabbards contained hooks or rings through which the leather belt was inserted and then it was either hung round the arms or slipped into the waist belt.[169]

[170]The development of fire-arms made the Mughal artillery effective. The first artillery consisted of tubes clamped to short wooden beams. These beams were transported by being loaded like logs in ordinary carts, unloaded on the battlefield and placed immovable each in its appointed position. Guns mounted each on a wheeled carriage of its own were later introduced from Europe and this convenient device was adopted in the Mughal army by Akbar. Wheels made the ordnance lighter and more mobile and thus the element of surprise in the concentration and shifting of fire-power became possible. Muskets were also greatly improved as a result of the constant care of Akbar in consequence of which increase in the power of hand guns, musketeers (*barkhandazes*) began to dominate the infantry arm and ultimately displaced the foot soldiers armed with sword and spear in the Mughal army.

[171]The Mughal bows were both single-curved and in the second variety two separate pieces were hinged with a metal grip. These were four to five feet long and made of wood, bamboo, horn, steel and sometimes of ivory. Mughal archer was generally known as *Tirandaz.* Their mace or *gada* consisted of a small steel rod with a single round head *Shasper* or lung-nearer an oval-shaped head. *Gurj*, a variety of *gada,* was having double head, one above the other. They are generally 3 to 4 feet long with head three inches in diameter. Sometimes, an octagonal steel shaft is attached on the top. This variety was called *dhara* and those having eight-bladed heads with basket were known as *gurguj*. Battle-axes of the Mughal period in general come under the name *tabar.* It consisted of a triangular blade with one broad cutting edge. The *jaghnol* variety of battle-axe of this period has a pointed head with two cutting edges. The shaft of the battle-axe measured 3 to 4 feet, head of the axe 3 to 4 inches horizontally and 3 to 6 inches vertically. The shafts were beautifully decorated with gold and silver work. Weapons like pistol, knife, long pointed blade, etc., were generally concealed within walking sticks (gupti) and profusely used during the period.

[172]Weapons like pistol, knife sand long pointed blade, etc., were generally concealed within walking sticks (gupti) and profusely used during the period. Body armours of the Mughal soldiers normally consisted of iron plates for breast, back and sides, helmet (top) for the head, *kantha sobha* (neckpiece), *kothi* (along coat of mail under

breast plate) and *angarakha* (ordinary quilted tight fitting coat of cotton up to the knee). These armours were invariably padded with red, green and yellow velvet or silk, *patka*, a kind of belt prepared of leather or cotton was wrapped round the waist to hold weapons.

[173]The horses engaged in regular battles were usually protected with armours. Kajim was a piece for the hind portion and was stitched over a quilted red cloth called *artak-i-kajim*. *Gardani* was a frontlet, *patta*, a headstall, *inam* reins, *zerband* martingle, *dumchi* crupper, *khogi* saddle, *ustak sharbrasque*, *bala* tang, ornamental tassels at corners of saddles, etc. The *mohra* was an armour piece to cover the face of the horse lest it may be frightened. The chained armour for the same purpose of wall called *andhiari*, the back was covered with *pakhara*.

[174]The armour for the hand was called *dastanah* and consisted of two separate steel pieces hinged together. The upper plate protects the hand from the wrist to the elbow. Velvet cloth was attached to the front to cover the fingers. Sometimes chains were stitched over a quilted velvet. It was worn round the hand fastened with hooks. Iron stockings were simply wrapped over the shoes for protection. Like horses, elephants, too, in the battlefield, are to be protected from the enemies. Several small steel plates were fixed to a carpet and tied on to the back with the help of thick rapes. Frontlets consisting of steel plates stitched to red cloth were also used. Wooden *howdahs* were generally placed on their backs. The hind portion was covered with chained armours.

[175]Mughal shields were extremely varied in nature and they come under the names of *chirwa, tilwa, phari* and *khera*. They are made of steel and hides of sambar, buffalo, nilgai, elephant, crocodiles, rhinoceros and tortoise shells. The shields were generally painted and figured with silver leaf and varnished with lightly ornamented with gold. Representation of stars and crescent on their outer portion was a common feature. Their diameter ranges from 18 to 26 inches. At times they are fitted with four or six steel bosses on their surface. Mughals introduced firearms in a late stage which came under the names of heavy cannons *(topa)*, light guns *(gajnal, hathnal, shatarnal, zamburak, dhamakah, deg* and *ghabarth*), matchlock and flint guns *(tufang)* and several varieties of pistols.

[176]We have a large number of Mughal weapons of war in the collection of the Orissa State Museum and its branch Museum at Dhenkanal. They include several varieties of swords like *tegha* and *dhup*, daggers like *jamadada, katara* and *chhura*, spears like *barchha* and *ballam*, shields, helmets and cannons. Some of them also bear Muslim inscription in them with aritistic finish in gold and silver. The armoury collection of several local Zamindars and feudatory chiefs preserves a large number of such weapons. For their effective use, artistic finish and quality many of these weapons under different names also continued to be in use by the Maratha soldiers and the army of the feudatory chiefs of Orissa in a later date.

Gupti, a stick with a concealed blade, was very commonly used during the Mughal and Maratha periods. Guptikard which was a knife concealed in a stick found reference in Mughal weapons. During the Maratha period walking sticks of many designs, which concealed blades inside, have been reported. A gupti could be divided into many pieces and sometimes a knife, pistol and a long blade, all assembled in one place and gave gupti its blade, all assembled in one place and gave gupti its real name.[177]

Taki Khan ruled Orissa from 1725 AD to 1734 AD. He was a bigotted Musalman, and in his time the Raja of Khurda found or affected to find it necessary to carry of the idol of Jagannath to the hills beyond the Chilika. Takikhan lie buried of Balaswar represented him as having spent much of his time in that town. He built the masonary tank, and reservior and the mosque and gardens known as the Kadam Rasul in Balasore. He is also said to have had a hunting place at Remna five files from Balasore under the Nilgiri Hills, a place still abounding with game, and whose name (Sanskrit Ramana a place of sports or hunting ground).[178]

Maratha Period

The Marathas wrested administration of Orissa from the hands of Mughals in the year 1751 and continued till they were finally repulsed by the British in the year 1803. The occupied portion of Orissa under their regime extended from the Bay of Bengal in the east to the Chhatisgarh tract in the west and the Chilka lake in the south to the districts of Jaleswer, Midnapur and Birbhum in the north. Orissa under the Marathas was divided into two political divisions one of which was distinguished by the name Garjat and the other a Mughalbandi. The Garjat was held by 24 tributary chieftains. The *Raja* of Khurda was the descendant of the royal family of Orissa. He was most powerful of all the chiefs. The Mughalbandi area was having the coastal strips of Cuttack, Puri and Balasore. The authority of the *Raja* of khurda in exercising regal privileges and conferring title on distinguished persons of both the Mughalbandi and the Garjat tracts continued even during the Maratha period. The lands of khurda held by the native prince were turned to be *Jagir* lands and placed under the *Jagirdars* who rendered some services to the *Raja* as per the terms of tenures. These Jagirdars as Dalbeheras continued to exercise some military powers. Next to them came the Dalees and following them the paiks. "Every state they possessed had a principal *garh* or fortress of brick stone or mud to which was attached a band of Paiks, a native hereditary militia. The Paiks were trained in the use of arms such as bow, arrows. The Maratha troops were generally armed, swords and also matchlocks; they were always ready to follow the command of their hereditary chiefs".[179]

[180]The Maratha authority appears to be generally averse to interfere in the internal administration of these chiefs. But they often acted as arbitrators in case of boundary disputes among local chieftains. The unruly conduct and insubordination of some of the ruling chiefs necessitated ruthless suppression in the hands of Maratha rulers. They had several engagements with the *Rajas* of Khurda, Mayurbhanja, Keonjhar, Kujanga, Kanika, Dhenkanal, Talcher, Hindol and Angul who became troublesome for them.

[181]The *Subahdar* of the province was at the head of both civil and military administration with his headquarters at Cuttack. Under him was a *Qiladar* incharge of the fort of Barabati with a reserve which was composed of musketeers, horse and foot. The number of the forces stationed at the fort of Barabati was not the same at all times. By the time Leckie travelled through the country the forces consisted of 1,000 Marathas and 150 Sikh horsemen and 500 irregular foot. From the information given by an Englishman who visited Cuttack in the later part of the eighteenth century the garrison composed of 300 musketeers and 20 or 30 horses.

[182]Under the control of the Subahdar there were a number of military stations each under the charge of a Faujdar with some horse and foot. There were some *Chaukis* under him; each of them consisted of a *Thanadar* with some men. Garrisons were placed in some parts of the country, one of them was in charge of a Faujdar commanding the fort of Aurangabad. A party of thirty-six horse and five hundred foot was usually stationed at Balasore. A strong Maratha station at Fulwarghat guarded the entrance of the town of Balasore. Some other important military stations that may be mentioned here were at Soro, Padmapur and Jajpur on the southern side of the river. According to Forster the number of cavalry stationed in Orissa was 2,000. It appears that when the British attacked Orissa the military strength was increased, 1,000 matchlock men at the command of Maratha chief were stationed at Guzurghat, Narasinghpur, Ramachandrapur and Kathipur in Mayurbhanja. One detachment consisting of 3,000 cavalry and infantry, under the command of Balaji, took post on the north bank of the Mahanadi to fight against the British. An army of about 5,000 infantry marched towards Manikpatna for the same of purpose.

[183]The Faujdar enjoyed both military and civil authority. He checked the disturbances in the frontier and also suppressed the rebellion in the neighbouring feudatory states. The Zamindars were required to attend the *Faujdars* with contingent of *Paikas* on all occasions for subduing refractory subjects. The *Khandaits* were responsible for maintaining law and order under the *Zamindars*. One of their chief duties was to seize offenders and produce them before the Zamindars. Under the Khandaits were a number of *Chaukidars.*

[184]As regards the nature of the Maratha army, the first point that came to our notice was its extreme mobility. The reason was that they were all horsemen, often with one spare horse for each trooper and they were not encumbered with baggage or tents, as they lived off the country and their hardy ponies fed on the wayside shrubs. They had no artillery, no workshop, no camp servants. The *Paindharis* who formed a regular appendage to the Mratha armies were not attendants on the fighting men, but looters, pure and simple; they were all mounted men and relieved the regular cavalry of some tasks like reconnoitering, causing distraction to the enemy by attacking his baggage in the rear while the soldiers were busy fighting in front and usually the pursuit and plunder of a defeated army while their

own regular troops were too fatigued after the battle.

[185]The second noteworthy characteristic of this army was that they always pursued enveloping tactics, intended to harass their enemy and cut off his supplies. They would not offer a stand up fight nor go forth to a pitched battle in reply to a formal challenge. The efficiency of the Maratha system lay in this that their vast hordes of horsemen could march long distances with extreme speed and secrecy, disperse for foraging or bewildering their enemy, and yet combine for striking a blow. This mobility also enabled them to break off engagement at any time they chose and vanish to a safe distance, without giving their enemy a chance of crushing them by pursuit.

[186]The Maratha Soldiers were exceptionally proficient in hurling spears. The *Pindharis* were equipped with spears of twelve to eighteen feet long. They are termed under the names of javelin, *barchha* and spear. The first two were hurled at the enemy while the third one was used as a thrusting weapon. They generally consisted of a steel blade attached to a wooden staff. At times complete steel javelins and *bachhas* are also available.

[187]Their mace generally had a knob on the round ball with sixteen ridges. The handle was cylindrical at either end and octagonal in the center. The variety of mace called garj or gurj consisted of a pike rectangular in section and with a globular head of seven leaves at the upper end of the cylindrical rod with knuckle guard surmounted by the tapering rod at the top. In certain cases the globular head of the mace was tipped with a quadrangular arrow head of steel and with many steel pikes projecting from the head. It was used to strike a blow on the head.

[188]The Maratha horseman as well as his comrade in the infantry were very lightly and scantily clad. The ordinary dress worn by these people comprises a turban, tunic, selah (loose mantle) and *janghtah* (short drawers) Officers, no doubt, were better protected with helmet (top) and an armour of chain.

[189]Cuirass or *Charaina* composed of four plates of steel was used for protection of the front. Complete suit of arms consisted of steel coat-mail, pair of armguards of embossed steel and a cuirass or

board belt composed of stripes of steel. The *zirh-bakhtar*, a steel skull cap from which chains hung completely of small steel rings, was commonly used.

[190]Several Maratha weapons of war like *dhup, khanda, tegha, talwar, targets, barchhas*, javelins, daggers, firearms including cannons, body armours are preserved in the Orissa State Museum and the armoury collections of ex-rulers of Orissa. Large hard of Maratha weapons of war used during the engagement between the ruler of Dhenkanal and the Maratha power and which find literary corroboration in the *Samara Taranga* of Brajanatha Badjena have been acquired from the Dhenkanal palace and displayed in the branch Museum at Dhenkanal. Weapons like *dhup, taalwar, jejjal, zambura, barchha, katari, yamadarh, gupti, dhal* are repeatedly used by Badjena in his work. In addition we can have wide knowledge as regards the military terminologies, tactics and equipments of the Marathas from the graphic narration of succeeding events of the said war in the book.

[191]The armoury articles presented in the Darbar hall of Jeypore Maharaja of Koraput district appears to be the best in Orissa. The rulers of the princely state have taken it as a pride to collect the best products of weapons of the period. The Darbar hall along with the military equipments also contains a rich collection of our cultural property. The doors of the Darbar hall are kept open during the *Dashara* festival each year for general view of the objects by the people of the interior parts of the state. The weapons preserved in the durbar hall may be classified as follows on the basis of information given by the palace authorities.

(a) Khanda-	Gupta Khanda	
	Khamanakhanda	
	Sureikhanda	
	Dhupakhanda	
	Karch Khanda	
(b) Kati-	Kaingari	
	Jamadadha	Soga
	Gagada	Katari

	Chaqu Burjuli
	Khangarkoti Batel
(c) Tangi-	Parsurama tangi, Chilapakhia tangi
	Mota tangi
(d)Tangia	Mundi tangia,Pharsa tangia
(e) Dhala	Patta dhala, Phari dhala
(f) Bhusana	Saveli, Pati chela,
	Mukundapuri chela,
	Bhala, Banati, Sibha
(g) Dhanu	Kasani dhanu, Batuli dhanu
(i) Khanda	KandaKena kanda, Kasani kanda, Bitakanda
(i) Chakra	
(j) Nali	Odia nail,Kepu nail, Jhamak nail, Barambai nail, bodinali, Pavan nail, Rifle, Magazine, Hand Martin, Sinder, Britchload, Command, Odia pistol, Kepu pistol, Revolver, Topa, Totatopa.
(k) Kada vindu	Topar, Patti Dostana

[192]In addition, helmets of iron and brass, *sanju, kamana, barchha, badau, bandhuka,* cannons, quivers filled with arrows, equipments of infantry, cavalry and elephant forces, *hawadas, tamjans*, whelled carriers of cannons, *bankachhuri*, gunpowder containers, light equipments, etc., are other most important objects of display in the Durbar hall.

[193]Similarly the armoury collection of the Orissa State Museum which finds place in the gallery and central store were mostly acquired from Khurda area, haladiagarh, Baramba and Narasinghpur palaces and Barabati fort and Lalbag palace of Cuttack town represent weapons and fire-arms of the Mughal, Maratha and Bhoi Gajapati period. They are *dhup khanda, talwar, kgadgas, jamadhar, katari, chhura, guptis, dhalas, bankachuras, ballams, barchhas, kuntas, bhalis, battle axes, kati,* axe, guns of various make, pistols, *jejjals, ganthias,* wheeled

cannons, *bandhukas,* helmets, goads, javelins, *sanjus, vadi bandhukas*,bows, and arrows of different make and gradations. Recently eight huge cannons from Barabati fort and two from Lalbagh palace. of cuttack have been added to the collection. Huge cannons are still lying in the premises of Ravanshaw College, Cuttack, S.D.O.'s office, Khurda, Chandavali bus stand of Balasore district, old palace premises of Jeypore *Maharaja* and Narayana Patna of Koraput district. The armoury stores of local *Zamindars* when explored thoroughly will add to our knowledge in this respect.

The Maratha soldiers, popularly known as Pindaris, were very proficient in wielding javelins, *barchha*, and spears of twelve to eighteen feet long. The first two types were hurled at the enemy while the third one was used as a thrusting weapon. They generally consisted of a steel blade attached to a wooden staff. At times complete steel javelins and brachhas are also available.[194]

By and large, the Maratha rule in Orissa was Military in character. The general administration of the province was in charge of a Subdar who was appointed directly from Nagapur. He led both the lives and the military administration with headquarters at Cuttack. The fort of Barabati was a garrison in charge of a Qiladar. The garrison contained artillery, cavalry and infantry forces. The province had several military outposts located at strategic places and faujdars. Baleswar in the north and Malud in the south were two most important strategic places where troops were stationed. To ensure quick mobilisation, the Maratha had as many as 2000 cavalry post in Orissa.[1 95]

[1 96]The Maratha troops were generally armed with muskets and matchlocks, swords and targets, spears and lances, daggers and clubs and bows and arrows. The muskets and matchlocks were used chiefly in bush fighting where when they have made a discharge they made the retreat in a hurry to their main body. But their chief dependence was their sword and targets. Their swords are, generally speaking, of an admirable temper and they are well trained up to the exercise of them, so that on al occasions in battle, they quit their musket and betake themselves to them with great success. As to their targets they are exactly round conveying almost to a point on the outside, light and covered with so smooth and hard a varnish or lacquer that if tolerably good, they will easily turn a pistol-ball and at hard a

varnish or lacquer that if tolerably good, they will easily turn a pistol-ball and at some little distance a musket one. They also have among them excellent slingers and archers.

[197]The Marathas continued the practice of using the bows and arrows which were generally of bamboo and steel. They often used cross bows. Their shields were mostly manufactured in raw hides or steel and designed in round shape.

In the cavalary charge swords were more reliable than muskets or bankbooks. Maratha swords were both straight and curved. Patta, a variety of Maratha sword, is double edged, straight and having a long knuckle guard. Sometimes narrow bladed straight repairs with gunlet bilts are found. The Khanda which the Marathas used had both board blades and curved blades[198].

At the time of Shivaji the great Maratha king, the love for indigenous physical culture reached the highest pitch. Almost all the gymnasiums were centres of military training. Even the valleys of the western military practice. Shivaji himself was an export in handling all weapons and in horse riding. Practically every Maratha was trained in handling weapons like sword, patta, spear, dagger etc[199].

British Period

The advent of British rule in India resulted in a rapid deterioration of the Indian system of physical culture and particularly the practice of sword fight, lance, Patta, jambia, farigada etc. The defence of the country fell into the hands of the alien rulers and they thought that their rule would be safe only of the Indians were prohibited from keeping weapons of war and were made clerks and teachers. Accordingly they passed the Arms Act and thereby prohibited the use of any kind of arms and banned the activities of the Akhadas and Vyayamshalas that were promoting the indigenous system of physical culture and military practice[200].

When British established their rule in south Orissa in 1766 and in North Orissa in 1803 the Orissan chiefs registered the establishment of British rule that is called the Resistance movement being the first phase of Indian freedom struggle. When the British took over the administration of Ganjam in 1766 the *Rajas* of Parlakhemundi, Mohuri,

Althagarh, Ghumsur, etc. rose against the British administration. Naturally they had to be put down. The insurrection of Orissan chiefs of Ganjam was temporary because there were risings in Parlakhemundi in the period 1799-1818 and in Ghumsar in 1801 - 1818. There were further serious troubles in Parlakhemundi and Ghumsar during the period 1821 - 1836. The trouble was so serious that Mr. George Russel was appointed as special commissioner for putting down the rebellion in Parlakhemundi and Ghumsur. After much trouble the rebellion was put down. 15 rebels were sentenced to death and hanged and 11 were sentenced to transportation in the Parlakhemundi rebellion.[201]

The Paika Rebellion of 1817:

In 1804 the Minor Raja of Khurda revolted against the British. The Key man of this rising was Jayakrishna Rajaguru, the guardian of the minor *Raja.* The rebellion of Khurda was ruthlessly suppressed and the leader Dewan Jayakrishna Rajaguru was publicly hanged. The *Raja* was dethroned and imprisoned. Khurda estate was confiscated by the British since 1805. The *paikas* fled away to the jungle and high land and carried on guerilla warfare for long time.[202]

Mahapatra Bhramarbur Ray, popularly known as Baxi Jagabandhu. The violation against British was popularly known as '*paika* rebellion' in Orissa History. The insurgents were of landed militia class consisting of *Paikas*, *Khandaits, Dalais, Dalbeheras* and *Rayats*. They were assisted by the *Kandhs*, *Savaras* and other tribal people, and were encouraged by the *Zamindars* and supported by a few Garjat chiefs. The rising was not confined to Khurda, Puri and other neighbouring areas, but spread all over the southern and eastern parts of Orissa. The '*Paika*' burnt the police thanas of Asureswar, Tiran, Hariharpur, and Gope and committed various atrocities in the surrounding localities. It was the first agrarian and popular rising in British Orissa.[203]

[204]The British rule in Orissa faced an explosive situation due to the imposition of Bengal Revenue, steady replacement of Oriya *Zamindars* by non-Oriyas, rapid deterioration of the economic condition of the Oriya *Zamindars* and the peasants, the tyranny and exploitation of the clerical staff, the soaring prices of essential commodities, non-availability of the approved legal tender, the coins and the widening gap between the people and their foreign rulers. A combination of

these factors precipitated an unprecedented crisis in 1817, which found expression in the rebellion of the *Paika of Khurda* under the leadership of Bakshi Jgabandhu Vidyadhara Bharamarbara Ray Mahapatra, the commander-in-Chief of the troops of the Raja of Khurda. He, like most of the people of Khurda, suffered because of machination of the *Amals*. He was driven to desperation by the wheel of injustice set in motion by the British authorities. Upon him fell the task of fanning the smouldering embers of discontent into open flame.

The rebellion was initiated by the movement of a body of the Ghumsara *Kondhas* into Banapur area who were thoroughly dissatisfied over the Company's administration and imprisonment of their king under false charge of murder. In the last week of March 1817 about 400 *Kondhas* entered Banapur, and indulged in large-scale looting of British property. The organised *Paikas, Dalaees* and *Dalbeheras* of Khurda rose almost immediately under their leader Jagabandhu. They marched to Banapur and joined the insurgents there.

[205]Immediately after this there followed looting of Government offices and properties, especially the *Thanas* and other Government buildings were made the targets of repeated attack. More than hundred people were killed at Banapur and the rebels carried of about Rs.15, 000 of Government money. C, Becher, the Salt Agent of the southern division, narrowly escaped but his boat on the Chilka Lake was captured and plundered. Then the rebels moved towards Khurda. On their way they were joined by hundreds of Paikas. This number swelled as they reached Khurda. Evidently, the Paikas were much encouraged and emboldened by the initial success of the insurgents.

[206]The rebels thus reached Khurda unopposed. The British officers without effecting any resistance abandoned their offices and moved away for safety of their lives. The treasury was sacked and only the Government buildings were burnt. Not a single house belonging to any private individual was touched. The rebels carried off one of the Barkandazes and killed another. A servant of the *Daroga* was slain and another person was wounded when the *Cutchery* was burnt. Another body of rebels marched to *Pargana* Lembai, entered the village Rathipur and killed Charana Pattanaik who had levelled false allegations against Jagabandhu in the past.

[207]The paika forces, being swelled to 3,000 by this time,

attempted several attacks on the British soldiers. Though much life was not lost in the earlier encounter the British camp had to abandon some of their baggage's in the confusion and decided to retreat towards Balakati. While preparing to resume their march in the night, the paikas again attacked them under cover of darkness. The British soldiers returned the fire and compelled the paikas to disperse in all directions. Impey returned to Cuttack after a most fatiguing march of day and night. When Prideaux reached Khurda the paikas numbering 5,000 attacked and plundered the house of *Rani* Mukta Dei of Panchagarh, captured her and her *Dewan* and were advancing under Jagabandhu to attack him. Captain Wallington who proceeded to Puri to prevent the outbreak of insurrection left instruction with Lieutenant Farris to attack Gangapara. Accordingly he proceeded with 50 soldiers. But as he reached there, he was attacked by the rebels and shot dead. A native *Subahdar* on the British side was also killed. Two messengers whom Lieutenant Farris had sent to Prideaux were also captured by the paikas who cut off their noses. Prideaux escaped with great difficulty to Cuttack via Pipli leaving all baggages behind.

[208]On April 7, 1817, 300 paikas with arms of various descriptions were joined by Raja Ballabha Chhotaray, the *Handmaid* of Garh Padmapur. They surrounded a village known as Hariharapur, to which the Tahsildar of Kothdesh sent an agent with a peon for the collection of revenue. The Paikas beat them, took away their clothes and destroyed the revenue papers. They also searched the Tahsildar. They plundered ten or twelve houses. They searched the *bund darogha*, looted his house and seized his uncle. Rebellion spread to the vicinity of Puri. The purchasers of the estates of Balarampur and Budhakera were violently dispossessed by the former proprietors.

[209]On April 12, 1817, about 200 *Choharas* assembled at Sukal village, at the south of Puri. In the same evening another body of Choharas, amounting to 2,000, arrived at Lokanatha Ghat at Puri. The Kachari at Lokanatha *Ghat* was set on fire at 9 o'clock at night. Several other houses were set on fire in the town including the house of the police darogha. About 150 people, variously armed, marched to the Judge's bungalow by the seashore while a part of insurgents consisting of about 3,000 or 4,000 stood at a distance from that bungalow. There was an exchange of smart firing for two

hours between the troops stationed for the protection of the Judges bungalow and the insurgents. By the time the insurgents came near the *sepoys*, the latter rushed forward, charged them and dispersed them in every direction.

[210]On 14th morning the main body of the Paikas numbering between five to ten thousand including Kondha from Ghumsar area entered Puri under the leadership of Bakshi Jagabandhu. The people of Puri at once joined hands with them. The Paikas from the *Rajas* private establishment also joined. The priests of the temple openly proclaimed the fall of the English rule and the restoration of the ancient line of sacred Kings. The Paikas had an action near the Jaganatha temple in which a European and some *sepoys* were killed. Captain Wallington's force was overwhelmed. Being thus hemmed in on three sides by the paikas and the sea, the British troops had beat a speedy retreat by the only road still open.

[211]Some Pandas of the Jaganath temple in collaboration with insurgents pillaged the treasure left behind in the tax treasury, taking away about Rs.3, 900.00. They also brunt a bungalow. The retreat of the British detachment made the insurgents master of the place for some time. They attempted to make the Raja of Khurda, now leaving at Puri, the acknowledged leader of the rebellion. But it appears that the *Raja* was not willing to take any active part in it because of his fear of the punishment which might be inflicted over him in case of failure. The town of Puri was strongly barricaded, various defences were thrown up in its vicinity and on the roads leading to it.

[212]Captain Le Ferre proceeded to Khurda with a large force and made a frantic search of Bakshi Jagabandhu in the adjoining areas but failed. He marched to Bajapur and set to fire all the Paika settlements at Bajapur and Kadalibari. Then he reached Kanas through Tapanga and encamped at Nuagaon after crossing the river Nuna. While continuing his march he met the rebels around one thousand at Dabonder and repulsed their attack. The Paika dispersed in all directions. He then reached Puri and drove away all the insurgents. On hearing his arrival the Jagabandhu fled away to the jungles of Banapur with some of his followers. The *Raja* of Puri who was on the point of making good his escape with 16 Paikas was soon taken into custody.

[213]Captain Hamilton who marched towards Puri met the insurgents

at Sarangagarh assembled under the leadership of one Dharamu Harichandana. With an encounter the insurgents retired with heavy losses. A body of Paikanumbering two thousand and five hundred made a feeble attack at Pipli on the British soldiers to rescue the Raja of Khurda but they were driven away by Captain Armstrong. Nineteen Paikas were killed and about eighty to one hundred were wounded. Captain Le Ferre reached Cuttack safely and the Raja was placed in close confinement in the fort of Barabati.

[214]The functions of the ordinary courts of law were suspended. Martial law was enforced at Khurda and Puri and then at Gop. Special care was taken to prevent the spirit of insurrection form spreading to the garjat states in the vicinity of Khurda. Rewards were offered to all who helped to capture the insurgents.

[215]In consequence of the movement of troops to various parts of the country, it appears that towards the end of May 1817 the insurrection was almost put down in Khurda, Puri and Pipli. But the situation in Kujanga and its neighbourhood could not be brought under control because the rainy season did not permit the march of troops in that direction. Taking this opportunity a body of 200 *Paikas* attacked the *Thana* of Pattamundai and wounded four of the *Barkandazes.* Another body of *Paikas* belonging to the Raja of Kujanga rushed into the *Kachari* of one Ramprasad who had the duty of transporting salt from Kujanga to the *Chauki.* They plundered it. They seized all the *Amlas* and carried them to Paradip. Eight *Barkandazes* who came to the assistance of the *Amlas* were similarly seized and carried away. Consequently the salt business of that part of the country was stopped. These *Paikas* destroyed the *Thana* of Tirun.

[216]S.C. Dc, analysing the various causes of the failure of the *Paika* rebellion of 1817, said that "The insurrection lacked organisation and cooperation between different groups operating in different regions. Nowhere did the insurrection make any impression on the British military force employed against them excepting at Puri where the British force had to retreat to Cuttack. But on the approach of the new force under Captain Hamilton, the insurgents left the town without even truing to strike once. However that may be we have to take into account the certain factors that led such sad failure of the *Paika*

rebellion. Firstly, the insurrection was not preplanned, it broke out on the spur of the moment, as such it could not be properly and efficiently organised. Secondly, it was confined to a few *Paikas* and their leaders and the mass remained passive spectators. Even the Raja of Tributary Estates did not come forward to join their hands, though Jagabandhu attempted to rouse them towards the end. Thirdly, the *Paikas* were accustomed to their own way of fighting, they had no idea of advanced military maneuvering and discipline nor had they the equipments and provisions to sustain them in their fight. In these circumstances any conspicuous achievement on the part of the *Paikas* was beyond expectation. That they mustered courage enough to make a bold and determined stand with almost no cooperation from any other quarter and without sufficient provision of equipment and faced the heaviest odds is deserving of highest credit. We cannot expect anything more of them in the circumstances."

[217]As regards to the charge that the rebellion was not a premeditated and preplanned affair and that it was just a sudden outburst of the spirit of revenge smouldering in Jagabandhu, P.K. Pattanaik observes that Jagabandhu had long before brooded over the execution of the scheme. The rebels had, at first, tried to place Gajapati Mukundadeva-II on the throne. They were perfectly aware of the strength which his name would have but to their cause and of the assistance they might have derived from the great body of the garjat chiefs in this regard. Even the refusal of the Raja did not deter Jagabandhu from pursuing his aims and objectives. The Rajas of Kanika, Kujanga, Nayagarh, Ghumsara, Ranpur and *Zamindars* of Marichpur, Harishpur, Gop and other places sided with the insurgents. The rulers of far distant lands in Balasore district were also contacted for the purpose Jagabandhu also maintained close contact with the Marathas.

[218]Commenting on the charge that the rebellion was confined to Khurda, P.K. Pattanaik observes that "Non doubt Paikas of Khurda were worst hit by the British policy. Their service land which they had been enjoying since time immemorial were resumed. Their land was assessed at the same rate as that of others. Steps were taken to obliterate them as a class. No wonder therefore they took a leading part in the rebellion in Khurda. But neither the *Paikas* alone had taken part in the revolt, nor had the Dalaees or Dalbeheras been the

leaders of the rebellion. It was the whole civil population of Khurda from Banapur in the South to Kanika and Kujanga in the north and from Puri in the east to the Baud-Daspalla area in the west that had participated in the rebellion. For it had been merely a work of disaffected Paikas or disgruntled Dalaees and *Dalbeharas* in the midst of unsympathetic and unaiding population a few decisive victories would have completely stamped it out. It was a rebellion long and deliberately planned, a rebellion which was nurtured and sustained by the whole population of Khurda or for that matter the whole *Mughalbandi* area and directly or indirectly sympathised and assisted by most of the *garjat* states.

[219]The failure of the rebellion may the attributed to the superior leadership, organisation, strategy and equipment of the British soldiers. Besides the indifference of a large number of feudatory chiefs, lack of open support by the Zamindars and Rajas in the course of rebellion, want of leaders except Bakshi Jagabandhu, the helpless condition of the *Gajapatiraja* and treachery of some local people worked against the interest of the rebels. The conciliatory measures and declaration of General Amnesty indirectly made it possible for early stamping out of the rebellion.

[220]P.K. Pattanaik has made an estimate of the organising ability and military prowess of Bakshi Jagabandhu in the following words: "The personality of Jagabandhu Vidyadhara is striking in many respects. His personal dash, courage, unflinching devotion and loyalty stand out prominently in the saga of the history of the rebellion of Khurda. No other person gave an example of resistance, so determined and so prolonged, as Jagabandhu to the British. He was subjected to all kinds of injustice, humiliation and degradation. The attempt to arrest him only steeled his heart and strengthened his resolution. The rebellion of 1817 was his handiwork. He not only organised the *Paikas, Dalaees* and *Dalbeheras* but also tried to enlist the sympathy and support of the people. He sent emissaries to chiefs of all states with a view to inducing them to join the rebellion. The extent of his activities was not limited to Khurda or to the district of Cuttack. Help was sought by him from the Raja of Berar to drive out the British from the part of the country. And the conspicuous thing was the secrecy with which this was being done under the very nose of the English officials

stationed at Khurda, Banapur and Puri. All these no doubt bear eloquent testimony to his great organisational capacity, vigorous drive and zeal. And when the appointed hour came he struck. He showed astounding military ability as well. The lightning rapidity with which the rebels won initial successes and the popular support they gained were a staggering blow to the British power and prestige. Of course he could hardly be a match for mighty and powerful adversary like the British and hence he could not succeed. Jagabandhu suffered defeat one after another. He, then, left the open front and took refuge in the jungle followed by a relentless foe pursuing in his tract. If on some occasions he fled it was with the hope of renewing his struggle with some chance of success on another day. In this way he continued his hopeless struggle for long eight years. One cannot but be astonished at the strength of his mind that sustained him throughout all his trials and tribulations during these years. Orissan history rarely provides such instance of iron will and determination. At last he accepted defeat when he felt that defeat was final. But then had he been born in an independent soil, his life story would have been depicted in other colours."

[221]Soon after the suppression of the rebellion, a committee headed by Walter Ewer was appointed to investigate into the causes of the rise of this revolt. He recommended several measures to the government in economic and political spheres. In order to quell the disturbance caused by the *Paikas* of Khurda. Ewer thought it expedient to strengthen considerably the number of *Barkandazes* to station several *Phandlies* in various parts of the interior and to establish an additional *Thana* at Banapur on the Chilka lake. The presence of a military force at Khurda and of detachments in Banapur would provide effective guarantee against the recurrence of any extensive depredations in the part of the country. Ewer did not like to restore the *Paikas* to their former possessions as he felt that would create problems for the government. They should be reduced to the class of common peasantry. Similarly he disapproved the idea of restoring the Raja of Khurda to his former position as this would enable the Raja to exercise some of his feudal rights over the tributary Rajas of the hills and the plains as his ancestors were accustomed to. Systematic attempts were made to disarm the *Paikas* and the *Khandaits*. Some *Khandaits* and *Dalbeheras* were killed during the rebellion. Some were sentenced

to imprisonment and transportation. Some even fled from the district. Ewer thought that elimination in this way of a number of discontented and dissatisfied *Khandaits* would be a very important step "towards securing the future in-offensive conduct of their followers."

In 1827 the Dalabehera of Tapang Garh, Madhab Samantaray rebelled against the British with the active support of the people, the Dalabehera resisted the British force for 7 days in a fight. At last he has imprisoned. The aboriginal people like *Kandhas, savaras* and other hill tribes of Ghumsar and Parlakhemundi rose in revolt against the British in 1815. The chief among whom were *kondhas.* The kandhas under the leadership of Dora Bisoyee continued the struggle for the two years. It also spread to the neighbouring areas like Banpur, Daspalla and Nayagarh.[222]

In 1849, a mass popular rising took place in Nayagarh under the leadership of Kamal Lochan Paikray. The rising was finally suppressed in 1851. The insurgents were imprisoned and the *Raja* was deposed. Before the great rising of 1857 Nayagarh came under the complete control of the British authorities.[223]

Orissa like other parts of India actively participated in the great Revolt of 1857 which is also described as the First War of Indian Independence. Of those great patriots who took the lead in the historic revolt, mention may be made of Ram Krushna samanta Singhar, Chaki Khuntia and Surendra Sai. Ram Krushna Samanta Singhar, the ex-zamindar of Balia (Pragana Burgan, Thana Jajpur) organized the Khandaits in August 1857 and rose against the British. So he and two of his principal followers were arrested and sentenced to 5 years rigorous imprisonment. Similarly Chaki Khuntia also called Chanan Hajuri played a pivotal role in the sensational drama of the great Revolt of 1857 in Orissa. He happened to be a panda of Puri by profession. Surender Sai of Sambalpur was yet another leader who kept the revolt burning for seven years (1857-1864) while in India it collapsed in 1858.In this connection, the secretary to the Chief Commissioner of the Central Provinces reported, "The Sambalpur District was perhaps the very last district in India in which the members of the disturbance of 1857 were finally stampad out." In fact it is no less a wonder that fighting with primitive weapons like bows-battle axes and countryside watchlocks Surendra Sai shook the very foundation of the British rule in Sambalpur while the British troops were fighting with muskets and howitzers. The other leaders like Madho Singh, Kunjal Singh, Hatee Singh and few other Zamindari of Ghess were also led the Great Revolt against the British rule in Orissa during 1857-1858.[224]

Establishment of Paika Company in Orissa:

In order to strengthen the newly established cuttack Legion, the Commissioner in Cuttack suggested for raising a military of local nature. Capt. Fraser, commanding the Cuttack Legion, urged the expendiency of a body of paikas for his troops as it would have offered him the opportunity of enlisting the local militia class. as the paikas were considered a fraternity bound to each other and their superious chiefs and the starts by a kind of feudal tenure first of all the willing individual were enlisted and then others were tempted through inducements to join Cuttack Legion.

Capt. Fraser observed:

[225]"the magic of thsat link by which they have hitherto clung to their Rajas, Zamindars, Kandytes, would soon be defeated, and their devotion to our government found nothing inferior to the corresponding race of men in the upper province".

[226]Thus a company of paikas was formed and attached as the 4th Branch to the Cuttack Legion. The components of this company consisted of one Subadar, two jamadars, seven Havildars, seven naiks and one hundred twenty sepoys. The British government brought, at last, this landed militia class to its fold and utilized their services in the best possible ways atleast for three decades. It reminds us how the East India Company after studying and watching the political situation in India, raised auxiliary and irregular forces which fulfilled their needs in acquiring power and territory these native soilders were clothed, drilled and equipped in the British style, which gave them a more martial appearance. The uniforms of the native Sepoys gave them a rock like steadiness of British infantry with an impossible figure on the battle field as their European counterpart.

[227]Consequent upon the transfer of the Cuttack Legion to the Brahmaputra Frontier under the orders of the Government of Bengal on 20 Dec,1822 the paika company was made over to the commissioner

of Cuttack to be employed under him. The authorities felt that these milllitia class would be useless and inefficient body of men if they were not trained and drilled by a European officer. It was the first important thing that they should always be effective the Government of Bengal approved of appointing a Europian officer on permanent basis to command the paika company. Lt. J. Waddilove a local officer of the Cuttack Legion, was appointed to the duty of superintending the discipline and the details of the paika company which was shifted to Khurda and hence forward it was known as Khurda Paika Company.

[228]The rules prepared for the guidance of the officers appointed to superinted the discipline and details of the paika company in cuttack appeared to the government of Bengal to be entirely proper and judicious and hence were approved and confirmed. Waddilove was instructed to explain those rules fully to the individuals attached to the paika company as well as to all others who might hereafter be entertained. The establishment of the paika company was for the present to be maintained according to the following statement which would give an augmentation of 5 privates at an additional monthly expense of 30 Rupees. Statement of the establishment of the Khurda Police Paika Company was as follows;

No	*Description*	*Pay*	*Total of each*	*Total*	*Grand total*
1	Subadar or	40	40	40	—
2	Jamadars	25	50	50	90
5	Havildars	12	60	60	—
5	Naik	10	50	50	—
1	Bugler	7	7	7	—
100	Sepoys	6	600	600	—
1	Laskar	5-12	5-12	5-12	—
1	Bisty	4-8	4-8	4-8	—
1	Pay habildar	5	5	5	—
				Rs 731.4	
	Establishment allowance for repair of arms =			Rs 22.1.4	
				Rs. 844.5.4	

Total Sika Rupees Eight Hundred and Fifty-four, Five annas, four pies.

[229]The duties of the Orissa paika company was heavy and burdensome. Detachments of the company were dispatched to different trouble spots to quell the disturbances. Their services were utilized in banapur, Ghumsar, Banki, Angul, Boudh,Nayagarh, Khondhmal,

Nilgiri, Kujanga, Mayurbhanj, Chainbasa and Sambalpur during the period for 1825-1857. they worked hard but got less pay compared with the regular sepoys. As they were treated as irregulars, they were denied pension. Even the services rendered by the man of the paika company could not be popular among the British authorities. Grievances of the disaffected men of the company were not redressed. On the other hand, they were warned and threatened of expulsion or dismissed. Gradually many of them were disarmed. The Government of Bengal declared that the paikas would no more be necessary and hence thought of dismantling the paika company. It was a death blow to the Oriya militia. At last, in march 1850 the paika company was dissolved but converted to the 8th Bangal Police Battalion.

The War Dance and Military Literature of Orissa

The *Paika* dance is a martial dance of Orissa. It is generally practised in Khurda, Nayagarh and Dhenkanal district of Orissa. The type of dance is performed by a warrior class known as *Paikas*. The primary aim of this dance is physical exercise and the infusion of courage in the dancing warriors. In ancient times this was a rehearsal for battle. It is a group dance. In the beginning the Paika dancers appear one by one in quick steps holding *khanda* (sword) and *dhal* (shield). Then they salute the presiding deity of war and begin dancing. All of them shout '*hai hai*' for excitement. They also utter some boli (rhythmical words) in order to raise the tempo of the dance which is accompanied by two earthen drums known as tikura. When the drums are played in high tempo the dancers dance and fight among themselves so quickly that any dancer committing the slightest error in timing is certain to be injured.[230]

The Naga Jatra or the dance sequences associated with the Sahi nacha or Jatra of Puri and its adjacent villages preserve even today the martial spirit of the glorious past when the empire was extending from the Ganges to Kauveri and when the Oriyas were really heroic people even today the marital spirit of the glorious past when the fight against the Muhammedan inroads for centuries. His feature, dress and dance are all heroic. He dances with a heavy load of weapons to the sound of battle-drums. He has ten main requirements for decoration on that occasion. They are shield (skin), sword, kukri, gun, round horn, iron shield, toilet box, bow and arrow, tighter skin and bell. His bow bears the face of a tiger and looks horrible. He possesses a long crown with a big flower at the end decorated with peacock feathers. He has a string of beads in the neck, feathers of Ara (a kind of bird with brown feathers found in the Chilka lake) in his hands, mirror and a string of beads on the wrist, golden rings, in the fingers, tiger's skin on the chest and waist, flags on the arrows, handkerchiefs tied to the hands, small bells attached to the thigh. He besmears his body with ramaraja (a powder of yellow colour) to save himself from the heat. He bears artificial beard and moustaehe. He decorate his forehead with Vermi in dress he looks like very ferocious indeed. The Jatra attracts thousands of people from villages and makes them heroic minded for the time. The dance is accompanied with no song.[231]

Ranapa nacha another traditional dance of Orissa, is often associated with its martial traditions. In this dance form the youths with the help of wooden or bamboo sticks dance in groups to the beating of war-drums and mahuri. Their dresses appear to be very scanty and uniform. The spirit and vigour with which the boys dance takes one to the glorious days of the past.It is no doubt performed in military camps to rejuvenate the fighting *Paika* soldiers.[232]

The history of Chhau dance is very ancient. It originated in the mock fights of the Oriya paikas who fought rhythmically to the accompaniment of a band of indigenous musical instruments to amuse as well as to keep themselves physically fit to meet any emergency. The origin of the ward 'Chhau' is still abscure. Some have found out an etymological meaning of the word chhau (from Sanskrit word chhaya, meaning shade-mask) and claim that the dance bears the name chhau for its use of the mask. This is the view of Seraikala school where mask is used. People belongs to Mayurbhanj school of the dance maintain that the Chhau has been derived from Chhauni, i.e., military encampment. The latter view seems to be more credible, as it is commonly admitted that this dance originated from the war rehearsals of the Oriya paikas. It is quite likely that Chhauni Nacha, in course of time, come to be called by the people as Chhau Nacha.[233]

Literature

Paika Akheda, a work in Oriya by Kanhei Campatiraya, is said to have been written during the rule of the Bhoi Gajapati Narasimhadeva in the early part of the 17th century. It is divided into twelve chapters dealing with different aspects of military affairs such as recruitment of soldiers, the weaponry divisions of an army, the medical corps. flags and their users, the navy and preparation for naval battles. military expenditions and construction of forts. He has given elaborate description of military costumes, equipments, traditional religious practices, organisation of battle-array and war music.[234]

Samar Taranga by Brajanatha Badajena describes the actual battles fought between the Maratha forces and those of the feudal chief of Dhenkanal. In this poem we come across for the first time in Oriya literature descriptions of real battles with the living protagonists on both sides appearing exactly as in-memoirs, war-plays or war-novels of today. Brajanatha's descriptions of the preparation for the war, the disposition of the cannons, the cavalry and the infantry, the emotions of the soldiers on the eve of the battle, the hideous shambles that a battle leaves behind with the piteous cries of dying and the wounded, the routed army's pell-mell flight for life are all depicted in matching words and colours without the least effort at exaggeration or for effect. The manly stirring address of the Raja of Dhenkanal to his courtiers who had advised him to retreat from his fort to avoid further reverses is worthy of being treasured in any literature.[235]

Rana Taranga by Bhagirathis, another unpublished manuscript preserved in the Orissa State Museum, describes the war that was conducted between the ruling Chiefs of Dhenkanal and Angul. The work has been divided into five chapters and although is a small kavya, the author has been very successful in illustrating the main events of the battle very intelligently. The cause of the war was border dispute and the rulers known as Raja Somanatha Singh of Angul and Raja Shyamsundar Deva of Dhenkanal. The battle took place at a place called Budhapanga located in the border area of the two estates.[236]

Phiringikali between by Madhusudan Vipra of Sanaputagarh in the district of Puri is yet another unpublished manuscript preserved in the Orissa State Museum. The work was prepared around the year 1835 A.D. It first refers to battle between Gajapati Mukundadeva of Khurda and Vajradhara Narendra Mahapatra of Ranpur. The cause of the war was due to plundering Khurda territory by the soldiers of the Raja of Ranpur. The author had also narrated the battles that ensued between the Gajapati Raja and the ruling chiefs of Dampara and Banki. The last phase of the work refers to the Garh Tapanga Yudha in which the *Paikas* of Garh Tapanga succumbed to the military powers of the British. The Tapanga soldiers under Madhava Routray showed exemplary courage and patriotic spirit for safeguard of their motherland. The author of the work claims to have witnessed the brave fighting of the Paikasoldiers.[237]

Khalikote Rajank Yasa Chaitanya Dasa contains the Account of the battle between the soldiers of Sri Narayana Mardaraja Deo, the Raja of Khallikote estate, and the army of Ramachandra Harichandana Jagadeva of Athagarh of Ganjam district. The cause of the battle between the two ruling chiefs was of boundary dispute. The British authorities interfered in this war and brought it to an abrupt end. The war appears to have been fought during the year 1850 A.D. The military weapons and fire-arms used in this engagement were *khanda, dholam chhura, katari bow, arrow, tarabari, pharikhanda, nail, chadak nail, topa, dhenuki*, etc. *Telengas* and Rajas were the main fighting forces of the army. *Changu* and *tamaka* produced the war music.[238]

Virasarvasva, another military treatise, was written by Gopinath Tunga, the Raja of Tigiria. The author has described the principles of warfare prevalent during the time along with the system of constructing forts of various categories, organisation of the army, arrangement of the fighting force in the battlefield, costumes and equipment of the soldiers, auspicious moment for commencement of the wars, nature of the king, minister and commander of the army, four-fold division of the army, use of war drums, recital of mantras during the time of actual engagements and so on. It is known from the colophon of the manuscript of Patanjaleya Yogasastra that Gopinatha Tunga of Virasarvasva was alive in the Saka Year 1710 or 1788 A.D.[239]

Viraparakrama by Vasudeva, another unpublished work on principles of warfare, has been preserved in the Orissa State Museum. This work seems to have prepared in the first half of the 18th century A.D.[240]

Budhapank Yudha, a military work by Nrusimha Rajaguru, refers to the military engagements of Raja Somanatha Singh of Angul with the formidable British power as well as with the ex-feudatory state of Dhenkanal. It provides vivid account of the bravery and fighting spirit of Raja Somanatha Singh and his ultimate imprisonment and death. This work is said to have been completed after the death of Raja Somanatha Singh in the year 1853 A.D.[241]

Yudhagita, another unpublished manuscript that finds place in the collections of the Orissa State Museum, describes the military engagement between the Rajas of Nayagarh and Ghumsara, the two adjoining ex-states of Orissa. The various weapons of war and fire-arms brought to our notice in this work are *ganthia, chadaka* and *jejjal*. The musical instruments referred to in this work are *dhama, damalu, damphanagara, bheri, turi, changu, bansi, kansala, telingi, manjara, mardala, virakahali and samkha. Khuntia Bhata* formed the non-combatants of this war.[242]

Fort or Strongholds of Orissa

It is an established fact that Kalingan Empire had a long temple and fort-building tradition since the 3rd century B.C., if not earlier. During these centuries many a fort rose to eminence, earned name and fame and ultimately be grimmed and dimmed by the passage of time leaving a remarkable history to the posterity. On account of constant attacks and vandalism of the enemies internal strifes between the monarchs they have been turned to dust but fortunately many a temple survived. Abul Fazal, the minister of Akbar, during his tour to Orissa mentioned clearly that Orissa was full of forts and each of five Sarkars (division) had forts with well garrisoned and trained armies.[243]

Durga means a fort in the Rigveda. It was used in the sense of a fort, or a stronghold.It was synonymous with pura meaning a rampart or fort or stronghold.The Brahmanas and Upanisadas also refers to the words pura and mahapura to mean the forts. In Devi Purana we find the construction of brick built walls which are indispensable in the artificial forts. The Ramayan furnishes us with a classified list of forts into river forts (*nadya*), the hill fort (*parvatiya*) the forest fort (vana) and the artificial fort (*krtrima*). They were protected by strong walls and ramparts and ditches were dug around for additional protection. Paikakheda gives us detailed information about forts like vana durga (forest fort), vari durga (desert fort), and giri durga (hill fort). The Mahabharata, on the other hand, reports different kinds of citadels in its Shantiparva. They are water citadels, human citadels and forest citadels. These citadels invariably contained an abundant stock of foodgrains and weapons and were protected by impenetrable walls and a trench. The walls were furnished with darts and missiles. The turrent along the walls were filled with armed men.[244]

Kautilya, the greatest authority on military science, classified the forts on the basis of their location. In his view they are of four kinds,viz; parvata (hill fort), audaka (water fort), dhanvana (desert fort) and vanadurga (forest fort). He explains a hill fort as one which is either perched on a rocky precipice or built in a valley in the midst of an encircling range of hills. A water fort, he says, may be situated on an island in the midst of a river, or on a plain surrounded by low ground or morass in which water is stagnated. Similarly a forest fort is either encompassed by many bogs and fens, interspersed with trees and bushes, or is grit by thickly set tall trees with undergrowth. Finally, a desert fort is one which is located either in the center of a wild tract dovoid of water or even of thickets or in a region sterilised by desert salt.[245]

[246]**List of the forts—**

Cuttack District

1. Barabati Fort — 2. Amaravati Kataka
3. Chauduar Kataka — 4. Chudanga Garh
5. Joduma garh — 6. Ratagarh
7. Teligarh — 8. Banki Garh
9. Baramba garh

Jajpur District

1. Baradiha Fort — 2. Jajpur Kataka

Angul District

1. Bataram prasad — 2. Puruna Garh
3. Tikarapara

Dhenkanal District

1. Bhimanagari — 2. Kodalaka
3. Dhenkanal Fort — 4. Motari
5. Kapilasa — 6. Bajrakota
7. Talmul — 8. Hadagarh

Puri District

1. Kalupada Garh
2. Kharagarh
3. Rathipur Garh
4. Sahajpari Kataka
5. Pipli
6. Maludagarh
7. Parikudagarh

Ganjam District

1. Jaugarh
2. Ganja Fort
3. Pratapagiri
4. Athagarh
5. Maltigarh

Khurda District

1. Sisupalgarh
2. Khurdagarh
3. Bhubaneswar
4. Bankadagarh
5. Kuhudigarh
6. Rameswargarh
7. Bualigarh
8. Kanjiagarh
9. Ghatikia Garh
10. Balabhadrapur Garh

Koraput District

1. Malkangiri
2. Jeypur
3. Papadahandi
4. Narayan Patna
5. Nandapur
6. Similiguda
7. Bissam Kataka
8. Boriguma
9. Gudari Kataka
10. Gunapur
11. Kotapad
12. Podagada

Mayurbhanja District

1. Hariharapur (Haripur)
2. Kusumia or Banakati Garh.
3. Rani Bandha
4. Santhilo
5. Mantri
6. Harichandra Garh.
7. Kurariya Garh.
8. Khunta
9. Bada belakunti
10. Koisari Garh.
11. Puradiha
12. Pathuria Garh
13. Itagarh
14. Dubigarh
15. Joshipur
16. Baripada
17. Mulapala (Ratanpur)

18. Khiching (Kichaka garh and Birat Garh)

19. Amarda
20. Similigarh

Balasore

1. Raibania
2. Jalesore
3. Karatasal
4. Kupari
5. Solampur
6. Ayodhya
7. Pratapagarh
8. Kans or Kanisali
9. Sujanagarh
10. Mughalmari
11. Gohira Tikra
12. Basta

Keonjhar District

1. Podasingidi Garh
2. Sitabinji
3. Bandhagoda

Phulbani District

1. Asuragarh
2. Gandharadi

Sambalpur District

1. Ambabhona
2. Baragarh
3. Bijapur
4. Kudopalli
5. Garhdwar fort
6. Sambalpur
7. Ullapagarh

Kalahandi District

1. Amathagara
2. Manikgarh
3. Jumlagarh
4. Garbhata
5. Gudahandi
6. Jhunagarh
7. Tanwanta
8. Asurgarh

Sundargarh District

1. Jagatagarh
2. Saraph Garh
3. Khadia Kudar
4. Jhunagarh

Bolangir District

1. Binka (Sonpur)
2. Patnagarh
3. Kharligarh

Raibania

Around nine miles north of Jalesore and two miles from the right bank of the river Suvarnarekha amidst dense grass and jungle stand the Rabania group of forts. They are four in number, the two larger ones being close to the village of Rabania and two smaller ones at the village Phulta (phulahatta). Of these two small forts nothing now remains save the outline of mud walls, with here and there scattered mass of laterite stones. All these forts are built of stone very loosely kept together. They are all hewn and of various sizes, the largest and most regularly shaped being found in the most important and probably most ancient portions of the work, the smaller and less carefully hewn in the walls and outworks. The largest stones are about 3 ft in length by a foot in depth and the same breadth. The mud fort located at the north-west angle of Raibania village is most interesting of the group. The shape of this fort is an irregular pentagon having the following dimensions:

Eastern wall	1,650 yards
Northern wall	1,650 yards
North-Western	880 yards
South-Western	1,550 yards
Southern	880 yards

There seems to be some sort of order even in the irregularity as the eastern and northern walls are the same length so also the north-western and southern. Though called the 'mud fort", the walls of the fort are not really of mud. The breaches made on these walls reveal the nature of their construction. The center consists of layers of stone gradually diminishing to a point and this is covered and entirely hidden with about four feet of earth closely rammed. The wall is surrounded by a deep and broad mote and a slight but continuous ridge, vidently artificial, runs parallel to the moat on its outer edge. Outside all this, at a distance, runs a nalla which by a little dexterous cutting and deepening has been made into a very efficacious outer moat lined here and there with a wall of laterite. The interior of the fort is a large plain covered with debris of stone buildings, tanks and patches of jungle.[247]

In the absence of tangible material evidence it is very difficult to assign any specific date to the great military stronghold in northern Orissa. John Beams[248] speculates the fort to have been built by Mukunda Deva, the last Hindu ruler of Orissa,who was responsible for the renovation of the great historic fort of Barabati and numerous ghats and tanks on the far off border areas. But the short reign of this monarch covering a series of Muslim incursions may not have given him sufficient time and resources to undertake construction of such formidable stronghold. It may therefore be reasonable to assign a date to this edifice some time during imperial Gangas whose illustrious rulers like Choda Gangadeva, Ananagabhimadeva and Narasimhadeva were credited with establishing several Katakas in different localities for efficient administration and successful fight with foreign aggressors. There is no doubt to the fact that the fort, originally built for military purposes, was subsequently by a series of rulers even after the fall of the imperial Ganga dynasty.

Barabati Fort

The fort of Barabati constitute the most important monuments of cuttack. According to Madalapanji or the palm-leaf chroncils of the Jaganath temple, King Anangabhimadeva of the Ganga Dynastey (1211-1238)built a new city in the of Barabati and named it as Barabati Kataka or royal camp of Baranasi. In the beginning of the twelfth century, Cuttack was the most important place of Orissa. Barabati fort witnessed the fortunes and the fall of the long line of the Ganga and Suryavamsi rulers. During the rule of the Muslims and Marathasit continued to be the capital of Orissa. The British army took possession of Barabati fort, the main seat of occupation of Orissa ruleras in october 1803.[249]

Abul Fazl[250] gives an account of the fort of Barabati. He possibly obtained the information from the report of Raja Mansingh who conquered Orissa in 1592 A.D. He wrote in Katak (Cuttack): "The city has a stone fort situated at the bifurcation of two rivers, the Mahanadi held in high veneration by the Hindus, and the Kathjuri. It is the residence of the Governor and contains some fine buildings. For five or six kos round the fort during the rains, the country is under water. Rajah Makand Deo built a palace here nine storeys in the hight: the first storey was taken up for the elephants and stables, the second was occupied by the artillery and the guards and quarters for attendants, the third by the patrol and gate-keepers, the fourth by the workshops, the fifth by the kitchen, the sixth contained the public reception rooms, the seventh, the private apartment, the eighth, the women's apartments and the ninth, the sleeping chamber of Governor.

In 1818 under the suggestion of Peckenham[251], the Commissioner, stones of the fort were used for repair of revetments and public roads and even sold to the moneyed persons at a price of rupees five to six per hundred pieces of dressed stones. The only remnants of the Barabati fort extant are a massive heap of earth supposed to be the site of the nine-storey palace in the centre, an arched gateway on the east and broad moat faced with stone masonry all round the fort. The gateway consists of an arched opening 9 feet 3 inches wide and 16 feet high, flanked by two square sloping towers to the right and left. A large banyan tree has taken root in the southern tower. The mote is crossed by a solid causeway flanked by short masonry walls. The fort walls were about 90 feet back from the mote and their site is marked by a low ridge of earth and stones running parallel to the moat.They appear to have been about 12 feet in thickness. The fort area including the moat measures about 2,300 feet.

Baramba Garh

The Raja of Baramba had his fortified residence located near the foot of a lofty hill, thus availing natural protection from its thick forests. The high walls of the fort on the other sides were added in subsequent dates. The four gateways of this fort were named as Champei dvara in the east, Gundu dvara in the west, Garh Khola dvara in the north and Khandamala dvara in the south. Each of these doorways has been associated with thrilling military operations of the incumbents. The Sunamuhin Vandha excavated by Rani Suka Devi once functioned as the moat on the southern side of this fort.[252]

Dhenkanal Fort

The magnificent fort of Dhenkanal is highlighted in the famous book *Samar Taranga* written by Brajanath Badajena, who was the eyewitness to the military engagements between the ruler of Dhenkanal and Maratha army. Singh Deo brothers transleted this book as 'War Waves'and quoted about this Fort as "This fort has been constructed on the middle of Pani Ohala hill with wonderful skill. From the outer gate you have to gradually ascend to get inside the premises of the Fort. If you look from the present 'Chandrashala' from a long distance you can easily notice the approach of the enemy from a long distance. The whole Fort was surrounded by a high wall. Under the cover of this wall many soldiers could effectively fire on the attackers. The gate of the outer wall and the Fort gate as well were built of very thick and high unbreakable wooden planks. To prevent the enemies advance from quite a distance outside the Fort, the great canons, *Chandi Prasad, Kalika Prasad, Mulaka Maidan* and others were kept arranged and ready. Then again 2000 cubits away from the aforesaid fort walls spreading to the east, north and west was another 7 cubits thick stone wall. Adjacent to the foot of this, was the 30- cubit-wide deep moat filled with water. On the opposite side of the moat was the two miles long unpassable thick bamboo jungle known as 'Ara', kept well preserved and well guarded. On the outer wall there were many buttresses for the soldier to fire long range guns and there are also many peep-holes in the wall for firing of muskets. Near the north-east corner of the 'Nrusingha Sagar' was a floating bridge to enable people to cross the moat. After crossing the moat by this bridge you arrive at the Torana of the aforesaid stone wall called 'Bamboo gate'. This was the first entrance gate to the Fort. About 1,000 cubits or more away stood the well-guarded 'Torana', the 'Jai Mangala' gate. After crossing this gate, one arrives just in front of the fort wall."[253]

This ancient fort of Dhenkanal is still noticed on the slope of the Pani Qhala (Jaladhara) hill, with the hill as its background commanding grand view for a long distance. With some modifications it is now the place of the ruling family of Dhenkanal. The old mud wall of the fort has been replaced by a stone wall. The advantage of the mud wall was, in the theory, that while a stone wall would crack and crash under heavy bombardment, shells and balls will just enter and be embedded in mud walls without crossing any damage. Small portions of the moat though partially filled up still exist giving evidence of its past glory. At two places portions of the moat have been converted into two tanks known as *Bali jhari* and *Utia jhari* (*jhari* means moat). The thick stretch of bamboo jungle , Ara, which protected back side of the fort, is no more to be seen. A busti by the side of this jungle which still exists is called the *Ara-Bullah Sahi* giving reminiscence of the Ara. The forefathers of the present inhabitants of this *Ara -Bullah Sahi* had been settled there with the purpose of keeping vigilance over this *Ara* jungle from the depredations of enemies, poachers, jungle fire, etc., by constantly roaming therein. The outer stone wall has been demolished and several buildings have been constructed from the stones that has been used there.[254]

Sisupalgarh

The ruins of Sisupalgarh are located about one and half miles to the east-south-east of the town of Bhubaneswar of Puri district. While going from Lingaraja temple towards the Daya river along the Puri road one sees about a hundred yards to the left the impressive fortification wall rising some 25-30 feet above the surrounding plains. The fort forms a rough square on plan. Oriented approximately along the cradinal directions, each of its sides measures about three quarters of a mile long, thus enclosing an area a little over half a square mile. The counters clearly suggest the existence of corner towers and eight large gateways, two on each side, besides about the same number of smaller openings distributed all over the perimeter. The gateways are so placed that if the distance between two corner towers of any side is trisected, a gateways will be found at or near each point of trisection. Such a disposition clearly suggests a rugular planning not only of the fortifications but presumably also of the streets inside, which are likely to have run east-west and north-south connecting the opposite gateways in a grid pattern. The fort is circumscribed by the waters of a streamlet called Gangua or Gandhavati. The main current which flows the past the western side of the fort has its source to the west of Mancheswar, some 6 miles north of Sisupalgarh, and joins the Daya river 7 miles further south. The builders of the fort, taking advantage of the proximity of this stream, trained its waters around the northern, eastern and southern sides of the fort, thus producing a moat with a perennial supply of water.[255]

The fortified area was excavated by the Archaeological Survey of India during 1948 and the excavator tentatively identified the site with Kalinganagar, the metropolis of Kharavela whose achievements have been recorded on the overhanging brow of the *Hati-Gumpha* of Udayagiri hill located at a distance of some 6 miles to west-north-west of Sisupalgarh. The gateway, constructed of large well-dressed laterite blocks, had a passage about 25 feet wide between the flank walls and was provided with two gates, one near the entrance and the other about 100 feet further back. Immediately behind the former gate was a guard room while adjacent to the lattter gate was an ancillary passage meant presumably for controlled admission at late hours.[256]

Ganja Fort

The fort of Ganja is located in Ganja town of the district. The construction of the fort which was commenced in 1768 by Cotsford, the First Resident of Ganjam, still forms an interesting ruins and recalls to mind the memories of former Residents and Chiefs in council who were engaged here partly in political and partly in commercial enterprises. The adjoining cemetery contains some interesting monuments which are gradually falling to decay. Due to unhealthy climate, lack of drinking water and outbreak of an epidemic fever compelled the residents to desert the place in favour of Berhampur in a subsequent date. This place was originally situated on the Rishikulya river which formerly emptied itself into the sea close to the fort, but its present mouth is nearly three-quarters of a mile further north. During the rains, the river is often in flood and its overflow causes severe damage to the surrounding areas. Once this was the chief port of the district in view of the fact that boats can be located in quite water and dragged up out of the surf conveniently.[257]

Khurdagarh

Originally a small village in *pragana* Dandimala. Khurda came into prominence when the descendants of the Bhoi Kings made it their capital during the Mughal rule. These Kings lived in a fort at the foot of the Barunei hill a mile to the south of the town. This site was apparently selected because it was protected on one side by the Barunei hill which was easily defended and on the other by dense, almost impenetrable, jungle. The fort was taken however by the Marathas in the time of Vira Kishore Deva and during the Khurda rebellion of 1804, it was carried by storm by the British troops after a siege of three weeks.The fort is now in ruins but traces of its walls and ramparts are still there.The earth mounds within the fortified area are known to have been sites for royal household. Goddess Barunei is worshipped in a temple on the northen slope of the hill. The caves on the hill have served the purpose of hideouts of the rebellious *Paikas* of the Bhoi rajas in the past. The British force after a period of siege demolished the main gateway and reached the inner area of the fort through ladders. They could not trace out the king as he, along with his trusted retinues, escaped through a secret door.[258]

Sambalpur

The ruins of the Sambalpur fort are seen at a place to the north-western direction of the town. This fort is said to have been built in the beginning of the 18th century by *Raja* Ajit Singh who was greatly induced by the repeated attacks of the Marathas. He extensively fortified the portion of the town in which his palace stood. He excavated a moat round the place, the two ends of which joined the river Mahanadi, one at the side on which the city police station stands and the other to the west of Samalai *gudi.* All round the palace thorny bamboos were planted to form a barrier against invaders and the bank of the Mahanadi from the Mohana *Durwaza* to the Samalai *gudi,* a length of 2,443 feet was defended by a stone wall. Towers or bastions with embrasures for guns were erected at intervals on the wall. They were 18 feet high and 72 feet in circumference and were faced with stone 3 feet thick and filled in with earth. Nothing now remains of the fort but the crumbling stone wall on the river face and a few smouldering bastions. One gateway only is left, that of Samalai near the temple of the goddess and though the remains of the moat are still visible, it is filled up here and there.[259]

Martial Arts of Various States in India

Kerala

Kalaripayattu—Kalari is the Malayalam word for a special kind of gymnasium, in which the martial art known as kalari payattu is practiced. Kalari payattu consists of various techniques and stages.

Stages:

1. *Uzhichil* or the message with gingili oil (sesame) is used for imparting suppleness to the body, but one person with a thorough knowledge of the nervous system and the human body, conduct the *Uzhichil.*

2. *Miapayattu* or Body exercise. After application of oil, students start with a series of body movements known as *maipayattu.* This includes twists and turns of the body leaps and jumps and poses, designed to gain control over various parts of the human body. One sequence of such an exercise helps make for easy movement of the body, along with sharp eye contact.

3. *Paliyankam* (Sword fight). Wielding the sword in an efficient manner is considered to be the peak of perfection in Kalari Payattu. Various methods in the use of the sword as a weapon of offence and defence, are being practiced today but the most one-inspiring and perhaps blood-curdling of these, is the Paliyankam.

Kalari Payattu demonstration includes physical exercises and mock duels armed and unarmed combat. Kalari Payattu is not accompanied by any music or drumming. It is a silent combat where style matters most. The spiritual atmosphere is always maintained. No performance or combat is began without duly propitiating the Gods. Character, fitness and courage are the demands of Kalari Payattu, which has about it an area of spiritual and historical association. Kalari Payattu is practiced by women also.[260]

Silambam in Tamil Nadu

Silambam had been used as a technique in warfare in the Sancam era of Tamil History. The origin of Silambam is traced to divine sources, namely, Lord Murga and also the mythological sage Agasthya. The etymology of Silambam is raced to the whizzing sound produced in the process of the play, from the practice of wearing anklets called Silambu in Tamil by the players and the agility and clearerness involved in practicing it. Usually the staff of soft wood, fairly uniform in cross section and of a height upto the forehead of the standing player is used.[261]

In India, staff-play is popularly known as Lathi in Maharastra, Dhal Lakadi in Gujarat, "Karrattam" in Andhra Pradesh, 'Neauvadi' in Kerala and 'Silambam' in Tamil Nadu. The use of long staff for self-defence or mock fighting was a highly organised in Tamil Nadu as early as the 1st and 2nd century AD. When Tamil kings resigned in Martial Majesty.

A three-type contest

1. Fight to the finish, when one of the combatants is dispossessed of his staff.
2. Totalling the number of 'touches' one makes on an opponent (indicated by appropriate marking on the body).
3. Superior skill shown in protecting pouch of money (kept at or in between contestant's feet).

The contestant who can register a mark on the forehead of his opponent is hailed as an outstanding victor in the contest.[262]

Nicobar Islands

Kirip (Nicobarese Wrestling)—In this wrestling, wrestlers grip each other from the rear with their hands, before starting the competition, and the grip may not be loosened till the end of the competition. The wrestler, using other parts of the body, including the leg, tries to put other on the ground. When the wrestlers back touches the ground, he is declared the loser. Three to five rounds of competition take place, between two wrestlers.[263]

Nagaland Wrestling

[264]Naga wrestling is very popular, especially among the Angami, Chakhesang, Zeliang, Rangma, and Mao tribes. Naga wrestling today has acquired an all Nagaland sports status and each alternate year a competition is held every year, however regional competitions are held in early January. These bouts commence with the contestants grasping each other's waist girdles. When the go signal is given both wrestlers attempt to throw each other. A number of leg tricks and muscle power are used to achieve victory but the use of the hands on an opponents legs is considered a foul, through the hands can be used to hold other parts of the body from the waist upwards. A wrestler is declared the winner if he succeeds in throwing his opponent and, in doing so, makes the trunk of the opponent touch the ground while he himself does not allow his own trunk to touch the ground. He can also be declared a winner if he succeeds in pulling or thrusting down the opponent or forcing him into a kneeling position with both knees and one hand touching the ground

simultaneously, or into a kneeling position with one knee or both hands touching the ground simultaneously, the verdict is normally adjusted out of three bouts, viz. two wins out of three.

Manipur

Mukna (Manipur Wrestling)—[265]Mukna is a form of wrestling which is as old as Manipuri society. The competitions are usually in the same weight category. Contestants wear a waist-belt and groin-belt. They hold each other belts and then the match begins. You are not allowed to hold your opponent's neck, hair, ear, private parts, and legs, with the hands. Boxing and kicking are also not permitted. The competitor who touches the ground first with his head, back, shoulders, knee, or the hand is declared the loser.The players of this game use some of the traditional equipments and dress. This is principally to protect the vital parts of a player's body. It also helps to identify the *pana* or yak to which the wrestler belongs. The waist belt is known as an *Ingra* the winner is called a *yare*. He is declared winner if he succeeds in pinning his opponent to the ground with the whole of his body or his back touching the ground. The contest in referred by a *yatra*. At the end of the contest, the winner is required to lift his opponent of the ground as a mark of strength, discipline and excellence.There are many techniques used in Mukna.

1. Kaplak-Kotpi
2. Khuto-Theibi.
3. Ninggong-Langba.
4. Chepching Chingba,
5. Heibong-Kangbi.
6. Longkhrouna-Leiba
7. Khudong pukhtpa
8. Khuchep-Haibi.
9. Khudong-Haipu.
10. Khudong - Awangba, etc.

Cheibi Gad-Ga : (A sword and spear game of Manipur)—This is one of the Manipur's most ancient martial arts. The fighting equipment is simply a sword and a shield, now modified to a stick encased in soft leather and a shield made of leather. The contestants fight a duel, and victory goes to the man who scores the most points. In ancient times the sword and spear were indispensable accessories to the equipment of a soldier from the royal household. Victory in this martial art, depends more on skill, than brawn and brute force.

This competition shall be held on a flat surface within a circle of 7m in diameter with boundary line of 7.5 cm to be marked in white colour. There shall be two lines of 1m lengths each in the circle, which shall be 7.5 cm in width and marked in white colour with a space of 2m between the lines. The cheibe stick covered with soft leather shall be 2 to 2½ ft. in length and the shield shall be 1 m in diameter. The edge of the cheibi shall have a coat of fresh liquid of white colour, which shall be replenished as and when it is considered necessary. For every interval stoppage, the durability of the colour shall be checked and accordingly be replenished. It is the only present method of counting of points.[266]

Thang-Ta and Sarit-Sarak (Armed and unarmed combat)—The history of Thang-Ta and Sarit-Sarak can be traced to the 17th century. Thang-Ta is mainly the technique of using a sword or a spear against one or more opponents but on many occasions there is a combined approach to the training of these martial arts. The Manipuri kings to fight against the British over a long period successfully used these martial arts. After the British occupied this region, martial arts were banned, but after, 1950' the rapid rejuvenation of martial arts began. Thang-Ta is practiced in three different ways the first in exclusively ritual in form, which is related to the *tantric* practices. It is believed that some forms of this ritual bring prosperity to the state while other forms bring destruction. The second way consists of a display of decorative sword and spear dances. These dances can be converted into actual fighting practices. The third way consists of actual fighting techniques.[267]

Mizo Inchai (Wrestling)—This discipline resembles wrestling in many ways like the popular Indian form of wrestling; physical strength and skill are once again the main attributes for success. Defeat can be registered in three ways.

1. When both shoulders are pinned to the ground for a count of six, in five seconds.
2. When a wrestler is lifted into the air and is kept suspended for a count of six, in five seconds.
3. When a wrestler in pinned down on the ground, in any position for a count of six, in five seconds.[268]

Traditional Martial art of Different Countries of the World

Thai Boxing—One of the most devastating arts ever to come out of Asia is that of mury Thai or Thai Boxing. This lethal Martial art is dedicated to pure fighting and is without forms of Kata. The training is hard, gruelling and intensive, usually beginning at around ten years old and exponents are noted for their art. When instruction commences in many thai, the first thing that is tought is footwork and leg movement. Co-ordination is vital because the pattern of the footwork dictates the range of the fighter's attack and defence. Both legs work together all the time, unlike many styles of karate and kungfu in which one legs can remain motionless for some of the time. The Thai boxer justifies the constant motion by commenting that a moving target is always harder to hit than a static one. At first sight mury Thai training is seen a little similar to that of western boxing, but any similarity quickly ceases with the introduction into training of the Thai fighter's secret weapon: the *yng knw* or long knee. This constitutes a defence and an attack all in one particular attention must be paid to balance and body posture. The long knee can be used to attack the stomach or sternum area. It can be converted from a short-range into a long-range weapon merely by extending the leg and suddenly it becomes a strong front thrust kick. The fighter learns to raise the knee when attacked so that it becomes an effective shield to guard the groin and lower body area with the hand held in a high guard, the Thai fighter uses the same leg to retaliate. The early records of Siam, as Thailand was once known, show that the unarmed art of Thai boxing has been practised since ancient times. There is evidence that it formed part of a military training syllabus. Throughout its 2000 years of history, this royal land has registered all attempts to conquer her, which probably gives a lot of credit to the fighting spirit of the people. Siam, in her geographical position of South East Asia, is bordered by Burma, Loas, Cambodia and Malaysia with warring tribes constituently biting at her heels. Siam had no maintain a tremendous will to survive.[269]

The Bondo system of Burma—Thailand's neighbour, Burma, has a Martial art called Bando, which means 'way of the disciplined'. The art is based upon twelve animals and practitioners usually select attributes of one or more of these animals and then train in that particular system. For example, in the Cobra Style lie all the lighting-like paralysing nerve strikes. The tiger system extols the ferocity and fighting power of that animal, whereas the boar form is famous for its hard locking techniques and close in fighting tactics. It is a complete martial system, which also incorporates weapons with exotic sounding names, it is perhaps interesting to note that some of the unarmed methods bear similarities to Thai boxing and also to muay Khmer, the boxing style of neighboring Cambodia. For instance, many of the kicks in bando are delivered with the shin.[270]

The Fillipino art of Kali—Hindu beliefs came to the Philippines by way of Malaysia about the time of Christ, but by the fifteenth century the Island's were composed of people from China, India, Arabia and other nations who mixed with the original Negritos settlers. In the southern Philippines live a largely Muslim community called the Moro, who use an amazing range of knives in their dances and martial skills on 6th March, 1521 the Spanish explorer Magellan arrived on the shores of the Philippines. By 27th April he had been killed in the Island of Mactan by the natives. His discovery of the Islands brought other Spaniards but these met great resistance from the Muslim Moro. In 1896 Tagalog people from Luzon, the largest Island of the Philippines, revolted against the Spanish occupation, which led to the provisional republic in 1898. It was from this race of people that the term Kali was derived to describe their Martial arts. One of the martial skills which comes under the general term of Kali is called arnish, which is known by other names in various provinces. This system is indigenous to the Philippines and utilizes two bladed weapons. Training was originally carried out in secrecy and sticks called Muton replaced the blades for both safety and secrecy. Modern exponents use two rattan sticks up to one meter (3ft.) in length and techniques involved either one or two sticks in a continuous striking action against vulnerable parts of the body.[271]

The Malaysian art of Bersilat—Bersilat is an ancient Malaysian art of self-defence, dating back to the early part of the fifteenth century. Today this art is generally referred to simply as Silat. It consists of many diverse forms which are also widespread throughout Indonesia. The art developed in the Agricultural areas, where most of its instructors lived and worked. It was introduced to Malaysia by the legendary hero and acknowledge father of Bersilat, Hand Tuah of Malacca. Hang Tuah is said to have gone into the Mountains for several years in search of a maha-guru (a grandmaster) to teach him the skills of this once most secret martial art. The knowledge he acquired through his vigorous training taught him how to face an enemy and defeat him. It was such a secret martial art in the old days, that in many villages the inhabitants could live their whole lives without ever realising that a guru or master of Silat lived and trained among them. Silat, like many of the martial art, delves deep into the spiritual aspects. Gayong, one of the major styles means "pure body and soul", which indicates that the practitioners must be physically and mentally clean. Harimau, the other major style means 'tiger'. A basic tenent of the system in that fighters must never over-estimate their own capabilities. Silat practitioners always stress that the art should not be used for initiating an attack. It is strictly for self-defence and for counter attacking when one is in danger. A skillful Silat fighter can pin-point with deadly accuracy the 12 vital spots or critical nerve centres on the human body. These are known as *seni sendi* and can be struck to cause severe pain at the slightest will experience a tremendous jolt through his body, reacting as through he had just suffered a severe electric shock. Malaysian silat incorporates many ground techniques and caters for the possibility of a defender being knocked to the floor and having to counter from a supine position. The most effective ground attack is to cripple the attackers supporting leg by smashing his kneecap or groin. As soon as they feel themselves falling, students learn to lash out with a type or short sidekick. The uniform that the practitioner wears a plain black short-lived cotton Malay shirt, with half-length-black trousers, and strip of black cloth tied around the student's forehead.[272]

The Capoiera of Brazil—One of the most overlooked martial arts in the world is that of Brazils capoiera. This art was born out of slavery, in personal defence of cruelty and persecution. Capoiera was invented by the blacks to fight the vicious slave owners and had its most terrifying results in the slave uprising. Many of the movements are highly acrobatic as the fighter performs a cartwheel on his hands. It is believed that the origins of the art lie in certain African folk dances and that the choreography was altered and adopted to suit the purposes of self- defence. It was through these dances that the slaves managed to hide the lethal aspects of this martial art from the landowners. In capoiera the emphasis is on muscular strength combined with joint flexibility and rapid movement. Making use of vary fast body reaction the capoiera fighter can deliver a blow with his feet that could smash a man's internal organs. In a fraction of a second he flips his body over, in a type of handstand, and delivers with tremendous force and accuracy a double foot blow to the aggressor's body they could well nigh cut him, in two without a doubt a capoiera man's feet are his deadliest weapons. He trains to kick as most martial artists train to punch. It has been said of capoiera, that it is one of the dirtiest formalised fighting styles known. Capoiera is not a complicated martial art. It has little more than 72 defined separate movements. Many of its techniques have colourful titles such as 'tail of the dragon fish', daddy's scissors and 'bannana plant'. Just like martial art the world over capoiera had one prime function: it was invented to kill.[273]

Taekwon do of Korea—During the fifth century Korea was divided into three Countries: Packche, Silla, and Koguryu. After much internal conflict Koguryu defeated Packche, but Silla obtained help from the Chinese T' ang dynasty and ruled supreme, setting up the capital in Kwangju. The Nobel families were well versed in martial skill and the young warriors were called hwarang. According to some traditions a school of martial arts were established by on kwang Bopsa which hwarangdo, a balance philosophy and fighting arts. The system of hwarangdo paralleled the Japanese teaching of Bushido and the Korean knights became formidable and awesame warriors. Their skilled included gun shin pup, which was similar to ninjutsu; kookup hwal bub, which was a form of acupuncture and medicine; nengong, which included internal and empty hand techniques; and a weapon skills system known as way-gong. By the thirteenth century hwarangdo had fallen into decline and only the essence of these skills has been preserved today. Through various invasions and occupations the Koreans adopted much from both China and Japan, however the empty hand skill date back to the union of Silla and the Tang dynasty. Chinese empty hand fighting was taught to the hwarang. This system became known as t'ang-su and from this original source and with Korean influence it developed into kwonpup. Based on the skills of the Kwonpop by the eighteenth century the system of tae kwon had sprung up in central Korea. In 1945 it became known as tae kwon do and has since spread throughout the world.[274]

Hapkido:

[275]Hapkido is another martial art, but distinctively different from tackwon-do. The word means way of co-ordinate power. The art exists almost exclusively for self-defence purposes. In hapkido there are no formalized patterns or sporting links. The art is unusual for the fact that it emphasizes a non-violent code of counter-defence. In an attack situation, the hapkido practitioner will remain clam until the aggressor has mode the initial advance and committed himself to a strike situation. The hapkidoist then simply applies a soft circular block to deflect the approaching blow. This is followed by an explosion of counter-offensive techniques, that can result in the attacker being annihilated. Hapkido combines the same principles found in aikido with the strong kicks and punches from Korea's indigenous tack Kyon. Some kicks are almost acrobatic in their delivery, with mid-air strikes using both feet at the same time. the art is composed of three primary skills, non-resistance when meeting force, circular motions in countering and attacking, and the 'water principle'. When the hapkido practitioner counters, he or she does it with ultimate strength and total intent of purpose. It is for these reasons that hapkidoists do not indulge in sporting competition. The art is also incorporates blows to the vital areas as well as locks and leverage holds.

The Sulsa of Korea:

[276]The sulsa were a warrior elite who can find their equivalents among the Japanese ninja. The secret sect, who stemmed from the hwarang-do, were masters of espionage and silent killing techniques. Their training was so extreme that other warriors often classed them as a type of one-man army. Students eligible to learn this art were picked from the cream of the Hwa-rangdo ranks. A modern parallel is the selection from special groups such as the Royal Marine Commandos in Britain, of entrants to the exclusive SAS. The sulsa's training guided him through martial art skills that could be geared to meet every encounter. They could walk on water using special boat-like shoes, scale sheer castle walls with ease and, with carefully adapted

kites, they were able to soar over enemy positions taking count of their fortificatations. Unlike the ninja, the sulsa were not picked and trained from birth. The principles of sulsa training have been adapted by many of the world's armed services, most notably the US Rangers, who were taught these skills by the late Mike Echanis. Echanis had been a student of hwarang-do under the grandmaster Joo Bang Lee. Lee taught him much of this ancient knowledge and Echaris expanded it with some of his own ideas. Modern psychology became involved and Echanis trained service personnel in thought- control and meditation.

Tang Soo do:

[277]Like so many of the present day Korean martial arts, Tang soo do is relatively new with roots reaching back into Koreas ancient fighting past. Its original name was Soo Bahk Do, but it was changed by its modern founder master Hwang Kee. In Korea, however, it is still known by its former name. Tang soo do is thought of as a way of life by its practitioners, rather than a means of self-defence, with the belief that the spiritual life must be balanced with physical life to create a harmony. Tang soo do places much emphasis upon kicking techniques, rather than on hand manoeuvres. Its ultimate tenet is self-important through the art. Tournaments and competitions are held on regular basis, with strict rules as regards behavior and the proper etiquette of fighting. Students being in the art by learning the five basic hyungs (patterns). Interestingly, these forms bear a remarkable resemblance to the Japanese Heian Katas. These are some people who think that Tang soo do, in past at lest, is really a disguised form of Japanese Shotoken Karate, with the addition of the indigenous Korean high kicks.

Africa—In Africa in the early part of the last century, the great Zulu ruler Shaka founded the first weli-trained Zulu armies. Shaka developed their combative skills as well as the assegai which was a flat iron spear with a wooden shaft made from a tree of the same name, which was used to great effect with long shield. Shaka used an effective spy network, drilled remarkably well disciplined troops, used effective battle strategy and had a complete system of martial arts. The shield was used with a long spear held point down behind it, while the short spear was held in the hand for close - quarter combat. The proud Zulu race used spiritual rituals before battle to make themselves invincible and wore an amulet on the arm which they believed protect them.[278]

Russian Sambo Wrestling—Russian Sambo wrestling has developed from many sources. The most distinct contribution has come from the country's central Asian provinces, where sport wrestling has been very popular for hundreds of years. In 1936 a prominent Russian wrestler named Anatoly Harlampief decided to do research into many of his countries folk wresting methods and combine them into a system not seen anywhere else in the world. The result of his endeavours was Sambo. In 1938 the Soviet Union's National Sports Committee officially accepted Sambo wrestling as an authentic martial art and part of the Russian national heritage and as such they designated it as bonafied sports. The word Sambo in a Russian acronym from 'self-defence without arms'. It has about 60 basic techniques. In sambo the wrestler can grip the belt of an opponent, but this is not permitted in Judo. Another favorite hold is the back of the Jacket and belt. The usual objects of attack are the ankle, knee, wrist and elbow. Pressure holds are applied to intensify pain force the opponent to submit, which he does by shouting 'yetsugi'. In competition there must always be a winner; there are no such things as draws or going into extra time. If both competitors have gained equal points at the end of about, then the match is judged by which fighter was the most aggressive.[279]

La Savate - kicking art of France—La Savate is a French Martial art chiefly concerned with fighting with the feet. The hand movements, apart from the open palms slapping the opponent across the face, hardly exist. There is no ground formed with both fists, as in western and Thai boxing. These kicks are executed from an upright position. La Savate is distinctly different from La boxe Franchise, which is the traditional from a French boxing. La Savate was a vicious type of fighting used primarily by ruffians and the French footpads (Muggers). One of the greatest teachers of the art was a Persian named Michel Pisseux. The system concentrates on going low kicks to adversary's shins, groin and knees. The few high kicks involved in savate are all targeted upon the head, attacking the eyes, nose and upper lip. An expert in the art can deliver a series of kicks, applied with clinical precisions. The feet move so fast, that even if a technique were to miss its target, another one would follow in just as quickly, giving the opponent very little time to retaliate. The savate man does not rely upon power in technique, because of the sensitive target areas.

La Savate is the only martial art with Asian origins that developed in Europe before the advent of Judo, nearly 100 years later.[280]

Japan

Weapon Arts the rise of Japan's Samurai:—In Japan's early history local landowners employed men to protect their property, hence the word 'Samurai' came into being from 'Sameru' which means to 'serve' and was used to describe these warriors. During the period of Yoritomo (1185 AD) military ruler of Japan became a golden age for the Japanese martial arts. The warriors became known as bushi - not samurai - and codes of ethics called the codes of Bushido were formulated. Unlike China, the Japanese bushi had a status at the top of the social scale; they had the right to bear arms, administer justice and even take life. Schools of martial study began to develop, called ryu, and these tought a variety of weapons and empty hand skills, instruction on battle strategy and other objects.[281]

Kendo—Kendo, meaning way of the sword, is a martial art developed from the classical Japanese Kenjutsu. Kenjustu had no sporting considerations; its sole aim was to kill an enemy. Kendo history is the history of the Samurai, the warrior class of feudal Japan, whose basic weapon was the Katana or long sword. The sword in Japan was held with such high regard, that it was sometimes known as the 'soul' of the warrior. Originally fencing was taught with a line (real) blade and then around AD 400 a training device was introduced called a bokuto. This was a piece a heavy red oak with the shape, weight a balance of a real sword and soon this became a popular weapon to practice with. Fencing in weapon those days was taught by means of kata, devised by the schools master, to simulate actual fighting situations. Although quite revolutionary for the times, training with the bockuto still caused injury. The next stage of development was the introduction of the shinai, along with protective armour. A shinai is made of four bamboo strips held together at strategic points by cord and of the ends by leather, one forming the handles. A hand guard protects the fingers with the equipments blows could actually be struck on the opponent. This allowed the student the facility to try complex multiple techniques time and time again, without the risk of the shinai smashing into his opponent's head or body if he failed.[282]

Naginata: women's weapon of defence

[283]The naginata resembles a pole with a short curved knive on the end, very similar to a halberd. It is about 6ft.6inches (2m) in length and is made of wood. Its curved blade measures about 20 inches (50cm) and is extremely sharp. Use of the naginata as a weapon on the battlefields of Japan dates back more than a thousand years. A man armed with one had a terrific advantage over a swordman. Not only could it outreach a sword, but it also had a tremendous sweeping capability. When an opponent evaded the razor-sharp blade, the user could whip the belt end around and sweep the opponent off his feet and then decapitate him. The bushi (Japanese feudal warriors) also found that the naginata had a distinct advantage over the spear (yari), because when used with a circular motion it could inflict deadly slashes on all parts of an enemy's anatomy. It became so effective that a shin protection was introduced as a standard part of the armour, as many a warrior in the past had lost his legs due to the slicing powder of this formidable weapon. With the modernization of battle weapons the naginata, like the bow, fell into disuse. Interestingly enough, it was the wives of the warriors who modified and used as a training weapon for teaching discipline to the girls of the bushi families. As the females mastered this shortened version of the weapon it was found to be of great use around the home, especially when their husbands rode off to participate in some war. Skill in the use of the naginata proved an excellent defence for the women when attacked or molested by the many roving bands of robbers and ronins (masterless samurai) during this turbulent era. Japanese homes of the period had low ceilings, so this shortened naginata could be used indoors as well as outside.

[284]At the emergence of Japan as a modern nation, the naginata was kept alive as an art form. Naginata training was deemed an essential part of the proper upbringing for a young lady. During the period of World War II, the naginata was eagerly encouraged by the government as a form of important military training for women. After the grate

conflict the naginata began its rebirth with the modification of some of the martial concepts, and sporting aspects were introduced. The naginata became a do. The live blade was replaced with an angled piece of plaited bamboo and naginata-do was soon a popular female sports. The kata in naginata-do are circular, not linear. The sport is said to be beneficial for a women's body because it develops the muscles evenly, providing the body with flexibility and suppleness, thus encouraging good all-round tone.

[285]There are two schools of naginata-do, the Tendo or heavenly way, and the Shinkage or new shadow school. The standard uniform for the women is the same as in Kendo: the Keikogi (the literal meaning of this is practice wear) and hakama- a kind of split skirt. In competition made Kendoka have pitted their sword skills against the ladies of the naginata, and nearly always came off second best. The female exponent cannot hope to match the strength of a male Kendoka, so instead she places emphasis on speed and flexibility. This combined with a high degree of skill through years of training, puts the men on the run, time and time again. Women's colleges through out Japan all have regular classes for training in naginata-do.

In the Japanese arsenal of fighting arts, a certain amount of confusion arises between 'Jutsu' and 'do', as in Kenjutsu and Kendo. A 'do' when used as a suffix to a martial discipline, such as in Karate-do or aikido, means a road, a way, and a path. Traditionally, when used in this context, it means the pathway to self-understanding and perfection through the training system of a particular martial art. Some of the old martial ways have been developed or adopted to place special emphasis upon such personal enlightment. If 'Justu' is the suffix, this indicates an art or skill, but refers to the warrior ways of the samurai class and the expression of their intentions in combat. The main difference between the old style and the new is that victory in combat was to the samurai an absolute priority.

Lai-do the Art of Drawing the Sword

[286]Lai-do is a twentieth century development of the art of iai-jutsu or batto-jutsu. The invention of the art of batto-jutsu as a distinction part of the wider study of swordmanship, kenjutsu, is generally attributed to Hayashizaki Jinsuke shigenobu. Shigenobu lived about 400years ago in the province of Oshu. Batto can be

translated as 'striking from the sheath' and the art of batto, or iai-jutsu as it became known, soon gained popularity as a specialization of a number of Kenjutsu schools (ryu). In the ancient iai-jutsu, the objective was both offensive and defensive. It taught the warrior to go into action instantly upon a sudden encounter. Striking on the draw distinguishes iai-jatsu within Kenjutsu; the earlier schools of sword fighting placed no grate importance on the drawing of the blade but rather on its effectiveness when unsheathed. The art of Kenjutsu fall into decline as the samurai turned to another areas of occupations for Japan had entered the modern era and was hungry for industrialization to catch up with the rest of the world. However although swords had been banned, the warrior did not need an opponent to practise iai-jutsu; this could be done alone. Slowly the combative aspects of the many schools of iai-jutsu became absorbed and students concerned themselves with training as a means of personal development of mind, body and sprit. Thus, iai-jutsu eventually became iai-do. Today in Japan there are many schools of iai, beet every school adheres to the basic principles which can be divided into four parts. First is nukisuke, which is the actual drawing of the blade from its scabbard. Then comes Kritsuke, the cut, followed by chiburi, or the symbolic shaking of the blood from the blade after a successful cut. Finally there is noto, the returning of the blade to its scabbard. The principle behind noto is to return the blade quickly without casting the eyes downwards, while remaining alert. This latter part requires perfect precision since the slightest mistake can result in damage to the hands on the razor-sharp blade. Novices may train with dual edged swords for years before progressing in to a live blade. From the time to time competition are held in which two contestants perform in parallel and comparative levels of skill are judged.

The Ninja

[287]During a period long ago there emerged in Japan a superb group of warriors whose skills were classed as being almost magical. These were the legendary ninja, the warriors of darkness, assassins of the night. Ninja training was designed to produce the complete fighting man. The art of ninjutsu wreaked death and havoc among the enemy, instilling fear into the local community, until the very

name, ninja, would send a cold shiver of doom down the spine. Feared throughout the land, the shadow warriors became legends in their own time. The ninja training began at birth. Barely able to walk, he would learn simple children's games that had ulterior motives. Before the child was five years old he would know the five exercises, consisting of balance, agility, strength, stamina, and what was termed as 'special skill' martial arts training was given almost immediately with weapons such as the boo staffs, sword, Kyu (the bow and arrow), shuriken (a star-shaped throwing implement), and other special weapons identified with ninjutsu. The unarmed combat method of tai-jitsu was practiced arduously. Before the age of seven, a ninja child would have been taught how to hold his breath under water for long periods, how to endure the rigours of inclement weather to climb trees and cliff faces, scale walls, survive for days without food and drink, learn to sleep on a tree branch without off, and dislocate his young limbs at will. This later exercise would aid the ninja to escape, in later life, if he was ever captured and bound. As the ninja child grew up, his life would be one long training programme. The simple nursery games would take on a deadly serious aspect, and the arts he was learning would be honed to perfection. As his youthful understanding grew, so too did the subject matter he was expected to embrace. He was taught always to expect the unexpected and he was schooled in psychology, so that when on a mission, weather it was to assassinate or purely spy for information, he could play on people's egos and use flattery and deception as formidable weapons.

The Tonfa and Kama

[288]The tonfa or tui-fa was another Okinawan farming implement that was adopted by the peasants as a weapon, to be used against their Japanese invaders. Originally it was a handle with the purpose of turning the wheel of a manually operated millstone that ground rice. Most commonly the tonfa is used like the *sai* as one of a pair, with one in each hand. The weapon consists of a long hardwood shaft with a cylindrical grip placed six inches (15cm) from the end at a right-angle with the weapon held by this projection each shaft lies along the underside of the forearm and is used to block and parry attacks. The grip can be revolved to allow the shafts to spin outwards to strike an enemy in the temple or throat. The kama is quite simple

an agricultural sickle and has been in use as long as man has grown crops. By itself it is obviously a formidable weapon, but in the hands of an expert it is quite lethal. The blade is attached to a long handle, which is flared slightly at the butt to prevent the hands from slipping on to the razor-shape crescent-shaped blade. As with most of these Okinawan weapons, the kama can be used either singly or pairs. The user can chop, hook and strike with various combinations, to put an adversary in deadly trouble.

Kyudo : The zen archery of Japan—As in the other arts Kyudo comes from a battlefield skill, that of Kyujutsu, but with the introduction of firearms in the sixteenth centuary the bow, or Yumi, became absolute as part of the arsenal of the Samurai. In Kyudo the archer pits himself against only one opponet - himself. The goals in zen archery are typical of all zen teachings. They are as elusive as trying to catch the wind in your hands, because in the end the archer can truly have no goals. The bow, arrow, target and archer must fuse together to become one. Then, and only then will the Kyudoka (one who practises Kyudo) release the arrow. Even in this stage, with the arrow in fligat, hitting the target is not important. The vital considerations are now the shooting is done, and the archer's state of mind when the arrow is released. Style and the method of preparation are important factors in Kyudo.[289]

Bow and Arrow—The bow in Kyudo is the largest in the world, measuring over six feet (1.8 M). The grip is not centred, but is approximately one-third of the distance from the bottoms of the bow. No other shaped bow can be found in either Europe or Asia that even remotely resembles the Japanese Yumi. Traditionally the bow was constructed entirely out of bamboo, with a pull weight of arround 80 pounds (36 kg). It is a compound bow, which means it is made up strips of word laminated, unlike the old English long bow which is classsed as a single stick and made from yew. With the grip of the kyudo bow closer to the bottom than that of its European counter parts, there is the added advantage of increased strength. These are two main school of Kyudo which are Ogasawara and Heki. All style divide the act of shooting into hassetsu or eight stages. The first movement is ashibumi meaning to step or tread. This is part of archer's stance. The next stage is dozukuri, the positioning of upper body, with the torso held straight but relaxed and breathing controlled. Then comes Yugamae, which is setting the bow in place with the arrow in a firing position. This is followed by Uchiokoshi, a double sectioned stage in which the kyudoka lifts the bow and looks at the target for the first time, then looks away; these movements are respectively termed monomi and daisan. Next begins the drow, called hikiwake, with the string hand pulling the arrow all the way back behind the ear. This position is held while the archer meditates on all the correct procedures; this is termed the kiai meaning the meeting. Now the archer waits for the arrow to shoot itself : the moment arrives when the strain is too great on the archers thumb holding the string. The hanare, or release, is then fulfilled. The archer does of willingly release the arrow; it just happens with the arrow in flight the archer watches it winging its way to the target, or not to the target. This motionless stance is known as Zanshin, the moment of knowledge. If the acquired skills are possessed by the Kyudoka, then it is at this stage that enlightenment takes place.[290]

The Sai is a weapon that resembles a trident, but with characteristics of a thick dagger. It is a three-pronged trucheon about 15-20 inches (38-50 cm) in length. Mostly used in defensive instrument against various weapons such as the sword the long itself. The Sai is used in pairs; sometimes a third in placed behind the back, wedged into the Karate belt. The weapon is used to block, strike, trust or ensure. In training with the Sai there is no competition and it is practiced according to classical traditions in order to keep its intrinsic values.[291]

Without Weapons (Unarmed)

(a) ***Aikido***—The literal translation of aikido is *ai* (harmony), *ki* (spirit), *do* (way), the way of martial spiritual harmony. This system of defense was originated by the late master Morihei Uyeshiba, who was born in 1883 at Wakayamana Prefecture in Japan. Master Uyeshiba devoted many long, hard years to the practice and study of several martial arts, before the development of aikido was realised. The new art was not only a form of physical defense and exercise, but also a deeply spiritual activity. The main schools of aikido philosophy maintain that the secret of this art is the oneness of mind, spirit and body and that the supreme state is to be at one with nature a spirit of the inverse. The technique of aikido are many and varied, each individual movement can be easily and swiftly followed by another. Essentially the techniques and Movements can be summarised as follows. Firstly the basic knowledge, such as *kmae* (posture), *ma-ai* (distance), *irimi* (entering), Ukemi (breakfalls) and chikari no dashikate (extension of power). These are followed by solo exercises (tandokudosa), which include movements such as breathing and wrist strengthening. After the tandoku dosa come the paired exercises, in which two individuals work with one another, turning and twisting their arms and bodies, in an effort to understand the continuous flow of power necessary for correct aikido technique the sequence continues with the wide range of throwing moves (nage waza), such as kaiten-nage (rotary throw) and shiho-naga (four side throw). Finally the last of the empty hand sections would include, katama waza (hold down techniques) incorporating ude-osae (arm pin) and kote-hineri (wrist twist). Self defense for an unarmed man against an assistant armed with a sword, knife or staff is another very important aspect of aikido technique. This type of training is called tanto-tori (knife taking), to-tori (stick taking) and token-tori (sword taking). Aikido is the perfect balance between physical and mental control, balance and perfectly timed relaxed movement.[292]

(b) *Shorinji Kempo*—Shorinji Kempo has often been described as a mixture of karate and aikido, though this is somewhat of an enigma. The art as practiced in Japan has a quasi-religious aspect about it, being greatly influenced by the Buddhist sect of Kongo Zen. The word Kongo means diamond and Zen is the school of Bodhidharma. The followers of Kengo Zen believe that the only power people should be guided by is knowledge of the world, and that a belief in one god simply divests man of most of his moral responsibility. Practice of this martial art is the west rests mainly on the philosophy and applied techniques, rather than adherence to religious principles. Shorinji is the Japanese translation of the Chinese word Shaolin-su, and Kempo is the Japanese translation of the Chinese word Chuan-fa meaning way of the fist. The fighting techniques of the Shorinji system comprise both soft and hard movements. Shorinji Kempo techniques are based firstly upon defence; attack is the last resort. The most important principle in the fighting system is the application of pressure to the vital points of the human body.[293]

The stick arts of Japan—In Japan there are basically three types of fighting stick. The bo staff is around six feet (1-8 m) in length and was an incredible 350 fighting styles in its repertoire. Next is the jo which is a little over 4ft zin (1.25m) long and has to fighting systems attached to it. Finally there is the hanbo, which is three feet (90 cm) long. Han means half, so it is half the size of the bo. One of the popular stick schools in Japan is that of *Shindo Muso Ryu.*[294]

(a) *Nunchaku - jitsu*—The nunchaku originated in southern Asia, where its primary function was as a flail in the cultivation grinding and polishing of rice. The agricultural workers of those are a could not afford, or in many cases were forbidden to carry, more conventional weapons, the nunchaku is constructed by simply joining two pieces of hand wood of equal length and weight, with cord, horse hair or chains, the weapon is then used like an extremely flexible whip. It is whirled around at great speed, employing a combination of techniques. It can be used by incorporating clubbing, poking and ensnaring techniques with the traditional flailing moves. In addition its flexible connection can be used as a vice.[295]

(b) *Jiu - Jitsu*—Among the many Japanese martial arts, probably the most misrepresented has been Jiu-Jitsu which is often described as the forerunner of Judo and the inspiration for aikido. Jiu-Jitsu in its fullest form was an art of the samurai warrior. Jiu-jitsu is constantly being confused with the art of judo, although both are distantly related. Jiu-jitsu is far more devastating than its sporting brother Judo. It is a combination, or series of combinations, of throws, holds and locks applied in most cases upon the limbs. They are carried out such a manner that by the addition and extra pressure, dislocation of a joint or actual breakage of a bone may occur. The art is based entirely upon a through knowledge of body balance, together with an accurate understanding of its construction.[296]

(c) *Kuatsu*-Kuatsu is the ancient art of resuscitation or revival, itself a branch of Jiu-Jitsu. It is so highly specialized that years of thorough training were given to instructors who had been carefully selected. They learned the art under a strict oath of secrecy. Kuatsu was considered to be the supreme knowdge in jiu-jitsu. Methods of Kuatsu are numerous and vary from school to school. One of the simplest methods used for resuscitating those who have been temporarily suffocated by choking involves grabbing the patient from the back and placing the edge of the palms on the abdomen, pushing upwards in a sharp movement. Groin injuries can be put to right using methods of Kuatsu, although complicated methods of recovery. It is thought that the knowledge of Kuatsu stems from the sister art of acupuncture, that of shiatsu.[297]

(d) ***Judo***—Judo was the brain-child of Dr. Jigoro kano, who established it in 1882 in Tokyo. It is a well-organised system of unarmed techniques, primarily based on thrown using leverage and holds. Judo means gentle way. It is nor Jets art; it is a sporting form partly developed from Jiu-jitsu. Judo is now practiced in almost every country in the world. Judo techniques are divided into three categories. Tachiwaza (standing techniques), newaza (ground techniques) and atemiwaza (vital point techniques).[298]

(e) ***Sumo wrestling***—Japanese sumo wrestling is thought by some to be more than 2,000 years old. Its origins lie in a mixture of folklore and myth. Japans oldest literary document, the Kojiki (records of ancient matters) penned in the early 700s, states that the goods fought for possession of the land. In 1684 official sanction was given to kanjin-Zumo (sumo) and it became a professional martial art and sprits. A series of rules and regulations were drawn up and supervisors were employed to see that they were carried out. In 1889 a man named Takasago petitioned for the re-instatement of sumo wrestling as a sport. Realizing great successor, the Tokyo Ozumo Kyokai was born (Tokyo Sumo Association). The complete recovery of sumo as a national sport in Japan came upon the competition of the Kokugikan, the hall of national sport. Today the art is controlled by the Japan Sumo Association. The highest award a sumo wrestler can receive is the emperor's cup. This was first given in 1926 to the ground champion Tsunenohana.[299]

China

The Chinese martial arts are divided into northern and southern styles. There are 'soft' and 'hard' style, which can be 'internal' or 'external'. There are also forms which contain a little of both. Northern and southern styles differ quite considerably, which is partly due to differences in geography between northern and southern China, and partly to differences in culture and traditions. Northerners are often bigger in stature than southerners and have strong legs, no doubt due to the many mountainous regions of their terrain. In the agricultural south the inhabitants are of slighter build and use their hands more in their work. There are also many other inherent factors that account for the southern style's predominant use of hands in fighting and the northern style's use of feet. Generally, northern style employ large movements with jumping kicks, while southern styles are more firmly based on the ground. The northern schools practise in prearranged sequences of technique, while southern schools encourage sparring in their training curriculum.[300]

(a) *The kung fu system*—Many kung fu styles have been based on the careful observations of animal fighting. An animal, having no interfering rational mind, moves freely and impulsively in an attack and defence situation. Therefore understanding the study of a martial system that is based on one particular animal, the underlying theme is to become like that animal, merging oneself through training to take on the nature of the breast. It is best explained as a kind of metamorphosis taking place, both mentally and physically, whereby the student completely identifies with the animal.[301]

The Chinese martial arts are usually separated into two distinct schools. The internal school comprises those three particular styles: they are tai chi chuan, pa-kua, and hsing-i. These 'soft' style, as they are termed, use the concept of yielding to an attack rather than meeting if head on. The second school consists of the external or 'hard' styles. These systems are associated with power strikes and hand body conditioning. They utilize force in straight lines with emphasis on kicking techniques. The Tai chi Chuan "form" is a continuous slow motion solo exercise whose primary objective is to teach practitioners how to attain spiritual and physical fitness, whereas the combat side of the art is secondary. The movements of tai chi are designed to allow the body to flow in a relaxed and smooth manner, without interruptions, and the structure of the form provides a method for claming the mind while concentrating at the awareness level.[302]

(b) *Karate*—Karate is the ultimate art of unarmed combat as well as being a super system of achieving physical fitness and control. Karate was born at Okinawa islands lying midway between China and Japan. The basic techniques of carate are punching (tsuki), striking (uchi), Kicking (Kesi) and blocking (Uke). After diligent practice of the Karate basis, the person then runs the principles of sparring (Kumite). Their are many stages like one step attacks and blocks, stepping punch to the face (oi Zuki Jodan) being blocked by a rising block (age Uke) etc. The student then progress to three step attack sparring by moving forward, while his opponent moves backward, counting the third block with a reverse punch to the stomach (gyakuzuki). Then followed five-step attack sparring (Gohon Kumite), which is simply an addition of two more movements. These must be practiced with as many students as possible to help build up confidence and ability, and to prepare each student for more advanced sparring training. The next stage in training is to vary the attacks and counters under the guidance of a teacher until the student is ready to apply techniques on his own in semi - free ore attack sparring (Jiyu Ippon Kumite). Finally, the student is ready to learn free style sparring (Jiyu kumite), one of the most advanced aspects of Karate. The traditional dress is known as a gi and consists of a loose pair of trousers and a double-breasted top held closed by a belt. A person just beginning to learn Karate wears a white belt. As the person become more skilled he used yellow, green, purple, brown and black belts.[303]

(c) *Skiamachia*—For more complete information on a formalized system of combat we must look to the ancient Greeks. The works of Homer (9th century B.C.), mentions Skiamachia, a sort of shadow boxing, which was eventually combined with wrestling to form an art called pancration meaning 'game of all powers'. A wide variety of techniques were allowed. So far as is known, pancration was the first recorded fighting discipline that incorporated a method of kicking with punches and empty-hand strikes. This art, or sports as it should be correctly termed, was introduced into the Olympic Games in 648 B.C. Indeed, some people believe that we could regard Alexander the Great (356-323 BC) as the founder of martial arts, who, through his invasion of India, brought with him the unarmed combat method of Greeks. However, it would seem somewhat presumptuous to suppose that Asia had to wait for that Macedonian conqueror to invade her borders before the martial arts were born. Recent archaeological investigation in southern China has unearthed paintings and artifacts suggesting that unarmed fighting methods were in operation long before his time.[304]

(d) ***Nanchaku***—It came into prominence with the advent of the Chinese martial art movies in the early seventies, and off course late Bruce Lee. The authorities, quick to notice their abuse in the hands of hooligans, brought in legislation and it was classed as an offensive weapon. Nanchaku have been part of martial arts scence for a few hundred year. Originally they were used for flailing rice from the husks, but later adopted as weapon. Nanchaku is practiced in kata from and has defensive and offensive techniques. Accuracy and control are the most important aspects of training and much time is spent perfecting these. In training, only the type with the cord is used, as the chain variety is deemed best used against other weapons for defence. Until quite recently the nanchaku was only over practiced for the improvment of the karateka, at a personal and individual level, but now a sporting element has been introduced whereby two exponents wearing special padded armour for protection actually goout on to the contest floor and do battle with each other. This is known as nanchaku de combet and organized in France. Its popularity has been far raching, and now many countries in Europe are staging regular competitions. The equipments consists of padded gauntlet gloves, a facemask not unlike that worn by kendoka, a padded breast plate and specially designed nanchaku that bend upon impact. These are constructed from a foam rubber material and are quite safe. Points in the contest are given for disarming (taking the nanchaku off your opponents by means of a strike-sweeps and take-downs are also included). By its very nature, nanchaku competetion is conducted at an almost lighting place.[305]

District and State Level PaikaAkheda Competition

The state government had organized paik akheda competition through the culture, sports and youth services department. The author scholar had gone through these departments and collected the data's. The total four times state level paik akheda competition were held in the year 1979,1990, 1992 and 1995. A district level demonstration programme of Orissan martial art was also organized on 15th August, 1998 at Khurda town. Total 17 teams were invited from Puri, Nayagarh and Dhenkanal district. Besides that, from the year 1991, the Surapratap

Sumrtipitha organised a district level paik akheda competition for the *Paikas* teams of the Dhenkanal district. Nowadays, every year more than 75 paik teams joins the competition.

The competition in the year 1979 (27th to 30th May)—In the year 1979, the competition was held at parade field (presently Indira park) at Bhubaneswar. Total 500 paikas, gurus, drummers and managers from 45 akheda participated in the competition.

The ceremonial offerings were held at Barunei hill by Sri Radhashyam Routray Dalabehara of Tapanga. Dalabehara handed over the torch to the horse rider. Torch rally starts from Barunei and reaches at Bhubaneswar parade ground. In the opening ceremony chief guest was late Sri Bijayanada Pattanaik the then union minister for steel and mines. The guest of honour was Hon' able Sri Ravi Ray union minister for health and family welfare. In the closing ceremony, the chief guest was Hon' able late Sri Nilamani Routray the then Chief Minister of Orissa.[306]

The competition in the year 1990—The competition was held from 14.06.1990 to 16.06.1990 at Gada Khurda. In the inaugural ceremony Hon'able Chief Minister late Sri Bijayananda Pattanaik inaugurate the competition. The puja rituals were conducted in Ramachandi Mandir at Gada Manetri. The total 60 number of paik brought the flame by road from Gada Manetri to Khurda. The Hon'able minister for pension and public grievances Mr. Prasanna Kumar Pattasahani received the flame.

The total 550 *Paikas*, gurus, drummers and their secretaries from 45 teams participated in the competition. The teams were limited to 13 numbers but more than twenty members (including drummers) joined the team.

The events were conducted as:

1. Mudugar chalana (eight compulsory techniques)
2. Lathi (single, dual and group)
3. Sword and shield (single, dual and group) (Patta and bana events were included in this category)
4. Banati (*chakra*, *rashi,* and *lathi* banati were included as individual events)
5. Ranapa (individual events)

6. Traditional war music's among drummers (Team twise)
7. The dress materials among the *paikas* (team twise)
8. Gada Bandana (team twise)
9. Individual best demonstration was held from the events like, (a)- lifting of big stone, wheel of the bullock cart, sagade (b)-nagaphasa, (c)-bankachura, (d)-singat chalana, and (e)-floor exercises.

The cash prize with a merit certificates were given the position holders. The prize money was Rs.200, Rs.150 and Rs.100 chaka for the first, second and third position holders respectively. All the participants including their guru got a merit certificates.[307]

The paik akheda competition in the year 1992—The competition was held from 10.04.1992 to 12.04.1992 at Gada Khurda. Total 87 teams from different districts applied to participate in the competition and 62 teams were joined in the competition. Hon' able Chief Minister Mr. Janakiballav Pattanaik inaugurate the competition.

The events were mentioned below.

1. Sword and shield (individual)
2. -Do- (dual)
3. Mudugara chalana (individual)
4. Traditional form of weight lifting like big stone and bullock cart wheel (individual)
5. Lathi (single)
6. -Do- (dual)
7. Ranapa (individual)
8. Patta (individual, dual and group)
9. Banatti (individual)

In the closing ceremony the cash prize was awarded including certificates of merit to the position holders. All the participants also got a merit certificate. The prize money was Rs. 200, Rs.150 and Rs.100 for first, second and third place holders respectively.[308]

The paik akheda competition in the year 1995—Every year 15 to 20 number of paik teams was invited to demonstrate the martial art in the Harekrushna Mahatab's Jayanti day by the organizing committee.

A rally was arranged from State Secretariat building to his residence near old town. On the processtion they demonstrates the activities.In the year 1995, Hon'able minister of sports and youth services Mr. Suresh Kumar Routray invited about 80 teams of different districts. Out of them total 65 teams participated in the competition. The competition was organized at B.N. High School field, old town, Bhubaneswar. Total 800 *paikas* including guru, drummers from different districts participated in the competition. The department of sports and youth services had organized the competition.

The events were mentioned below.

1. Mudugara chalana (individual events)
2. Lathi (individual events)
3. Sword and shield fighting (dual)
4. Banatti (individual event)
5. Patta chalana (dual)

The prize money was awarded at the end of the competition. The first, second and third position holders receives Rs. 500, Rs. 300 and Rs. 200 respectively. Apart from these events, a cash prize Rs. 500/- was given to a team, related to wearing traditional paik dress. A best team was selected and awarded cash prizes Rs. 500 on the basis of good demonstration programme on the road. A drummer was awarded cash prize Rs.500 on the basis of his best individual performance among all the teams. All the *paikas* and their guru also got a participant certificates.[309]

District Level Competition at Dhenkanal—The district level paik akheda competition was started in the year 1991, at Surapratap Smurtipitha, Dhenkanal. The aim of the competition was to revive the traditional martial art of Orissa and to create interest among the militia class of Dhenkanal district. Hon'able Sri Kamakhya Prasad Singhdeo (M.P and hereditary chief of the Royal Dhenkanal Palace) take initiative action to start this martial art competition. In the year 1988, he gave financial assistance to six-paika teams and a demonstration programme was organised at Dhenkanal stadium. The next year the same programme was also organiged without any financial assistance by the Government. Then the executive bodies and Sri Singhdeo, president of Surapratap Sumrtipitha took a decision that a martial arts competition was highly essential among the *paikas* and from the year 1991 onwards the same competition was organised. In the year 1991, only eight teams participated in the competition. In the year 1992, total twentythree paik teams participated in the competition. For the first time, two ladies teams were included in this competition. In the year 1993, total twenty four paik teams with four ladies team participated in the competition. In the year 1994, total forty teams participated in the competition. In the year 1995, total forty eight teams participated in the competition. The total fiftytwo and Sixtyone paik teams participated in the year 1996 and1997 respectively. In the year 1998 and 1999 total sixtyeight and seventyfive teams from Dhenkanal district participated respectively. The details about the teams represented year was are mentioned in the graphical designs.[310]

Three to five judges observed the competition. All the teams got twenty minutes time to demonstrate the martial art. The judges evaluated the team on the basis of physical fitness, paika dress, stepping, techniques, drum beats, *paik thani*, *paik boli* etc. All the teams were got information about the rules of the competition from the judges.

Rules of the Dhenkanal District Competition are mentioned below.[311]

1. All the paika teams are bound to wear traditional paika dresses at the time of competition and demonstration programme.
2. Discipline is highly essential at the time of demonstration. Within their time limit (20 minutes) they are supposed to demonstrate according to the direction of their guru. At a time they are not allowed to demonstrate all the activities like sword, lathi, banka chhura, ranapa, mudugara etc.
3. The height of the lathi (steff) should be their nose height.
4. At the time of demonstration, the participants should not forget to demonstrate stepping, *chahani* (aggressive facial action) etc.
5. *Kuhata, boli* etc. should be pronounced clearly.
6. Traditional drum beat is highly essential at the time of demonstration.
7. The judges also observed the physical fitness of all the teams.

Prize Ceremony—At the closing ceremony the meeting was presided by the president of the organization. Then the Guest of honour, Chief Speaker and Chief Guest deliberate their speeches. Then prize distributions were conducted team twise and individual wise. Three best teams were selected from men section and first, second and third prizes were given to them. Similarly three best team from girl's teams and three from boys side were distributed first, second and third prizes. Individual prizes were also distributed to the *paikas* in different activities like sword, lathi, patta, ranapa, etc.

Incentives to the Paika Gurus from the Governments—[312]In the financial year 1996-97, four paika gurus from Puri, Nayagarh and Khurda districts got sports person pension Rs. 300 per month.From the year 1997-98 another six paika gurus belong to Cuttack, Dhenkanal and Khurda districts got the same pension. Now, the government has revised the sports person pension from Rs. 300 to Rs. 500 per month which will be implemented with effect from 01.03.2000. The government further decided to grant pension for maximum five paika gurus in each financial year. Now, total ten paika gurus (two from Puri, one from Nayagarh, two from Khurda, two from Dhenkanal, three from Cuttack district) receives the sports persons pension.

Criteria to receive the pension:

1. The Paika Guru should be 60 years of age.
2. He should participate five times State level Orissan Martial Arts competition or ten times district level competition.

The relationship of *yaga ghar* of Puri town with Paika Akheda—Puri or Purusottam Ksetra of Orissa has got its names and fame for Lord Jagannath all through the world. This Ksetra on the basis of the cult of Jaganath has been described in Puranas as the most sacred place in Bharata Varsa. It is a place, where the God Purusottam (Jagannath) has made his perpetual abode like Vaikuntha Bhuvana[313]. This was a meeting place of Hindus, Buddhists and Jains and had unique advantage to systematize and assimilate the essence of these three spiritually intellectual disciplines.

[314]Puri mainly consists of seven *sahi* (colony) and forty-two *kandi* (lane). In each *sahi* there was one akheda and under the akheda many Yaga ghar were located. Sadasiva Rathsarma quoted the details about sahi and akheda as follows.

1. Matimandap Sahi	— Matimandap Sahi Akheda
2. Dolamandap Sahi	— Janhimundia Akheda
3. Kundheibenta sahi	— Pathara Akheda
4. Markandeswar Sahi	— Makandeswar Sahi Akheda
5. Harachandi Sahi	— Chamundamundi Akheda
6. Bali Sahi	— Bali Sahi Akheda
7. Goudabad Sahi	— Goudabad Sahi Akheda

Sadasiva Rathsarma quoted the yaga ghar to their respective Sahi of Puri as follows.[315]

1. Matimandap Sahi	—	Bhoga Jaga
2. Dolamandap Sahi	—	Jadutiadi, Bajragada Amin, Amin Champagada, Jagatapratihari Nua Tota
3. Khundheibenta Sahi	—	Sundara, Bisuni, Gopali, Marichikota, Malligada, Aleikota, Ganeshguruja, Bramha, Majana, Mali, Jadu, Indradumna Kota, Kandara Kota, Khaki Kota, Makar Dhwaja, Balabhadra Ballav, Narasingha Gada, Bada Jaga, Bhagabata Kota, Gopinath Ballav, Dibyasingha Kota, Beladala, Sudanga Kota.
4. Markandeswar Sahi	—	Duari, Satabakhara, Bhatta, Rahasamahanty, Panda, gadasahan Badapokhari , Muduli, Badapokhari.
5. Harachandi Sahi	—	Bada Akheda, Barabati, Tapanga, Nrushingha Ballav, Jamikhuntia, Dhwaja Gada, Sankha Kota, Iswar Ballav, Kusan Khuntia, Muduli, Dekhit Badapokhari.
6. Bali Sahi	—	Khuntia, Hinjala, Kadam Gada, Luha Gada, Naga Kota, Panchuati, Gurujanga, Dubei, Kalika Kota.
7. Goudabada Sahi	—	Adanga Tiadi, Khasu Kota, Jaban Gada.

All these Yaga Ghars, mentioned above are of four types:[316]

1. Raja Angila that is functioned and managed by the King.
2. The Bakshi and Parichha managed Bakshi Khanja. (Bakshi and Parichha were the title given by the king).

3. Badati types were functioned and managed by religious people like Sadhu, Santha, Sanyashi and Baistambi.
4. Bahumana categories were managed by the local Jamindar.

The term *Guruja, Kota*, and *Gada* were all associated with *Jaga*. However the meanings were little different. A *Yaga* consists of 200 members called *Gada* and 500 members called *Kota*. All these gadas were controlled by Raja. *Guruja,* it is also known as *Buruja,* a meeting place of higher officials of Raja. The place is in circular type and sometimes God and Goddess of the respected jaga like *Durga, Nrushinha, Salya, and Ganesh* shining there. The most important thing is the members of the jaga ghars are not called paika. Most of the members belongs to *Sebayata* class of Lord Jagannath Temple.[317]

Debadatta Samantasinghar[318] quoted that on 11th century A.D. under the direction of Maharaja Choda Gangadeva four *Kota* were established to protect Lord Jagannath temple from foreign invasion. These kotas were: *Naga Kota* at south side, *Marichi Kota* was in east side, *Bhagabati kota* was in north side and *Endradumna Kota* was in south at Puri town.

These Akhadas of the respective sahis were mint for local administration of their respective sahi's, promoting the culture of Sangeeta (singing, playing and dancing); and organization of 'Sahi Yatra' comprised of various physical activities like sword fighting, Lathi fighting, Banati (Fire Play), Gada mudgar, Naga dance etc accompanied by *Vira Vadya*. These activities were to be presented publicly at the time of Sahi yatra. This festive occasion is related with Jagannath temple. The Sahi yatra starts from Sri Rama Navami day and it ends the day of Abhiseka Utshav of Sri Rama. The 'Jagas' were the centre for physical education and music. The members of the Jaga gharas regularly do physical exercise like danda, baithak, wrestling, gada mudugar etc. The *sahinayak* (chief of their respective sahi) were incharge of the Jaga ghar.[319]

References

1. D.C. Dasgupta, '*Educational Psychology of ancient Hindu*', Calcutta, Calcutta University Press;(1949): p. 85.
2. C.Tirunarayanan, S.Harinarasarma, '*An Analytical History of Physical education*, Karaikudi, South India Press, (1972): p. 6.

3. R.S Tripathy, *'History of Ancient India'*, Varanasi, Motilal Banarasidas, (1960): p.30.
4. S.N Das, *'Physical Education, Games and Recreation in early India'*, Lucknow; The Upper India Publishing House, (1985), pp.10-12
5. R.C. Majumdar and A.D. Pusalkar, *'The Vedic Age'*, London, George Allen and Unwin Ltd, (1957): p. 517.
6. *Chandogya Upanisad*, Quoted by F.Max Muller, Motilal Banarasidas, (1969), Vol.1, part 1, p. 96.
7. *Mundaka Upanisad*. III, 2,4 (Quotated by) F. Max Muller Vol.XV, part II,Varanasi: Motilal Banarasidas; (1969): p. 40.
8. Maxmuller, F., *Brhadaranyakopanisad* (trans), S.B.E., Vol. XV, Varanasi: Motilal Banarasidas, (1965), V.14, 4.
9. A.S Altekar, *'Education in Ancient India'*,Varanasi, Nand Kishor and Bros. (1957): p.7.
10. V. Sitasamiah, *'Valmik Ramayan'*, Sahitya Akademi, New Delhi, (1972), p. 54.
11. Keay.P.E., *'Ancient Indian Education'*, London, Oxford University Press, (1918): pp.61-62.
12. *Valmik Ramayan*, VI, pp.28-30, Quoted by, S. N. Das, "Physical Education, Games and Recreation in Early India", p. 22.
13. *Valmik Ramayan* V 48-5, Ibid, p. 23.
14. Dikshitar, V.R.R, *'War in Ancient India'*, Madras; MacMillan Ltd., (1948), p. 380.
15. H.C Das, *'Military History of Kalinga'*, (Calcutta, Punthi Pustak, 1986): p.71.
16. *Bhagabat Gita*. VI.17., Quoted by, B. K. Majumdar, *'Military System in Ancient India'*, (Calcutta, World Press,1955):p.88.
17. *Mahabharat*.1, Quoted by, B. K. Majumdar, *'Military System in Ancient India'*, p.35.
18. Keay, P.E, *Ancient Indian Education*, London, p. 61.
19. S.N Das, *'Physical Education, Games and Recretion in Early India'*, p.50.
20. *Ibid*. p.51.
21. P.C Chakravarti, *'The Art of War in Ancient Iadia'*,Calcutta, Abinas Press,(1941): p.99.
22. H.C Kar, *'Military History of India'*, Calcutta, K C M Pvt. Ltd.; (1980):p. 96.

23. S.D Gyani, '*Agani Purana A Study*', (Varanasi, Chowkhanba Publication,(1964): p. 280-81.

24. Agni Purana, Quoted by, P.C. Chacravarti, '*The Art of War in Ancient India*' p. 93.

25. Bhagbat Gita, Quoted by B.K. Majumdar, "*Military System in Ancient India*", p. 89.

26. P. Sensharma, *Kurukshetra war : A Military Study*, Ganganagar, Darbari Udjog, (1975), pp. 93-94.

27. Sabhaparva - Mahabharat, Quoted by B.K. Majumdar *Military System in Ancient India,* p.7.

28. Eraj Ahamad Khan, *History of Physical Education,* Varanasi, Narendra Bhargava, (1964), p. 316.

29. Mahabharata, Udyoga Purana (100. 16-17), Quoted by B.K. Majumdar, *Military System in Ancient India,* p. 34.

30. D.C. Dasgupta, *Jain system of Education*, Calcutta, Sri Bharat Press,(1942), p. 62.

31. C.H. Tawney, *Somadevas Kathasarit Sagar*, Varanasi, Motilal Banarasides, (1968): p. 200.

32. S. Beal, *The Romantic legend of Sakya Budha*, Trubner Co., London, (1875), p. 71.

33. H.M. Johnson, *Trsastisalaka-Purusacarita by Hemacandra*, Vol. II, Baroda, Baroda Oriental Institute, (1931), p. 71.

34. H.C. Rai Chawdhry, *Political History of Anicient India*, Calcutta : Punthi Pustak. (1959): p. 249.

35. R.K. Mukherji, *Ancient Indian Education*, Varanasi : Motilal Banarasidas, (1960): p. 347.

36. D.C Dasgupta, *Jain system of Education*, Calcutta, Sri Bharat Press, (1942): p. 60.

37. P.L Vaidya, *Lalita – Vispara*, Bhuddhist Sanskrit Text, No.l, Dearbhaga: Mithila Institute, (1958) Chapter, III.p. 67.

38. Keay, P.E. *Anicient Indian Education*, p. 102.

39. M.N. Das, *Ancient and Medieval Empires and Kingdoms,* History and Culture of Orissa , p. 87.

40. H.C Das., *Military History of Kalinga*, p. 86.

41. D.C Sircar, "*Inscriptions of Ashok*", p. 37. Quoted by H.C. Das Military History of Kalinga, p. 88.

42. H.K Mahatab, *History of Orissa* Vol.1 (Cuttack, Prajatantra Prachara Samati, 1960): p. 19.

43. M.N Das, *"Indian History"*, (Cuttack, Vidyapuri, 1986): p. 55.
44. *Kautilya Arthasastra*, Translated by R.Shamasustry, Mysore, Mysore Printing and Publishing House, (1923): Ch. I.p. 120.
45. R.P Mohapatra, *Military History of Orissa*, pp. 12-13.
46. *Ibid*,p.13.
47. D.R. Bhandarkar, *Comprehensive History of India*, Vol. II, Ed. N.K. Sastri, Varanasi, Motilal Banarasidas, (1956):p.224.
48. B. Mishra, *Orissa Under the Bhauma Kings*, Calcutta,Vishwamitra Press, (1934): p. 43.
49. H.C Das, *Military History of Kalinga*, pp. 93-94.
50. R.P Mahapatra, *Military History of Orissa*, pp. 22-23.
51. *Ibid.* p.23.
52. Hirananda Sastri, *Brahmi Inscription on a Wooden Pillar from Kirari.* E.I. Vol. XVIII, p. 152-157.
53. N.K Sahu, *History of Orissa*, Calcutta, Nabajiban Press, (1980): Vol.I, p. 343.
54. Nagendranath Pradhan, *Rise and Fall of a Powerful Hindu Kingdom of India*,Souvenir on Utkal at a Glance, Bhubaneswar, Published by Shiksha Vikash Samiti, (1998): p. 46.
55. Harish Chandra Panda, Military History of Orissa, Ed, by P.K. Mishra, Comprehensive History and Culture of Orissa, vol.1Kaveri Books, New Delhi, 1997,p.588.
56. Harish Chandra Das, Military History of Kalinga, p.96.
57. R.P Mohapatra, Military History of Orissa, p.26.
58. *Ibid*, p. 27
59. *Ibid*, p. 28
60. H.C Das, Military History of Kalinga, p.96.
61. *Ibid*, p. 96.
62. R.P Mohapatra, Military History of Orissa, P. 33.
63. *Ibid*, p. 33
64. *Ibid*, p. 33-34.
65. *Ibid*, p. 46
66. *Ibid*, p. 46.
67. *Ibid*, p. 47.
68. *Ibid*, p. 48.

69. Yuktikalpataru, verse, 24-29, quoted by R.P. Mohapatra, Military History of Orissa, p. 48.
70. B.R Das, Bhaumakaras and their times, p. 133.
71. R.P Mohapatra, Military Histiry of Orissa, p. 49.
72. E.I, Vol. XV, 1919-20, pp. 363-364.
73. K.C.Panigrahi, History of Orissa, p. 67.
74. R.P. Mohapatra, Military History of Orissa, p. 49
75. U.K. Subudhi, Bhaumakaras of Orissa, Calcutta, 1978, p. 85.
76. R.P.Mohapatra, Military History of Orissa, p. 53
77. B.Mishra, Orissa Under the Bhauma Kings, p. 28.
78. B.Mishra, Orissa Under the Bhauma Kings, p. 48.
79. *Ibid*, p. 58.
80. R.P Mohapatra, Military History of Orissa, p. 55.
81. *Ibid*, p. 55.
82. Harshacharita, Text 68 (translation 55) Qut.by R.P. Mohapatra, Military History of Orissa, p. 55.
83. E.I., Vol. II, p. 1-12.
84. Watters, Vol. I, p. 171.Qtd. by R.P. Mohapatra, Military History of Orissa, p. 56.
85. Harshacharita, Text 68 (translation 55).
86. B.R Das, Bhaumakaras and Their Times, pp. 137-138.
87. JBORS, Vol. II, P. 419ff.
88. B. Mishra, Orissa Under the Bhauma Kings, p. 46.
89. *Ibid.*, p. 97.
90. E.I.,Vol. XXIX, pt. IV, p. 85.
91. B.Mishra,Orissa Under the Bhauma Kings, p. 98.
92. R.P. Mohapatra, Military History of Orissa, p. 56.
93. *Ibid.*, pp. 56-57.
94. *Ibid.*, p. 61.
95. Ibid., p. 69.
96. E.I,Vol, XXXIII, pp. 263-274, Verse 30-31.
97. R.P. Mohapatra, *Military History of Orissa*, pp. 69-70.
98. *Ibid.*, p. 70.
99. *Ibid.*, p. 70.

100. *Ibid.*, pp. 70-71.
101. K.C Panigrahi, *History of Orissa*, p. 118.
102. R.P. Mohapatra, *Military History of Orissa*, p. 71.
103. R.P. Mohapatra, *Military History of Orissa*, p. 77.
104. *Orissa History Research Journal*, Vol. V, No. 6., pp. 1-100.
105. SII,Vol. V, No. 1347. Verse 5 and 23. Quoted by R.P. Mohapatra, *Military History of Orissa*, p. 79.
106. *O H R J*, Vol. V, Nos.1-2, p. 69.
107. K.C. Panigrahi, *History of Orissa*,Cuttack, Kitab Mahal, (1981): p.167.
108. R.P. Mahapatra, *Military History of Orissa*, pp. 88-89.
109. *Ibid*, p.91.
110. C.V.Ramachandra Rao, *Admnistrative and Society in Medieval Andhra,1033-1538 A.D.*,p. 185.
111. R.P. Mohapatra, *Military History of Orissa*, p. 91.
112. *Ibid*, p. 92.
113. *Ibid*,p. 98.
114. K.S. Behera, *OHRJ*, Vol.XXVII; Nos. 1-4, p. 8
115. K.C. Panigrahi, *History of Orissa*, p. 414-415.
116. R.P. Mohapatra, *Military History of Orissa*, p. 94.
117. R.L. Mitra, *Antiquities of Orissa*, Vol. II, p. 255.
118. R.P. Mohapatra, *Military History of Orissa*, p. 96-97.
119. *Ibid*, p. 98.
120. R.L. Mitra, *Antiquities of Orissa*, Vol.I, p. 255.
121. R.P. Mohapatra, *Military History of Orissa*, p. 85.
122. M.N. Das, *Glimpses of Kalinga History*, pp. 207-208.
123. K.C. Panigrahi, *Histroy of Orissa*,p. 259.
124. *Ibid*, p. 259.
125. Account of Duarta Barbarosa, Vol.II, P.133, Qted. P. Mukherji, *The Gajapati Kings of Orissa and their Success*, Calcutta, General Trading Co.(1953): p. 136.
126. Rayavachakam, 72-81, Qted V. Ramchandra Rao, *Administrative and Society in Medieval Andhra (1033—1538 AD)* pp. 270-271.
127. K.C Panigrahi, *History of Orissa*, p. 260.
128. *Ibid.*, pp. 286-287.

129. *Ibid.*, p. 286-287.
130. P. Mukherji, *The Gajapati Kings of Orissa*, p. 120.
131. P.K. Pattanaik, *A Forgotten Chapter of Orissan History*, p.127
132. R.P. Mohaputra, *Military History of Orissa*, p. 180.
133. *Ibid.* p. 181.
134. W.Ewer to Government: 13th May, 1818, *Orissa History Research Journal*, Vol. IX, No. 3 and 4, Para 187.
135. C.D Mohapatra, *Utkal Itihasara Eka Agyanta Adhyaya*, p. 322.
136. P. Acharya, *Studies in Orissan History*, Archaeology and Archives, p. 255.
137. P.K Pattanaik, *A Forgotten Chapter of Orissan History*, pp. 80-81.
138. *Ibid.*, pp. 69-70.
139. R.P. Mohapatra, *Military History of Orissa*, p. 181.
140. K.N.Biswal, *Princily State in the District of Dhenkanal During the British Rule*.p. 74.
141. *Ibid.*p. 68.
142. R.P. Mohapatra *Military History of Orissa*, p. 182
143. P.K Pattanika, *A Forgotten Chapter of Orissa History*, p. 80-81.
144. R.P. Mohapatra *Military History of Orissa*, p. 182
145. G.Toynbee, A Sketch of the History of Orissa, *History Research Journal*, Vol, IX, No. 1 and 2, p.13.
146. *Ibid.*, p. 93.
147. Barabati Kaifiyata (Ed.), S.N. Rajaguru, Jhankar, Vol. iv, p. 418 (Oriya)
148. R. Sewell, *A Forgotten Empire*, p. 277
149. R.P. Mohapatra, *Military History of Orissa*, p. 184.
150. Sadasiva Rathsarma, *PaikaKheda* Ed.p.71.
151. Kartikeswar Patra, *The Port of Orissa*, Bhubaneswar, Panchasilla, (1988): p.18.
152. M. Mansingh, The Sage of Land of Jaganath, p. 47.
153. Rayasingh, L.N., "*Oriya Samar Sahitya*", Unpublished Thesis (Oriya) Utkal University, (1991) p. 226.
154. R.P Mohapatra, *Military History*, p. 184-185
155. M.A. Haque, *Muslim Administrate in Orissa*, p. 257.
156. R.P. Mohapatra, *Military History of Orissa*, p. 180.
157. B.C. Ray, *Orissa Under Mughals*, Calcutta, Punthi Pustak, (1981): p.190.

158. M.A Haque, *Muslim Adminstration in Orissa*, p. 257.
159. R.P. Mohapatra, *Military History of Orissa*, p. 190.
160. *Ibid.*, p. 190.
161. *Ibid.*, p. 190.
162. *Ibid.*, p. 191.
163. *Ibid.*, p. 191.
164. *Ibid.*, p. 191.
165. J.N. Sarkar, *Military History of India*, pp. 146-147.
166. *Ibid.*, p. 147.
167. G.N. Panth, *Studies in Indian Weapons and Warfare*, p. 149.
168. Baidyanath Gochikar, *Sahijatra Ra Sanyashi*, Oriya, Souvenir, p.16.
169. R.P. Mohapatra, *Military History of Orissa*, p. 192.
170. J.N. Sarkar, *Military History of India*, p. 152.
171. R.P. Mohapatra, *Military History of Orissa*, p. 192-193.
172. *Ibid.*, p. 193.
173. G.N. Panth, *Studies in Indian Weapons and Warfare*, p. 168.
174. R.P. Mohapatra, *Military History of Orissa*, p. 194.
175. *Ibid.*, p. 194.
176. *Ibid.*, p. 194.
177. *Ibid*, p.103.
178. N.K. Sahu, *History of Orissa*, Calcutta, Nabajivan Press, p. 300.
179. B.C. Roy, *Orissa Under Maratha*, Calcutta, Punthi Pustak p. 128.
180. R.P. Mohapatra, *Military History of Orissa*, p. 195.
181. B.C. Ray, Orissa Under Marathas (1751-1803), p. 128.
182. *Ibid.*, p. 140.
183. R.P. Mohapatra, *Military History of Orissa*, p. 195.
184. J.N. Sarkar, *Military History of India*, p. 155.
185. *Ibid.*, p. 157.
186. *Ibid.*, p. 196
187. G.N. Panth, *Studies in Indian Weapons and Warfare*, p. 186.
188. R.P. Mohapatra, *Military History of Orissa*, p. 186.
189. G.N. Panth, *Studies in Indian Weapons and Warfare*, p. 187.
190. R.P. Mohapatra, *Military History of Orissa*, p. 197.
191. *Ibid.*, 179.

192. *Ibid.*, p. 180.
193. *Ibid.*, p. 180.
194. B.C. Roy, *Orissa Under Maratha*, p. 130.
195. N.K. Sahu, *History of Orissa*, (Nalanda, Cuttack,1980): pp.227-278.
196. R.P Mohapatra, *Military History of Orissa*, p. 196.
197. *Ibid.*, p. 196
198. *Ibid.*, p. 196.
199. C. Tirunarayan, S.Hariharasarma, *An Analytical History of Physical Education*, (South India Press, Karaikudi, 1985):p. 7.
200. *Ibid.*, p. 7.
201. K.C Mohapatra, "Anti British Movements of *Paikas* 1776-1836", (*Souvenir on Paika Akhada Competition and Martial Tradition of Oriyas*,1979):p.66.
202. P.K Mishra, "Freedom Struggle in Orissa", *History and Culture of Orissa*, Ed. by M.N. Das, p. 259.
203. K.M Patra, *Orissa Under East India Company*, New Delhi, Munshiram Monoharlal, (1971):p. 22.
204. S.C Day, *Guide to Orissa Records*, Vol. III, p. 196.
205. Toynbe, OHRJ, Vol. IX, Nos. 1-2 (reprinted), p. 15.
206. R.P Mohapatra, *Military History of Orissa*, p. 155.
207. *Ibid.*, p. 155
208. B.C Roy, *Foundation of British Orissa*, p. 270.
209. *Ibid*, p. 271-272
210. P.K Pattanaik, *A forgotten Chapter of Orissan History*, pp. 183.
211. B.C. Roy, *Foundation of British Orissa*, p. 273.
212. R.P. Mohapatra, *Military History of Orissa*, p. 156
213. R.P. Mohapatra, *Military History of Orissa*, p. 185.
214. B.C. Roy, *Foundation of British Orissa*, p. 276-277.
215. *Ibid.*, pp. 279-280.
216. S.C. Day, *History of Fridom Struggle in Orissa*, Vol. I, p. 145.
217. P.K. Pattanaik, *A forgotten Chapter of Orissan History*, pp. 205.
218. *Ibid*, p. 207.
219. R.P. Mohapatra, *Military History of Orissa*, p. 161.
220. *Ibid*, p. 203-204.

221. OHRJ, Vol. III, No. 4, Paras-237-238.
222. P.K. Mishra, "Freedom Struggle in Orissa", *History and Culture of Orissa,* Ed. By M.N. Das, (Vidyapuri,Cuttack,1977): p. 259.
223. *Ibid,* p. 260.
224. Jagannath Patnaik, "Role of Orissa in the National Movement", *Souvenir on Utkal at a Glance,* p. 91.
225. P.K. Mishra, *Last days of the Oriya Milita,* S.S. Printers and Publishers, Bhubaneshwer, 1999, p. iv.
226. *Ibid,* p. iv-v
227. *Ibid,* p. v.
228. *Ibid,* p. 9.
229. *Ibid,* p. vii.
230. K.D. Das, *A Study of Orissan Folklore*, Cuttack, Nalanda, (1953): pp. 86-87.
231. N. Senapati, *District Gazetters*, (Cuttack, Survey and Map Publication, Orissa,1981):p. 165.
232. R.P.Mohapatra, *Military History of Orissa*, p. 188.
233. Durga Charna Kuanr, "The Chhau Dance of Orissa", *History and Culture of Orissa.* Ed. by M.N.Das. pp. 755-756.
234. R.P.Mohapatra, *Military History of Orissa*,p. 176.
235. M.Mansingh, *The Sage of the Land of Jaganath*, p. 44.
236. R.P.Mohapatra, *Military Histry of Orissa*, p. 177.
237. *Ibid,* p. 178.
238. *Ibid,* p. 178.
239. K.K. Bisoi, *O H R J,* Vol.XVI. Nos.1-2, p. 76.
240. *Ibid.*, p. 76.
241. R.P. Mohapatra, *Military History of Orissa,* p. 178.
242. *Ibid,* p. 179.
243. Dipak Kumar Basu, *The Magnificent Fort of Barabati*, p. 41.
244. L.N Rayasingh, *Oriya Samara Sahitya*, p. 89.
245. R.P Mahapatra, *Military History of Orissa*, p. 242.
246. Ibid., p. 247.
247. R.P Mohapatra, *Military History of Orissa,* pp. 252-253.
248. John Beams,*IA,* Vol. 1,1872, pp. 33-36.
249. R.P Mahapatra, *Military History of Orissa*, p.257.

250. *Ain-I-Akbari,* Vol. VI, No. 1, P. 55. Quoted by H. Blochmann, Royal Asiatic Society of Bengal, 1939, H2.12.
251. R.P Mahapatra, *Military History of Orissa*, p. 259.
252. Srivatsa Dash, *Baramba Itihasa*,Oriya, (Cuttack,Saraswata Press,1940): p. 79.
253. S.P Singhdeo & G.P. Singhdeo, *War Waves*, 1980, pp. 9-10.
254. *Ibid,* pp. 11-12.
255. R.P Mohapatra, *Military History of Orissa*, p. 269.
256. B.B Lal, *Sisupalagarh, An Early Historical Fort in Eastern India*, No.5, pp. 60-105.
257. T.J Maltby, *Ganjam District Manual*, 1918, pp. 96-97.
258. R.P Mohapatra, *Military History of Orissa*, p. 271.
259. *Ibid,* p. 286.
260. Sports Authority of India, *Indigenous Games and Martial Arts of India*, Vol. 1, p. 8.1.
261. David Manuel Raj, *Silambam Techniqu and Evaluation*,Unpublished Thesis, Jiwaji University, Gwalior,(1967): p. 870.
262. Sports Authority of India, *Indigenous Games and Martial Art of India*, Vol. 1, p. 9.1.
263. *Ibid.*, p. 10.3.
264. Sport Authority of India, *Indigenous Games and Martial Art of India,* p. 6-24.
265. *Ibid.*, p. 10.4.
266. *Ibid.*, p. 10.3.
267. *Ibid.*, p.1 0.4.
268. *Ibid.*, p. 10.4.
269. Peter Lewis, *The Way of Martial Arts*, p. 125.
270. *Ibid,* p. 129.
271. Michael Finn, *Martial Art a Complete Illustrated History*, London,Mackenzie Publishing Ltd, 1988, p. 187.
272. Peter Lewis, *The Way of Martial Art*, p. 129.
273. *Ibid.*, p. 130.
274. Michael Finn, *Martial Art a Complete Illustrated history*,p.188.
275. Peter Lewis *The way of Martial Arts*, p. 122.
276. *Ibid.*, p. 133.

277. *Ibid.*, p. 133.
278. Michael Finn, *Martial Arts and Complete Illustrated History*, p. 194.
279. Petter Lewis, *The Way of Martial Art*, p. 133.
280. *Ibid*, p. 135.
281. Michael Finn, *Martial Art a Complete Illustrated History*, p.17.
282. Peter Lewis, The Way of Martial Arts, p. 79.
283. *Ibid.*, p. 78-79.
284. *Ibid*, p. 78-79.
285. *Ibid*, p. 78-79.
286. *Ibid*, p. 78.
287. *Ibid*, p. 103.
288. *Ibid*, p. 84.
289. *Ibid*,p. 80.
290. *Ibid*, pp. 81-82.
291. *Ibid*, p. 83.
292. Jim Wilson, *An Illustrated Introduction to the Martial Arts*, p. 55.
293. Peter Lewis, *The Way of Martial Arts*, p. 97.
294. *Ibid.*, p. 87.
295. Jim Wilson, *An Illustrated Introduction to the Martial Arts*, p. 62.
296. Peter Lewis, "*The Way Of martial Arts*", p. 91.
297. *Ibid.*, p. 91.
298. *Ibid*, p. 93.
299. *Ibid*, p. 101.
300. Micheal Finn, *Martial Arts A Complete Illustrated History*, p. 52.
301. Peter Lewis, *The Way of Martial Arts*, p. 15.
302. *Ibid*, p. 16.
303. Jim Wilson, *An Illustrated Introduction to the Martial Arts*, p. 18.
304. Peter Lewis, *The Way of martial Arts*, p. 90.
305. Peter Lewis, *The Way of martial Arts*, p. 83-84.
306. *Souvenir on Martial tradition of Orissa.*
307. Records from the Office of the *Directorate of Sports and Youth Services*, Government of Orissa, Bhubaneswar.
308. *Ibid.*
309. *Ibid.*

310. P.Barala, "Paika Akheda Competition of the year 1993 and Statements of the Judges" *Souvenir on The Orissan Martial art*, Dhenkanal, Surapratap smurtipitha, (1994): p. 17.
311. *Souvenir on Orissan Martial Art*, Dhenkanal, Surapratap Smurtipitha,(1994): p. 27.
312. Records from the office of the *Directorate of Sports and Youth Services,* Government of Orissa, Bhubaneswar.
313. Gopinath Mohapatra, *"Jagannath During the Rule of Gangas and Suryas"*, Ed. by, M.N. Das "History and Culture of Orissa", p. 409
314. Sadasiva Rathasarma,Souvenir on "*Utkaliya Paramparika Sanskrutika Mahautasava*" (Oriya) Puri, Srikhetra Hanuman Jayanti Committee, (1983) pp. 5-6.
315. S.Rathsarma, "*Akheda and Jaga Relation*", Souvenir on "Utkaliya Paramparika Sanskrutika Mahautasava" (Oriya): pp. 10-11.
316. D. Samantasinghar, "*Srikhetrara Sanskrutika Pranakendra Jagaghar*", souvenir on "Utkaliya Paramparika Sanskrutika Mahautasava" (Oriya): p. 30.
317. S. Rathsarma,."*Akheda and Jaga Relation*", Souvenir on "Utkaliya Paramparika Sanskrutika Mahautasava" (Oriya): p. 5.
318. D. Samantasinghar, "*Srikhetrara Sanskrutika Pranakendra Jagaghar*", Souvenir on "Utkaliya Paramparika Sanskrutika Mahautasava" (Oriya): p. 29.
319. Damodar Hota, "*Orissi as a form of Indian Classical Music*", Ed. By, M.N. Das, History and Culture of Orissa, pp. 774-775.

3
Methodology

The survey method of research was used to gather necessary data to critically analyse the Orissan Martial Arts. The present survey method applied in this study includes questionnaire, textual information, interview and observation of various techniques used in martial arts. The purpose of this study is (i) to gather data of martial art in Orissan literature, (ii) to collect various techniques and tactics of the Orissan martial arts, (iii) to collect information regarding the various age and sex groups involved in different akhadas, (iv) to get relevant information about location, financial supports and facilities, etc, available in different akhadas in Orissa and (vi) analysis of various weapons used by paika.

Questionnaire. A questionnaire was framed to collect relevant data regarding location, facilities, interest of various age and sex groups, and financial status of different paika akhadas of Orissa.

The draft questionnaire was framed and submitted to the guide. The suggestions received were duly incorporated in the questionnaire. The opinion and suggestions of the guide helped to restrict the number of questions in the questionnaire up to 25. The unnecessary and irrelevant questions were strucked out from the content of the questionnaire.

Then the questionnaire was put to a pilot test before sending to secretaries of five akhadas to ascertain its validity. After establishing the validity of the questionnaire, adequate copies were printed. The printed copies of questionnaire were then dispatched to 116 akhadas of our state. The addresses of the paika akhadas were collected from the Directorate of Sports and Youth Services and Surapratap Smrutipitha, District Dhenkanal. Out of 116 akhadas requested to respond the researcher through questionnaire, 48 akhadas replied within the time limit given by the researcher. Further the rest of the non-respondent akhadas were requested by sending one more copy of the questionnaire each and self addressed stamped envelop was sent to send the questionnaire duly filled in within a month.

The above attempt resulted in receiving another 33 questionnaire by the research scholar. Thus the researcher was able to gather 81 questionnaire in total for the study. The data collected through the questionnaire were then analysed and interpreted through percentage statistics.

Books and Journals—The textbooks and journals of the History of Orissa were referred to extensively to give the study a comprehensive coverage. In the light of results obtained from the study, the research scholar's suggestion and recommendations were made. The original materials examined in the course of this research, were collected from the Orissa State Library, State Archives, Orissa State Museum, Kedarnath Pathagara, Utkal University Library, Kanika Library of Revenshaw College Cuttack and the library of the Govt. College of physical education, Bhubaneswar.

Observation and Interview. The observation and interview technique had adopted for the collection of various data. Observation is one of the most important techniques of obtaining the objective data particularly at the time of their occurrence. This technique was also used for the final validation of the scientific conclusions drawn through the scientific methods by the scientists. Goode and Halt[1] have therefore made a comment that "science begins with observation and most ultimately return to observation for its final validation". In this technique the researcher attentively, carefully and consciously collects the data with deliberate use of the senses, attention and perception, which can be considered as the most distinguished components of the observation technique.

Sturat Chaplin[2] also appreciates the importance of precision tools of observation and states, "observation instruments are important and accurate just as truly as one the thermometer or the stethoscope of the physician".

Many Paika gurus even today in various villages of Orissa are teaching Orissan martial arts in the traditional way where a few people still appreciate this art. As it has still not been incorporated in any programme of physical education, any where in the state, no manual, describing the techniques of Orissan martial arts seems too available.

However, after observing the Martial arts from different districts of Orissa and discussing with their Palika Gurus, necessary steps had been taken to analyse the techniques of Orissan Martial arts.

The secretaries of the various akheda and their team members had extended their full co-operation to the scholar for the collection of data. In some areas, they had also arranged demonstration programme of the martial art exclusively for the research scholar. In some festive occasions like Raja Sankranti, Dola Yatra, Durgapuja, Makar Sankranti, etc the scholar had the opportunity to witness some traditional Martial art that are specially demonstrated by youths and paik gurus at their villages. The photographs of various activities were also taken in a 35mm camera in the festivals.

The author had the opportunity to observe the district and state level paik akheda competition. Every year, a district level Orissan martial art competition was organised at Dhenkanal district of Orissa. Every year the martial art competition was also organised among 15 to 20 teams of Orissa in late Dr. Harekrushna Mahatab's birth aniversary day at Bhubaneswar. The research scholar had the opportunity to observe the state level martial art competition, which was held at Gada Khurda in the year 1990 and 1992. The author was the member of the jury committee of the martial art competition, which was held at Bhubaneswar in the year 1995.

The interview was exclusively conducted only for the paik gurus of different paik akhadas of Orissa. The purpose of the interview was to get first hand information regarding the present status of the martial arts in the society, the interests and attitudes of the participants and villagers. Since the research scholar belongs to Puri town and acquainted with all the jaga ghars, conducts the interview programme for the secretaries of all the yaga ghars. He has also visited all the akheda and yaga ghar of Puri Town observed their facilities and equipments etc. The research scholar was also interested to get first hand information about their motivational aspects, financial support, organisational set up, etc.

Martial Arts of Orissa

The paikas of Orissa know many types of floor exercises, which are their major part of physical training. Before learning the skills of various weapon fighting, they first keep their body fit with the help of *Danda, Baithak* and other floor exercises. Then they learn the types of stepping, which is called *Ghar*. They practice four types of stepping namely one step, two steps, three steps and four steps. These stepping exercises are major part of their training before learning the various skills of the weapons. Their traditional floor exercises are almost similar with modern gymnastic stunt and floor exercises. The floor exercises can be divided into two parts namely, (a) With arm support, (b) Without arm support.

Danda—The performer takes a dips position. He keeps both hand wide (more than his shoulder level), hips upward and goes down with a forward and downward swinging movement. Then the entire body weight comes to his palms and toes. He comes to his original position lifting his hips with arm and toe support. The paika practices sixteen types of danda. These dandas are called as *(a) Sada Danda, (b) Chakra, (c) Lahadia, (d) Chhatibadia, (e) Chalatalia, (f) Gala, (g) Baghachahani, (h) Bagha Chata, (i) kimbhiria, (j) Bahubadia, (k)Bahujhinka or Dena, (l) Kolajhinka, (m) Pithichhat, (n) Chamaka or Parauḍa, (o) Benta Bhanuri, (p) Kenchuamoda.*

Baithak—Starting position: standing with feet apart about six inches, toes pointed forward and fists, closed.

After this position, the paika takes a full knee bent position with heels raised, then straightens the knees and returns to the starting position. This exercise is very important for the beginners.

Floor exercises with arm support (Front side)

1. ***Kudapaka (Forward role)***—From a squatting position, the paika places the hands on the floor about shoulder width apart. Then he places the chin on the chest and leans forward pushing with the feet and bending the arms. The paika allows the back of the shoulders to touch the floor first as the roll is executed and continues rolling on over the back. When the shoulders touch the floor, he takes the hands from the floor and grasps the shins with pulling the body into a tight tuck. In this way he rolls forward continuously for four to five times.

2. ***Kandhapaka (Shoulder Roll)***—The paika stands at one end of the floor with the feet spread slightly. Then he leans forward and throws the left arm towards the floor looking between the legs as the arm is thrown. Then he strikes the floor at the elbow first and rolls up the arm, across the shoulders and back and ends up on the feet facing sideward. The right arm can be used to push the performer to his feet. They also practise this exercise (stunt) from a run.

3. ***Mankadachit (Head Spring)***—The performer takes a slight run, then he places both hands on the floor with the top of the head about 6 inches in front of the hands as through doing a headstand. He pushes up the feet keeping the body in a deep picked position with the legs straight. The hips are carried over the head until the body weight falls off balance down the floor. He whips the legs overhead from the waist and on toward the floor in one continuous arch, simultaneously pushing with the hands. Then he lands on the feet with the knee bent slightly depending on the height of the headspring.

Thieaphopada (Hand Spring)—The performer takes a good run, skips on the right foot and brings the left foot forward. He places left foot on the fulka, bends forward at the waist and places both hands about 24 inches ahead of the left foot. He kicks the right foot overhead followed by the left. As the feet are being carried overhead, he keeps arms straight and the eyes are fixed on a spot about six inches in front of hands. As the body passes through the handstand position, the paika push off the fulka with the shoulders and wrists without bending the arms. This is continued over to the feet and with the knees flexed.

Olata Chali or Hanuman Chali **(Handstand with Moving Forward and Backward)**—The performer stands straight on both the hands by the side of the body. Then he skips on the right foot and brings the left foot forward. He places the left foot first on the floor or fulka bending forward at the waist and places both the hands according to his shoulder level ahead of the left foot. He kicks the right foot overhead followed by the left. As the feet are being carried overhead, he keeps the arms straight and the eyes are fixed on a spot about six inches in front of the hands. He maintains in this position for few seconds and try to move both the arms alternately forward and backward.

***Saulia Kudapaka* (Dive and Roll)**—The performer starts from a standing position, leaps forward and dives forward making an arch of the body in the air. His body lands on the hands and he continues a forward roll.

***Adachira* (Cart Wheel)**—Adachira may be performed either to left or to the right. The performer starts with the left side facing down the floor with the legs and arms out stretched and apart as in the spokes of a wheel. He rocks to the right side by placing the body weight on the right leg and lifts the left foot off the ground. Then he rocks back to the left by placing the body weight on the left leg. With the momentum established by this rocking motion, he bends to the left side at the waist and places the left hand on the floor about 2 feet to the side of the left foot. He forces the right leg overhead and simultaneously pushs off the floor with the left leg. As the feet approaches the handstand, he places the right hand on the floor about shoulder width apart from the left hand. As the body passes through the handstand from the side, he brings the right foot down on the line established by the left foot and hand by bending to the right at the waist. The left foot will follow to the floor and one finishes facing the same direction as at the start. The paika also performs one hand cartwheel (Ekahata Adachira).

***Pachha Kudapaka* (Backward Roll)**—The performer starts from a squatting with the hands on the floor and the knees between the arms. He leans forward slightly and then backward into the roll. He pushes with the hands, sits down and starts to roll onto the back. He places the hands above the shoulders with the fingers pointed back and the palms up. Then he keeps the chin on the chest thrust the roll. He rolls over the top of the head and onto the hands, keeping the knees tucked into the chest, pushes with the hands and continues the roll to the feet, finished in a squat position.

***Pachha Thiea Phopada* (Back Hand Spring)**—The performer starts from a standing position with the feet about shoulder width apart, and the arms, held straight out in front of the body. He swings the arm downward, simultaneously bends the knees and sits back as through sitting in a chair. As the body falls off balance backward swings the arms upward overhead, simultaneously forcing the head backward. He straightens the legs and pushs off the floor with the toes. As he pushes off with the toes, he forces the hips upward and makes a swing circle with the hands. As the hands land on the floor the body approaches to a handstand position. From this position, he snaps the legs down from the waist as in the snap-down and lands in a standing position on the feet.

Agali or Akashi (Front Somersault)—The performer takes a good run, skips on the left foot, swings the right foot forward, simultaneously raises both arms overhead, and lands on the fulka with both feet at the same time. When the entire body is in the air he places the chin on the chest and continues the circular motion with the hands by grasping and pulling at the shin into a tuck position. The chest remains close to the knees and heels close to the buttocks. After completing the somersault, he shoots out of the tuck and lands in a standing position.

Pichhili (Back Somersault)—The performer starts it from a standing position with the feet about shoulder width apart and the arms hanging in a natural position at the sides. He bends the knees, drop the arms backward and jump up swinging the arms overhead as through catching a horizontal bar. He throws the head and arms backward hand simultaneously bringing the knees unto the chest. He makes a small circular motion clockwise with the hands into a tuck. In the tuck position he pulls the knees to the chest hand and forcing the head backward then he lands on both the feet.

Double Forward Roll—It starts with one partner lying on the floor with his feet in front in the air while another stands at his head in a straddle position. They grasp each other's ankles. Then the top man dives forward into a forward roll taking the bottom man's feet down towards the floor. The roll brings the bottom man up onto his feet and he in turn dives forward. The other man is on top again does the same, and they continue in a steady roll down on the floor. The paikas perform this activity only for demonstration purpose.

Double Backward Roll—It is started in the same position as the doubles forward roll. The top man sits down pulling the bottom man's feet back with him. The bottom man executes a backward roll pushing up vigorously with his hands. Thus, the positions of both the paikas are now reversed, and the activity may be continued in a steady roll.

Pithi Chakra **(Back to Back Toss)**—In this activity, one person tosses the other person over his back. They start standing back to back with the hands clasped over the shoulders. One person bends his knees and he leans forward and proceeds to lift the other person over his back. The thrower or bottom man should be sure to dip slightly with his knees so that the top persons buttocks and rests against the lower back of the bottom man. The thrower should stop his forward lean and raise up as he feels the top man rolling off his back.

Kandha Olatathia **(High Arm to Arm Balance)**—The partner stands facing each other with arms raised and each grasps the other person's upper arm. The top man then leaps towards the bottom man and encircles his legs around the bottom man's waist. He then swings down between the bottom man's legs and then back upward towards the upper man to arm position. The bottom man swings the top man up and tries to move under him, so that the final part of the activity can be done in a slightly press motion. The top mounter swings freely upward into the upper arm to arm position allowing the bottom man to move in and hold him up over his lead.

Kandha Agali and Pichhili **(Back and Front Somersault)**—The partners start facing in the same direction with the bottom man's hands resting just above his shoulders and the top man behind him, grasping the bottom man's hands as in a handshake. The top man then moves to the side of the bottom man and the bottom man squats down a little. From this position, top partner places his right foot on the bottom man's thigh and proceeds to climb upward onto the shoulders. The bottom man pulls with the arms and keeps both arms firm and strong while the top man approaches to the final position. Then the top man takes a front or back summersault. Sometimes the research scholar finds at many places the top man moving a sword artistically. After demonstration he handed over the sword to other person and takes a back or front summersault.

Bhuin Kandha Teka **(Low Arm to Arm Balance)**—The bottom man is in a supine position with the arms up and the legs straight out on the floor while the top man straddles the bottom man's waist and leans forward and places his upper arms in the bottom man's hands. The top person grasps the backside of the bottom man's arm, he then jumps upward into a tuck position and continues to press into a low arm to arm. The research scholar also finds that the position can also be reached by kicking upward with one leg followed by the other.

Martial Arts (With weapons)—Before the paika performs the weapon art, he first learns types of steps. There are four types of steps called *eka ghar* (one step), *dee ghar* (two steps) *tin ghar* (three steps) and *chari ghar* (four steps).

Banka Chhuri—*Banka* means curve and *chhuri* means knife. It means a curved knife. It is similar to dagger. This is one of the important weapons of paika used to meet an emergency in which one may be attacked. Now a days it is also practiced by paika gurus almost in all the villages. Now it is not so popular compared to lathi and sword. The paika gurus teach their students in a systematic manner. He divide the group into pairs and in each pair one is designated as offensive person say for example (A) and the other (B) is defensive person. Each is given a banck chhuri (sharp less) or a bamboo stick for the practice. The competition is also organised in an understanding manner. Both paikas demonstrate the attacking and defensive techniques with the beat of drums.

Head Stroke—The offence paikas for example A takes the right foot forward, lunges on it and tries to hit straight on B's (defensive paika) head with full force.

Defensive paika 'B' avoids it by bending down and passing under the right arm of 'A', keeping on the right, stepping forward with the right foot, turns round and faces the same direction as A. B holds A's right ankle with the left hand over it, pulls the foot up and holds the toes with the right hand (partner facing A's side of the right foot).

Side Strokes (Throat, Chest and Ribs)—Sidestrokes are usually aimed at the temple, throat area and any part of the trunk including the chest. The attacker with the bank chhura in the right hand will move towards the left side of the opponent. All the strokes (chest, ribs, throat etc.) is practised with same artistic footmark with drumbeats. Sometimes both challenge with *kuhata* and slapping their right thigh with right hand.

Defence

A attack B—B holds A's right wrist with his left hand. A now tries the same stroke on B and holds B's right wrist with his left hand.

B throws away his banka chhura quickly and before A has anytime to stiffen his joints holds his left wrist (Now B has held both of A's hands). B pulls his right arm upward and turns left about. (If this is done with same force and quickly, A automatically turns about). Now both are standing back to back position. B lifts A over his back and throws him over, keeping the grip on A's hands. Then A loses his balance and falls down on the ground. Now B can lock his throat.

Sometimes both the paikas lost their Banka chhuris and try to seize each other.

Release from Rear Waist Hold

(a) When the hands are free, the paika bends sharply downward and holds opponents front leg in between his legs, then pulls it upward and sits firmly on his knee and at the same time pulls his leg upward. In this case the opponent loses his balance and he releases from his rear wrist hold.

(b) When hands are free, with a sudden jerk, he spread his elbows a bit; then he turns his body a bit either to the right or to the left and takes his rear leg behind opponent's knees from the rear. He bends a bit, grasps both of opponent's knees and lifts him upward.

Release from Front Waist Hold

When the opponent seizes the paika from front with both hands round his waist.

In this case of both the hands free, the paika holds his hands tightly and turns sharply to any side placing opposite leg behind his knees and pushes him backward.

If hands are free, he gives a jerk, spreads his elbows a bit and holds his body. Then he tries as in above when the opponent seizes from the front with both hands round opponents waist.

Release from Single Wrist Hold—Sometimes opponent seizes the right hand with his right hand. In this case, the paika turns his right hand towards opponent's left hand to press his right thumb downward to release his hand. He also gives a sudden jerk downward to release opponents grip.

Release from Double Wrist Hold—Sometimes opponent seizes the right wrist with his left hand and left wrist with his right hand. In this case paika turns both the hands inward, bends the wrists inside and turns them downward and outward to be released from the opponent.

Lathi—It is one of the ancient martial skills of our country. It has different types of names in various regions like Maharashtra where it is called lathi, in Andhra it is popularly known as knedubadi, Tamilnadu Silambalm.

In Orissa it is known as Gaudabadi or badi khela. At present, the paika performs many skills, techniques and tactics in single and double lathi. He moves his hands in an artistic manner. Simultaneously he moves his arm and legs forward and backward rotating the lathi in his hand. However, fighting is conducted both among team and dual type in an understanding manner. The team conducts no actual fighting. However they perform same attacking and defensive techniques at the time of fighting.

Grip – Many Types of Grips are used by the Paika

Two Hands close Grip—In this types of grip the performer holds the lathi (staff) at one end with the palms of the both hand.

The performer holds a lathi in one hand or in both the hands and sometimes he performs keeping two lathis in both the hands, so the grip depends upon the performance level of the paika. At the time of fighting the grip is changed according to the offensive and defensive techniques of lathi.

One Hand Close Grip—In this variation the performer holds the lathi (staff) at one end, in the palm of the right hand. The left hand remains silent and assists according to the movement of the body.

One Hand Grip at the Centre of the Lathi—In this grip the performer hold the lathi in the palm of the right hand at the centre of the lathi.

Two Hand Wide Grip— In this type of grip the performer holds the lathi with the left palm at the proximal end and right palm remains one foot away from the left palm.The lathi is pointed to the opponent's chest.

Two Hand Close Grip (Palm Open Down the Staff)—This grip is to enable the staff rest on the 'V' position so that it can be slide along the staff as exigencies demand.

Right hand–End and Left Hand–two Fingered–Grip—In this grip, the lathi is kept in between the first phalange of the left thumb and the first phalange of the index finger while the right hand grips it at the end.

Two–Hand–Reverse–Midi Grip: (Left Palm Opened Over the Staff)—Sometimes the 'V' position of the left hand is slide across the staff keeping the fingers stretched as required in the manoeuvre. This variation is called Two-hand reverse grip palm opened over the lathi. These types of grips are mainly used for defensive purpose.

Two Hands Reverse Wide Grip at the End of the Lathi—The lathi is not always held by one end only with single hand or both the hands. Sometimes, as situation demands both the palms slide over the lathi at the end of the lathi.

Swing

Aga Chakri (Front Swing)—The lathi is held with two-hands close grip at the proximal end. The lathi is swung with the wrist, the distal end first rotates a clockwise circle on the right followed by an anticlockwise circle in the left. The swing may also be done with the distal end rotating first on anticlockwise circle on the right followed by a clockwise circle on the left.

Pachha Chakri (Back swing)—The lathi is held with a two hand close grip. Swinging the staff with the distal and describing a figure of eight in front, the hand is gradually lifted higher and higher till the hands reach over the head and beyond, the elbows pointing to the front and continuation of this swinging in that position is the 'Back Swing'.

Overhead Swing (Munda Chakri)—The same swinging action over the head in a horizontal plane is called "Over head swing".

Bahu Chakri (Underarm and Over Arm Swing)—The lathi is held in the front at the proximal end with a two hand close grip, with the elbow kept flexed at approximately 90'. The lathi is swung in such a way that the distal end describes a clockwise circle in the sagital plane, the elbow on the side of the swing keeping close to the body.

Banati (Fire Arm)—It is an unique type of armament used by the paika at the time of Gorilla war. This comes under fair armaments. Now a day's paika uses it only for demonstration purpose. In a rashi length about 4 feet, clothes are attached to both the ends in round shape with equal weights. The beginners use it for learning purpose. After he learns it properly, then only he demonstrates banati with fire. The paikas himself prepares it. At both the ends, clothes are tied with the iron rings. So at the time of movement, the small particle could not sleep from the ring and the cloth is used with castor oil. After fire lit on both the ends, the performer starts moving the banati the both hands with various types of techniques. Guru Rama Chandra Suar of Shree Jagannath Samarakala Academy is proficient in this martial art. His teaching process is fine and every year he conducts a district level banati competition at Puri town. The author also finds at many places the paikas demonstrating banati with the help of lathi. At the both ends of lathi, an iron is attached to knot the clothes. They use oil in the clothes and lit the fire at both ends. The paika uses double lathi banati and demonstrates the skills.

Gada Mudgara:(Indian Club)—This equipment is not included in arms and armament of Orissan army. But the paikas use it to get strength. The paika knows that the strength is an important factor and they practised various types of exercises to develop strength for the major muscles of the body. The wrestlers also practised various types of exercises to keep fit and to get maximum strength. The exercises with mudgara helps to develop the trapizeus, deltoid, biceps, triceps and muscles of the forearms. They also perform exercise like baithak keeping two mudgaras in their hands resting to their shoulder to get strength of their quadricep and hamstring muscles. The techniques are called do dasti, chau dasti, and bagha nisha etc. The mudgara is built by seism wood. It has a handle and it is in round shape.

Do Dasti (Two Step Movements)—The paika holds the handles and lifts the mudgara up with the power of his wrist and the tail is pointed upward. Then he rotates the mudgara clockwise over his head with two-step movements of his left and right arm alternately.

Chau Dasti (Four Step Movements)—The movements remain the same as above. With four steps movement of his feet he performs the activities alternately moving his left and right hand.

Bagha Nisha (Tiger Mustach)—The paika lifts both the mudgaras up by flexing his elbow; the tail of the mudugara is pointed upward. He lifts his arm and brings both the fists near to his mouth and turns his wrists laterally, both the tails of the mud gara are pointed to the opposite directions. He holds the position for few seconds then keeps the mudu gara on the floor.

Patta—It is also an unique types of equipment. Many akhadas use this equipment. The research scholar finds that the term 'patta' is used as a technique of sword in Puri town. In almost all the yaga ghars of Puri town the term *addapatta* is used. This is the variation type of sword. Instead of a hilt, a forearm guard is attached at the bottom of the straight sword. There is also a handle fixed inside the forearm guard. The forearm guard is made of brass with some decorative works. All the movements of shoulder and elbow joints are possible. The paika gurus modify the same equipment in wooden form for learning purposes. The forearm guard is constructed in wood with some artistic work. A wooden stick (two and half to three feet) is attached at the forearm guard. The paika use it in the right arm and holds a stick (2.5 to 3 feet) in length in his left hand. The left hand stick is called Pasara. The beginners are used to learn in wooden form with their partners. The research scholar observed that there are two types of techniques namely *pancha ghar kainchi* and *sataghar kainchi* are practiced by the paikas sometimes they individually demonstrate the skills and techniques of the patta. However, in the competition, they select their partners and fight each other in an understanding manner. The research scholar also finds some places like Maluda, Parikuda and Rbenanuagaon of Puri districts where the fighting is arranged among four to eight paikas. The paika gurus those who are proficient enough in this skill also challenge the opponents that he can mark vermilion at a specific part of the opponents body with the patta or passara. They both use vermilion on their patta and passer. With their stipulated time fixed, they try to mark their opponents body. Whoever has marked first is declared winner.

Sword—The sword movements of the paika deal with to protect four sections of the body called *Shir* (head), *Chumour* (upper body), *Kamar* (waist) and *Kati* (Hips) region. They hold the tilt of the sword then salute their Gurus which is called *Guru Bandana* or *Salami* and then with the stepping movements (two, three and four steps) the sword is swung with the wrist in clockwise movement on the right, the tips move to down then up, followed by an anticlockwise movement in the left side. The movement continues for four to five times then he changes his steps. This is the most common movement of the sword. The other techniques are called *Dhalpa*, *Palta, Binchhini, Belara, and Chanara* etc. In *Dhalpa* movement, the paika moves his sword taking a step and rotates his entire-body clockwise in the air and then lands on other foot. The reverse movement of the body is called Palta. The paika moves his sword and steps forward with rotating his body clockwise direction. In this way he moves few steps forward and comes to his original position. This movement is called *Binchini*. Some times the paika moves his sword and rolls on the floor. This is an artistic movements and only few paika Gurus and senior most paika can demonstrates the technique. This technique is called *Belara*. The overhead swing of the sword is called *Chanara.*

Kadalikata: (Banana Cutting with Sword)—This is the artistic movement of the sword and only senior guru having proficiency in sword can demonstrates this techniques. One person lies down on the floor in supine position. Two bananas are kept on his left and right shoulder. Two bananas are kept on his left and right thighs and one banana is kept on his neck. The paika Guru moves his sword and with the drum beats he moves towards the paika who lies down on the floor and cuts all the bananas kept on his body. Guru Kasinath Nayak of village Bachhera district Khurdha, is proficient in this art.

Haladi or Chandan Pochha:(Cleaning Sandalwood or Turmeric Paste)—First of all the paika puts sandalwood or turmeric paste in his upper and lower body. Then he holds two swords on his both hands and with the drumbeats he moves both the swords in his body carefully. From the swords he tries to remove all the paste from his body. Within few minutes he removes all the paste from his body with the movements of his sharp sword on his body. Guru Sri Durjyodhana Das from Maluda is proficient of this fine art.

***Ranapa:* (War Foot)**—It is the combination of two terms. The term Rana means war and means foot. The paika use it at the time of Guerilla war particularly in the forest area. It is made of wood or the bamboo stick. The footrest is attached with stick. The length of the bamboo or wooden ranapa varies from one and half feet to six feet. The beginners use small ranapa for the practice purpose. The foot is tied with straps. Sometimes they tie it near the knee joint. After using it, the paika walks and runs speedily. Then they demonstrate sword, lathi etc. The mock fight also arranged in groups and individual basis. This demonstration programme attracts all the spectators. Guru Sri Niranjana Samal of Dhenkanal is proficient of this art.

***Nagaphasa:* (Cobra knot)**—It is one of the oldest weapons used by the paikas of Orissa. In Ramayana and Mahabarata the same weapon was used. The paikas apply the Nagaphasa when he wants to keep him as a Prisoner. It is very difficult to open the *phasa* or knot. It looks like a *naga* or cobra. At present the paika demonstrates it. This is made of *Beta* a particular root of the tree. There are five circles in the Nagaphasa. The paika holds it in his left hand and takes a back somersault and puts his head in the top circle of the Nagaphasa and lands perfectly on the floor. Then he opens it and again takes a back somersault. This time he tries to enter his head in the top circle and both the hands in the two side circles and lands on the floor. Lastly he tries to enter his head, both the arms and both legs into five circle of the nagaphasa when performing the back somersault. This demonstration is unique and the paikas particularly from Maluda and Parikud villages of Puri district are proficient of this art. Guru Sri Kedarnath Das of Maluda is proficient of this art.

Akalana and Sagadachaka—The literary meaning of the Akalana is beyond our imagination. It is a big stone, which is lifted by the paika in various ways. The big stone is circular shape and semi circular types. The paika lifts it from the floor and keeps on his shoulder and back. In this way he moves front and backside of the arena and demonstrates to the audience. Sometimes he also lifts the stone from the floor and in the forward bending position immediately he throws it over his head. The risk factors are very high. The stone falls down just backside of the paika.

The Sagadachaka (bullockcart) demonstration attracts all the spectators. First of all the paika put his head inside the rims of the wheel. Then with both arm support he tries to lift it from the floor and moves both clockwise and anticlockwise directions. In the last phase, he removes both the hands from the wheel and the entire weight of the wheel comes to the neck portion. Then he rotates his body speedily on the floor.

Pyramids—It has been found that many paika teams perform pyramids for demonstration. The performers are arranged in a line or in a circle. The heavier and stronger member of the group stands on the floor to form the foundation. The other members climb with the help of bottom man's thigh to their shoulders. The top person demonstrates a sword or lathi techniques. In the past, it was essential to climb the fort wall.

Description of Weapons

Weapons were the best friends of the brave, the symbol of authority and token of command, the visible sign of force, strength and domination. The history and development of weapons go back to a very early date. In the earlier phases axes, spears, daggers, bows and arrows, maces and slings were extensively used. In the subsequent centuries numerous other varieties along with defensive equipments came into practice. These weapons underwent a gradual process of evolution. The Agni Purana categorized weapons into five distinct varieties, viz; those thrown by machines (*Yantra mukta*), those thrown by hand (*Panimukta*), those thrown and drawn back (*Mukta Sundharita*), those not thrown (*Amukta*) and natural weapons such as fist. The Yukti Kalpataru of Bhoja divides weapons into deceitful and non-deceitful. The *Nitiprakasika* on the other hand divided the arms according to their nature into *mukta* (thrown) *amukta* (not thrown), *Mukta-mukta* (thrown or not thrown) and *mantramukta* functionally into (1) weapons of slashing or cutting, like the swords, axes, etc., (2) weapons like thrusting like trident, spears, etc., (3) projectiles like arrow, javelins, fire-arms, etc., and (4) weapons for smashing like the mace. Indian soldiers also knew elaborate and comfortable equipment for self-defence.

Weapon can be divided into two main categories. The first, indirect weapons, that contain those which either fire a projectile to destroy their pray, or are the instrument of destruction themselves. These include stones, catapults, spears, bows and arrows, throwing sticks, light and heavy artillery, and finally rockets and bombs. The second category contains those weapons which are normally included by an individual in close combat. They could also be thrown but this would greatly reduce their effectiveness. This second group is known as direct and included clubs, knives, swords, sticks, fails and bayonets. In the course of the history of weaponry, the weapons in these categories have been both individually employed and used in conjunction, with equal effect.

Many of these skills and weapons, created out of necessity, have become obsolete in modern times. It is only now that there is a general revival of interest in mastering combat techniques. Some of the weapons, such as the rifle, bow and arrow and pistol, have been adopted for use in modern sporting competitions and have thus continued to develop and improve, but many others have fallen into disuse and the skills forgotten.

Bow—Bow is the oldest, the most used and most widely distributed of projectile weapons. During the Moghal period, the bow in general was called Kamana or Kaman. The string was called either *Zih* or *Chillah.* In Hindi the string was called *panach*, *punchak,* or *pratyancha*. Another local name given to it was *dori;* ordinary thread or rope. The simplest and commonest kind of bow or a piece of wood tapering in both direction from the middle and having the ends connected by a string shorter than the wood. The side of the bow away from the archer when shooting is called the 'back', and is generally rounded. The shaft is called the 'stave' and it's two curved sides are called limbs. The middle of the bow is known as the 'grip' or the 'handle', and the ends, the 'tips'. The latter are frequently made of horn. The 'notches' for the string are termed 'nocks'. 'Rudra' is the most god of Hindu Pantheon. He is the first preceptor of the science of archery.

In the Sanskrit literature various names have been allotted to a bow. According to the Amarkosha, it can be called *dhanusar, chapa, sharasana, kodanda, karmuka, ishuwasa, kalaprastha, gandiv* etc. The common name found a bow in the works of Kalidash is *dhanu*. Other words found are *kodanda, druna, chapa, sharasana* and *sharanga*. The last one was made entirely of horn.

In India three bows are regarded as supreme. These are (i) Pinaka or Ajagara of Shiva, (ii) Sharanga of Vishnu and (iii) Gandiva of Arjuna. Other famous bows were Kodanda, the personal bow of Rama and Vijaya the favorite bow of Karna.

A bow made of a single piece of wood or bamboo is called a 'self' or a simple bow. These are very easily available, are easy to make and very often are quite effective. The composite bow, at its best, is in front superior to all forms. Such bows are built up of a wooden core that is merely a support to hold the other parts together, a horn belly and a sinew back.

Arrow—Ancient Indian Literature refers to arrows of many types. The common name of Indian arrow is *teer* or *tir* and *bana*. The point was called *paikan* in Parsian and *bhal* in Hindi. The shaft was termed *kilk* in Parsian and *Sari* in Hindi and feather were called *par* in Parsian and *pankha* in Hindi. So far as the arrow used by paika called *sara* or *tira*. The upper part was called *muna* the middle part shaft was called *Sareni* and the end part is called *para*.

The Atharvaveda specifies the parts of an arrow as shatya (shaft), pirandhi (shaftment) the area on the shaft to which the feathers are attached is termed as 'shaftment', sharanga (point) kulamala (the nock or notch) and apaskanibha and apastu. The last two terms mean the upper and the lower part of the shaft respectively. The Aitereya Brahmana describe the different parts of an arrow as anika (point), shalya (shaft), tejana (nock) and parani (feathers).

Jamadhar—Jamadhar is one of the oldest weapon. It has a V-shaped hilt consists of two horizontal and two vertical bars, trangular blade, gradually tapering to a point, bears a mid-rid at the lower end. During Muslim period it was very popular in Orissa.

Dagger—Dagger, triangular blade with a small mid-rid tapers to a point the hit consists of a bow like recurved pommel and a cylindrical grip with a globular knob in the centre.

Sword—Sword is a hard weapon characterised by a longish blade of metal and a small grip to hold it. It is different from the thrusting weapons like spear, Javelin and pike on one hand and slingers like arrows on the other. In case of arrows etc, the blade forms either a small portion of the effective length or is tied to a staff.

A sword has two main division: called the hilt and the blade. In Oriya the hilt is called *mootha*. There are various kinds of hilts available on the swords. A blade generally has two main divisions, i.e., the *tang* or the portion of the blade that fits into the hilt and the blade proper. The thick part, opposite to the edge, is called the back or the back-edge. Edge is the sharpened part, running from top to bottom. The swords having blades sharped on both the sides are called double edged or two edged and those having sharpening on one side are called single-edged. In Oriya it is called *dhara.*

Tang is the upper most part of a blade, not visible in a sword since it is inserted into the hilt. The tang, generally a rectangular flat piece (sometime circular), is cemented and thrust into the hollow lift. Locally it is called *dumala.* The lowermost part, the tip of the blade is called the point. In Oriya it is called *Muna.*

Dhupa—It has a broad, straight, long, double-edged blade and in generally made of flexible burnished steel. It is considered as an emblem of sovereignty and high dignity and was therefore, displayed on state occasions, being carried in gorgeous velvet covering by a man who held it before his master.

Gupti— Literally it means a 'concealed weapon'. It is a sword-cane or a sword in the shape of a walking-stick.It is also called sword stick. Egertun describes one gupti as "a long fluted, flexible and very slender blade, fitting into an ivory stick-sheath". During Maratha rule, this weapon became popular in Orissa.

Patta—Patta was perhaps the most favoured weapon of the marathas. These Pattas were invented by the marathas in the west Deccan and were latter diffused by them into the areas which they penetrated. The Patta has a long flexible, regularly tapering, straight steel blade, almost always double-edged in shape. The gauntlet covers the arm almost to the elbow, and has an iron strap hinged to the upper end that goes around the arm. The grip is at right angles to the blades. The gauntlets are generally embossed, inlaid or otherwise decorated with tiger's head, human face, dragon's face, foliage and acrobats in laid with gold and silver, head of a monster smallaring an elephant and the trunk of the latter extending down the blade, and so on. The blade of the patta is attached to the gauntlet hilt by a pair of seatings which run down the face of the blade, on both sides, for a few inches; and to which it is riveted. "The hilt is in the form of a combined fist and vanbrace forged of a single piece of steel; across the interior of the fist is a transverse grip, and at the top of the vambrace is a metal loop through which the forearm is thrust" The interior, into which the back of the arm fits tightly, is generally padded. Sometimes the bar is also padded. In Orissa this weapon is very famous.

The patta is held by thrusting the hand through the loop with the back against the metal and grasping the bar (or bars) with the fist. It is wielded directly by the strong muscles of the fore and upper arm, and through the wrist.

Katari—This weapon is very popular in Orissa. It has a broad, heavy, single edged blade, less wide at the end than at the hilt and sharp on the concave side. The top of the weapon is slightly curved and more wide than end part. The hilt is very simple and made of wood. The maximum length of this weapon was 20 inches and the minimum of 18 inches; the width of the blade was 1.5 to 3.5 (from the thinnest to the widest part) inches (approximately).

Straight Double Edged Sword—It is one of the oldest and most typical of Indian swords. The Khanda was used by the Rajputs, Mughals and Marathas but it was very popular in Orissa and central India. Some of the khandas of Orissa and central India were mounted in the old Indian hilt and were generally flat-bladed.

The greater number of surviving khandas are even located at Khurda, Dhenkanal and Ganjam district in Orissa. It has both single and double edged. In single edged khanda, it has a strengthening plate with ornamental. It has a broad, straight blade, usually towards the point, which in generally quite blunt.

Singhata—It is also spelt as a Maru, Madu, Maroo or Singauta (literally 'to kill'), as G.N. Pant describes. It is a typical Indian, especially

Maratha, paring and thrusting weapon consisting of a pair of horns fastened together with their points in opposite direction. The horns generally used are that of a buck. Usually the horns overlap but sometimes they are fastened to the opposite ends of a short handle. In the centre, for the protection of the arm, is fitted a small circular shield of leather or metal. It was the favourite weapon of the Marathas but was also used by the Bhils and other tribes.

The author had located such types of weapons at Maluda District Puje. At the time of interview he also came to know that these weapons were used by the tribal people of Orissa. Such types of weapon were located at Dhenkanal district and perhaps during the Maratha rule, these weapons were used by both the Maratha soilder and paika of Orissa.

Knife—It is perhaps the most used weapon in all ages and in all countries. Its varieties are infinite. It is most used as a convenience, a tool and a domestic instrument, than as a weapon. As prof. G.N. Pant describe, during the medieval ages in the heat of the battle, midst the armoured warriors, the knife was practically useless but once the adversary was knocked down with a sword, spear, axe, club or other fierce weapon, the victor, climbing on the chest of the fatter enemy, found it easier to thrust his dagger or sever the neck with his knife which was always dangling by his waist-band. In Orissa it is popularly known as Banka Chhuri. The paika keeps this weapon on his waist belt.

Spear—Spears and Javelin were among the most ancient weapons and were specially favoured by the horsemen. The attendants, guards, foot soldiers of Orissan army carried the spears. Spear, in fact, is a long shafted weapon intended solely for thrusting. It is a class name and includes many named and unarmed thrusting weapons. In Orissa the term Verchha, Tenta etc. was used for spears.

Bhala—It consists of a long wooden or bamboo shaft with a long and pointed iron blade. The blade, generally leaf shaped, is with or without a medial-rib and has a hollow shank into which the shaft is interested. It is a thrusting weapon and was seldom hurled. It was generally used by the foot soldiers and operated with both hands.

References

1. W.J.Goode, P.K.Halt, '*Methods in social Research*', (New York, MeGraw Hill Book Co, 1952): p.119.

2. Sturut Chaplin, "New Trends in Social Research" *Journal of Education Sociology*: 565-566, quoted by P.V.Young "Scientific Social Surveys and Research", (London, Asia Publishing House, 1554): p.169.

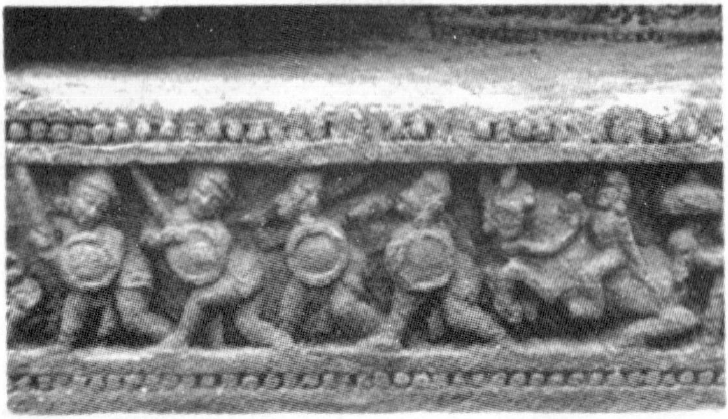

Fig. 1. Marching scene of the foot soliders Konark Temple, Puri.

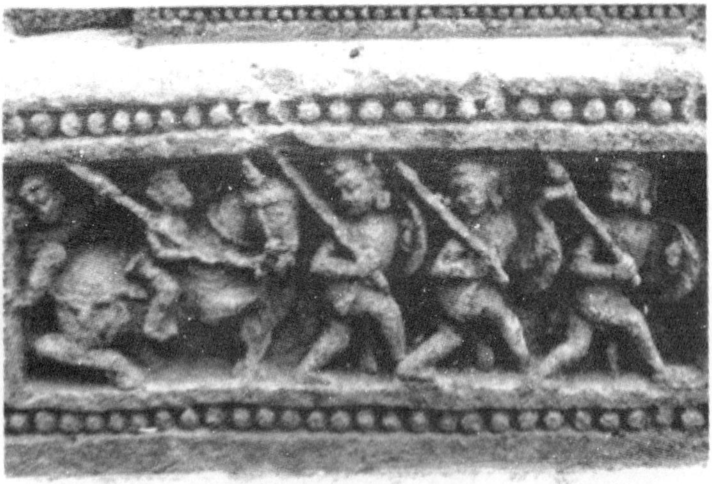

Fig. 2. Marching scene of the foot soldiers Konark Temple, Puri.

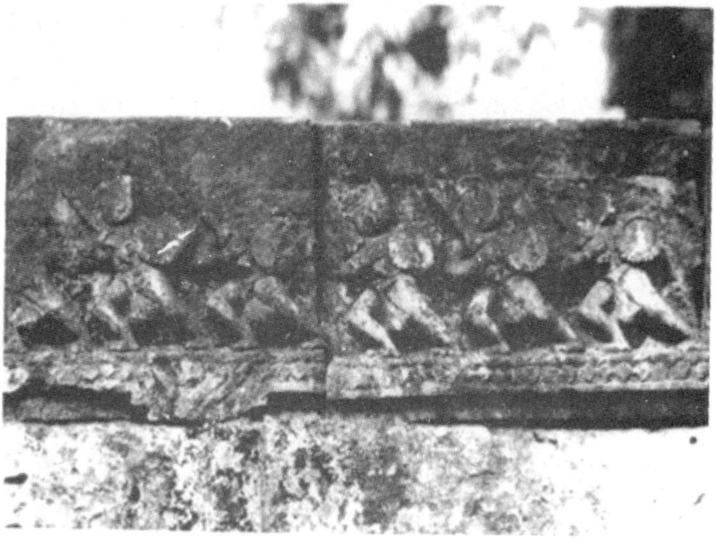

Fig. 3. Marching scene of the foot soliders Telegarh, Orissa State Museum.

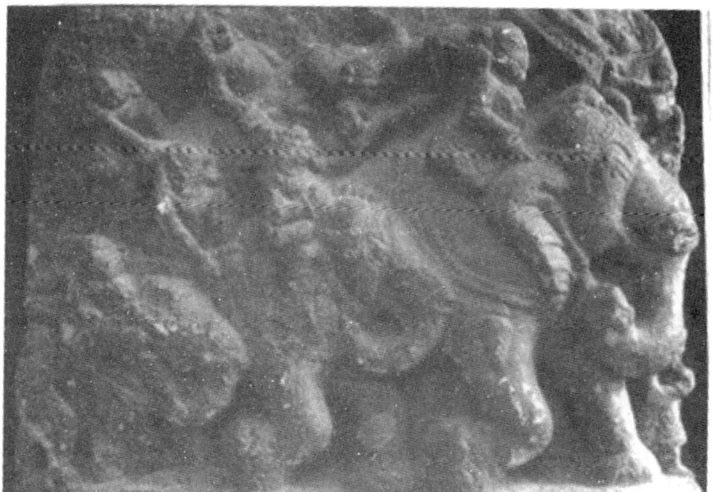

Fig. 4. War Elephant, Orissa State Museum Gallery.

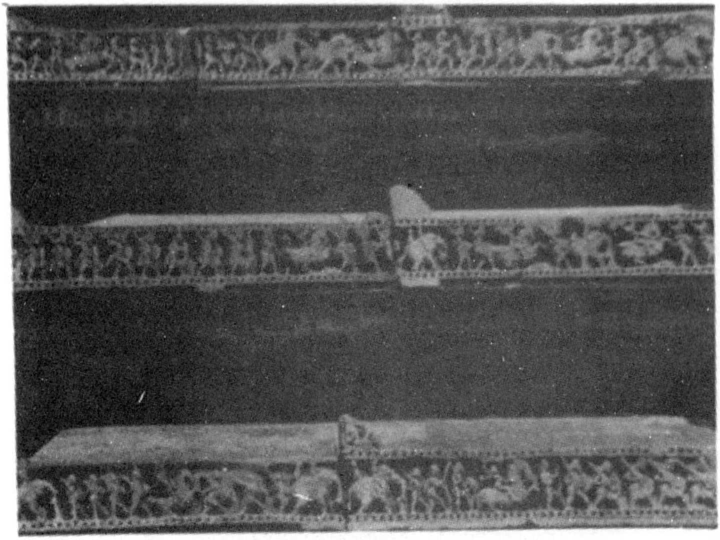

Fig. 5. Cavalry with foot soliders, Lingaraj Temple, Bhubaneswar.

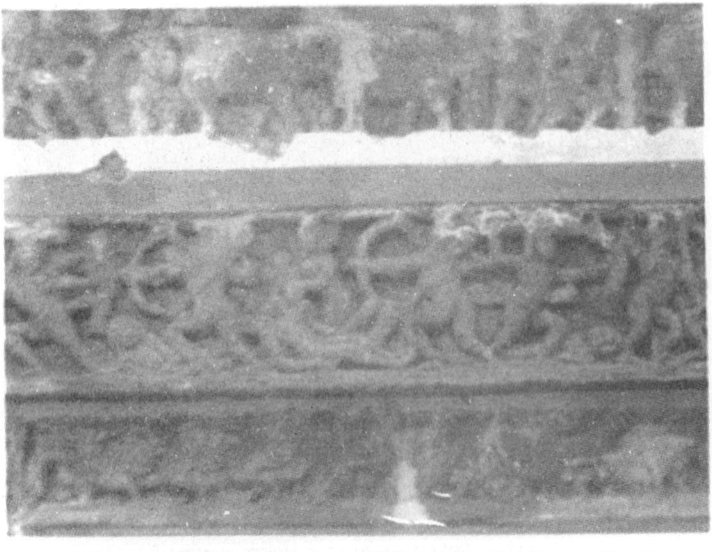

Fig. 6. Mahabharat scene, Singhanath Temple, Baideswar, Banki.

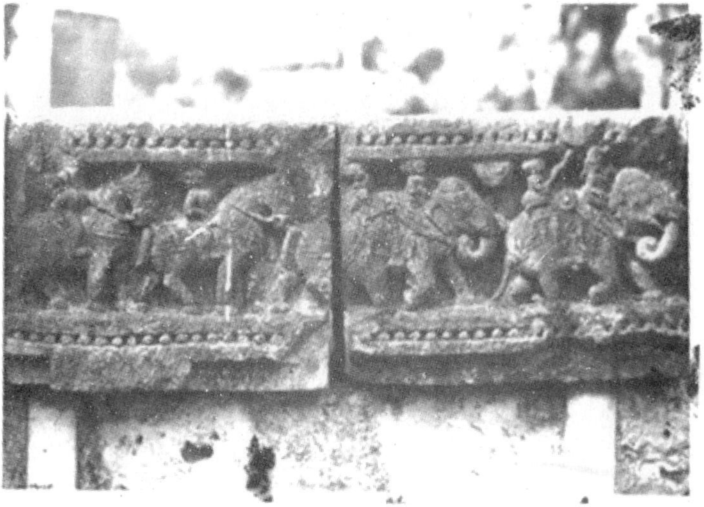

Fig. 7. War Horse and Elephant Telegarh, Orissa State Museum.

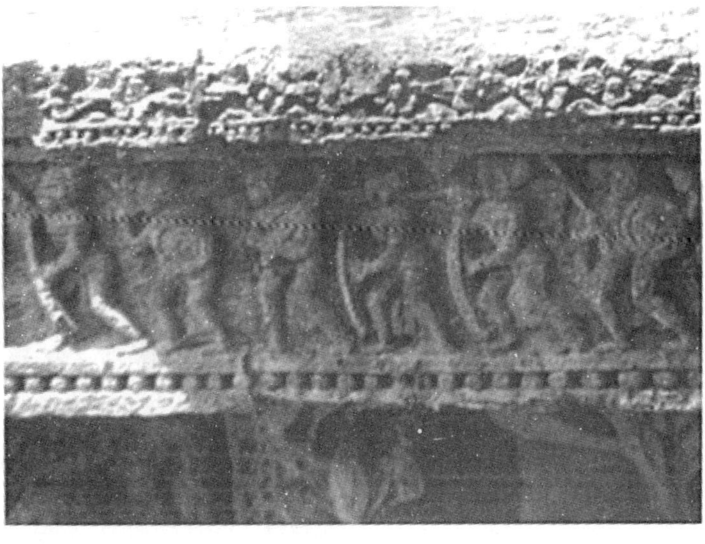

Fig. 8. Marching scene of the foot soldier, Konarak Temple, Puri.

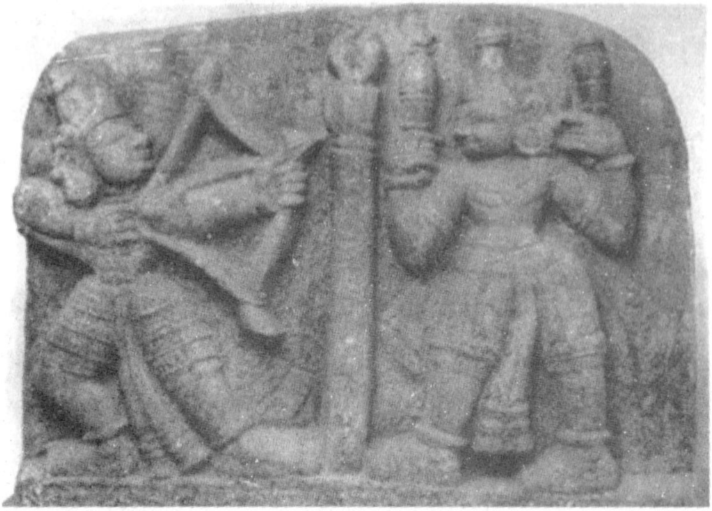

Fig. 9. Lakhabindha (arrow hit) and Gada mudgara scene, Orissa State Museum.

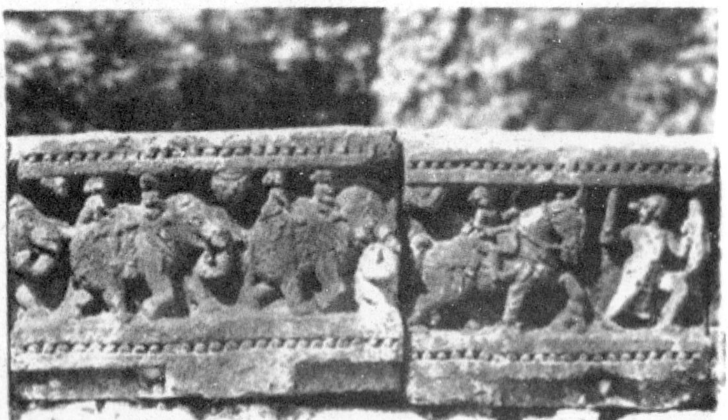

Fig. 10. War Horse and Elephant scene Konark Temple, Puri.

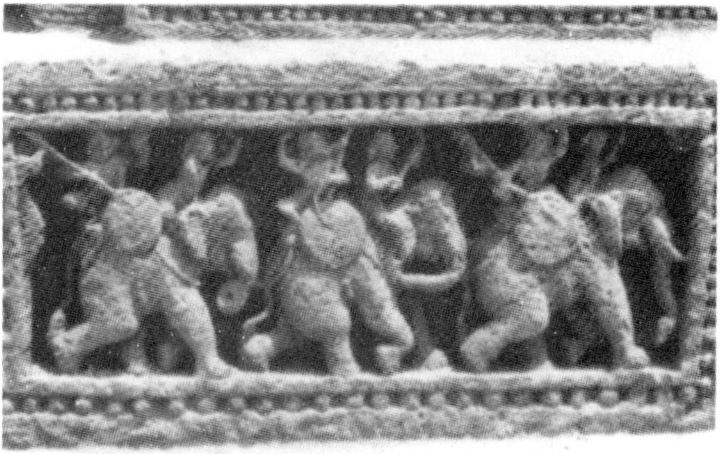

Fig. 11. War elephant Konark Temple, Puri.

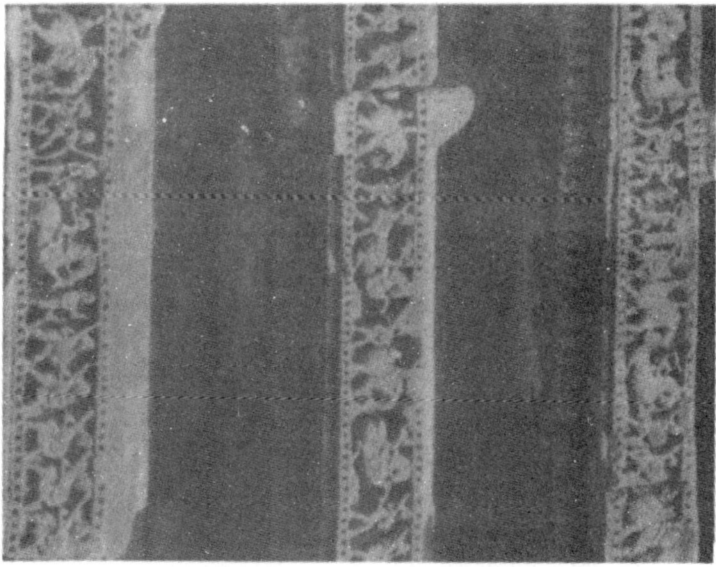

Fig. 12. Cavalary and Foot soldier, Lingaraj Temple, Bhubaneswar.

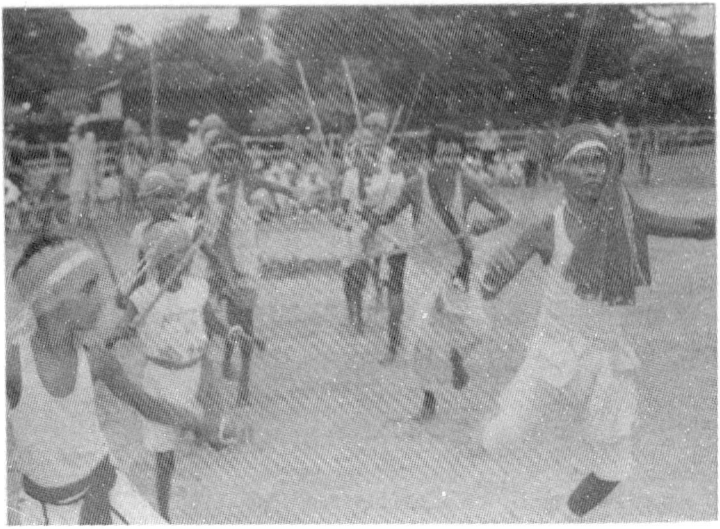

Fig. 13. Marching scene of paikas.

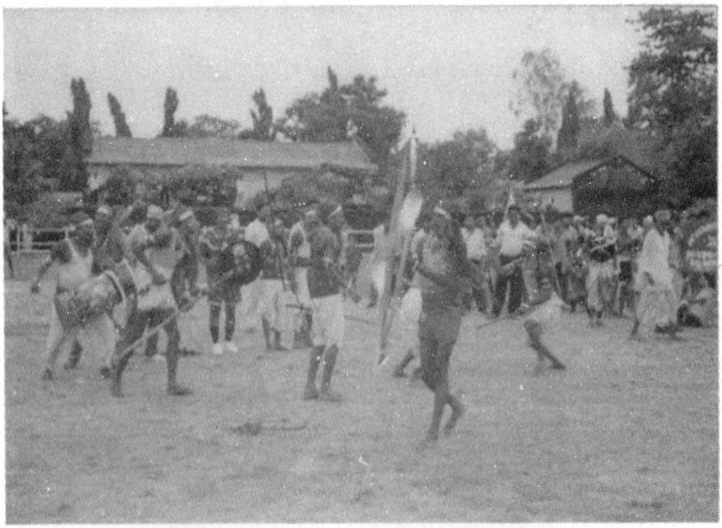

Fig. 14. Group demonstration of various martial arts of Orissa.

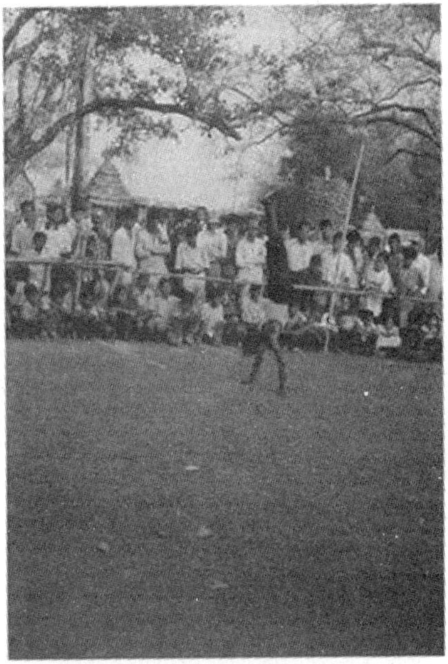

Fig. 15. Demonstration of Floor exercise (Dola festival).

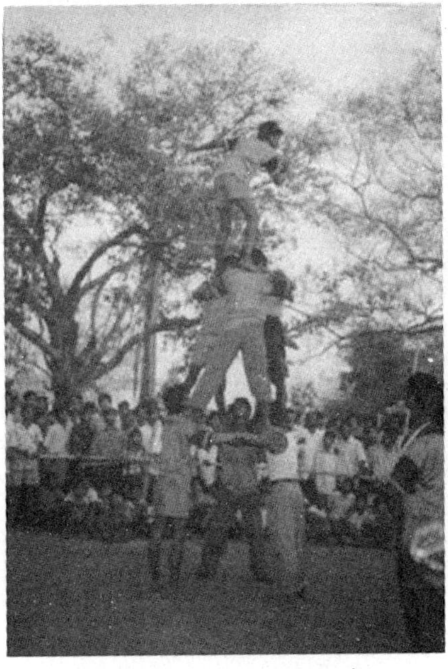

Fig. 16. Pyramid demonstration.

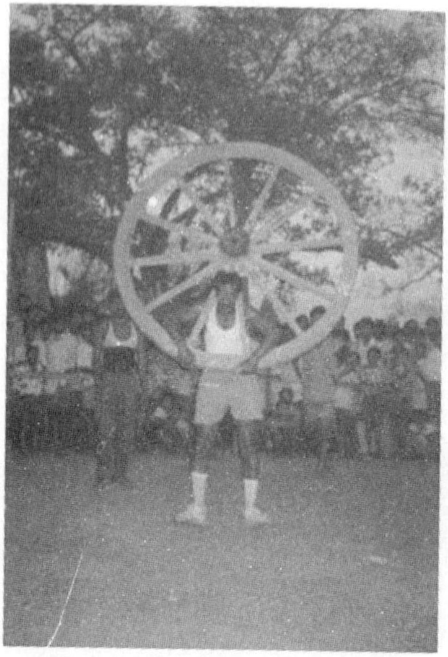

Fig. 17. Sagadachaka demonstration.

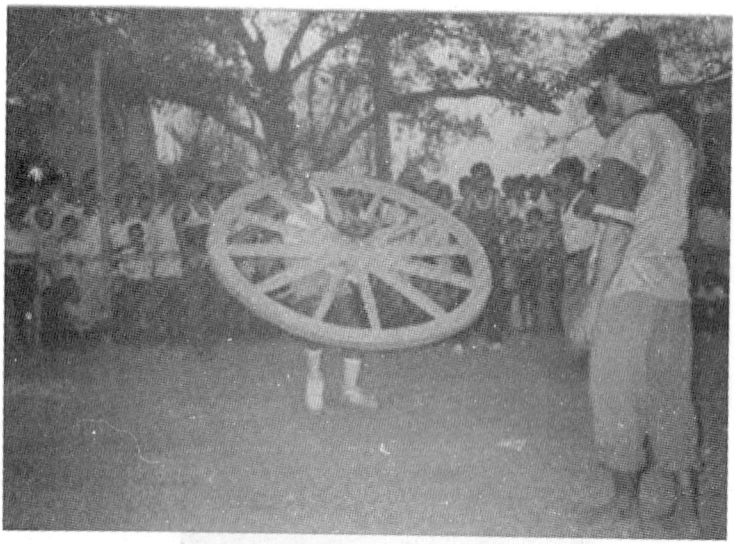

Fig. 18. Sagadachaka demonstration.

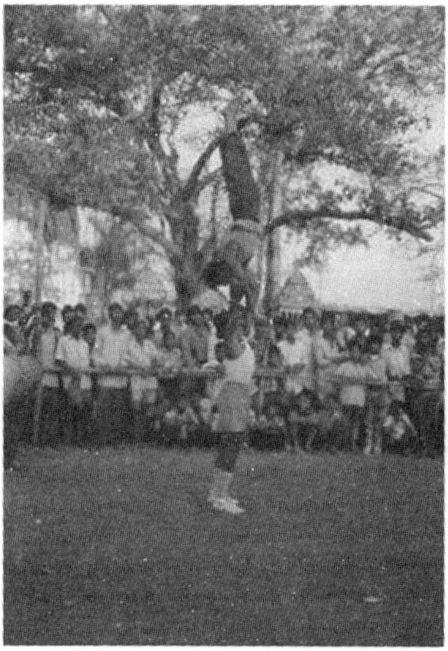

Fig. 19. Handstand over the shoulder.

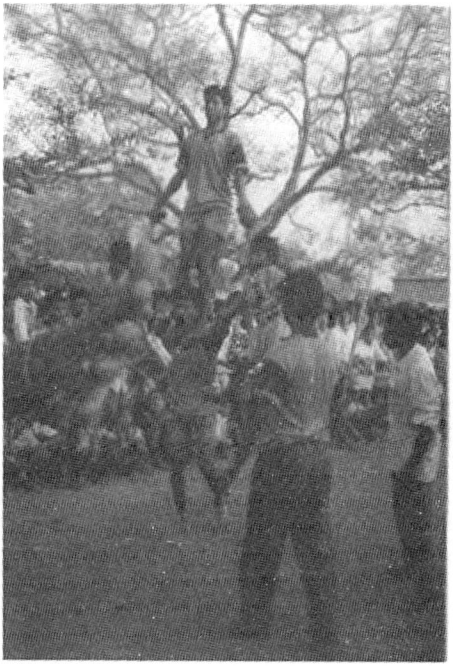

Fig. 20. The paika is going to perform front somersault from the shoulder of a paika.

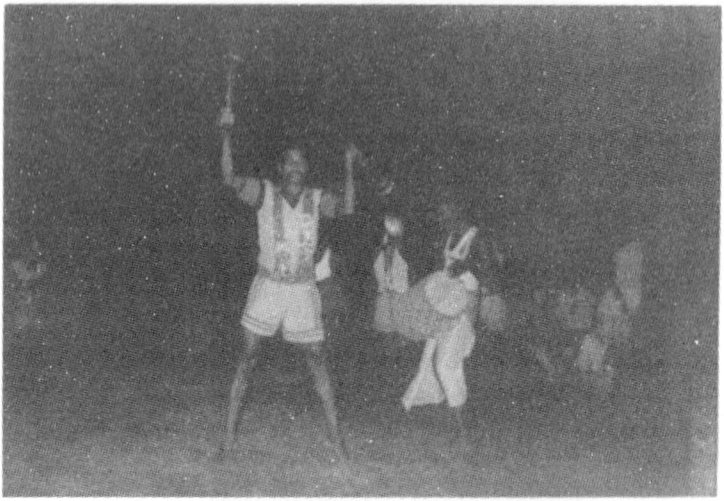

Fig. 21. Demonstration of Gada Mudgara (Do dasti)

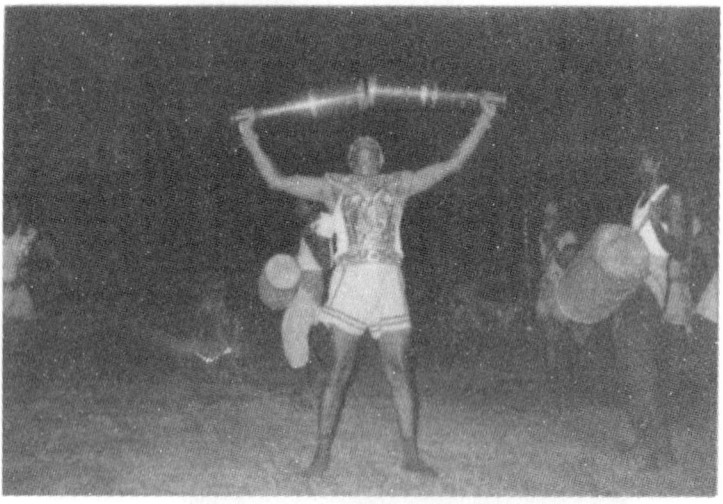

Fig. 22. Demonstration of Gada Mudgara (Baghanisha).

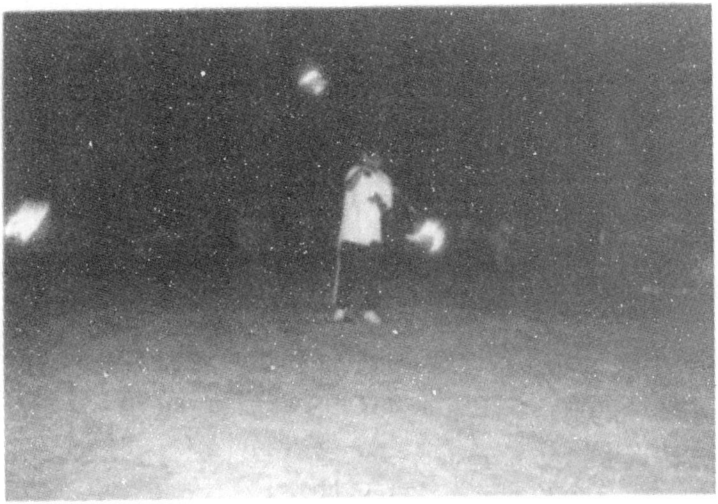

Fig. 23. Demonstration of Banati (Fire arm).

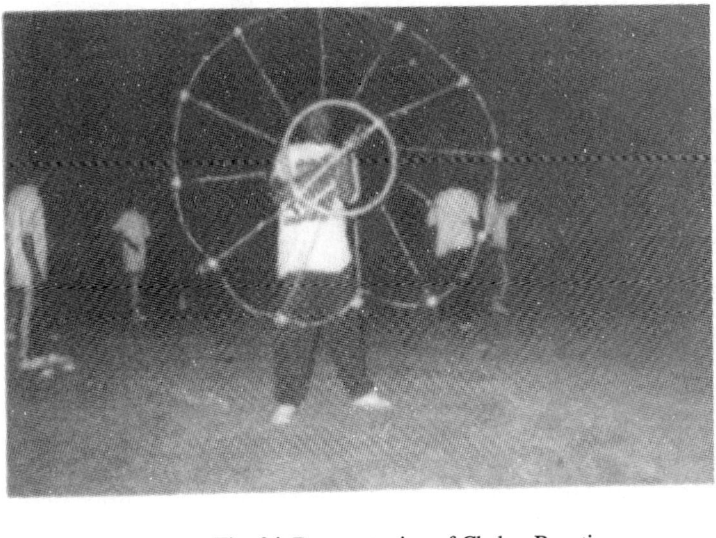

Fig. 24. Demonstration of Chakra Banati.

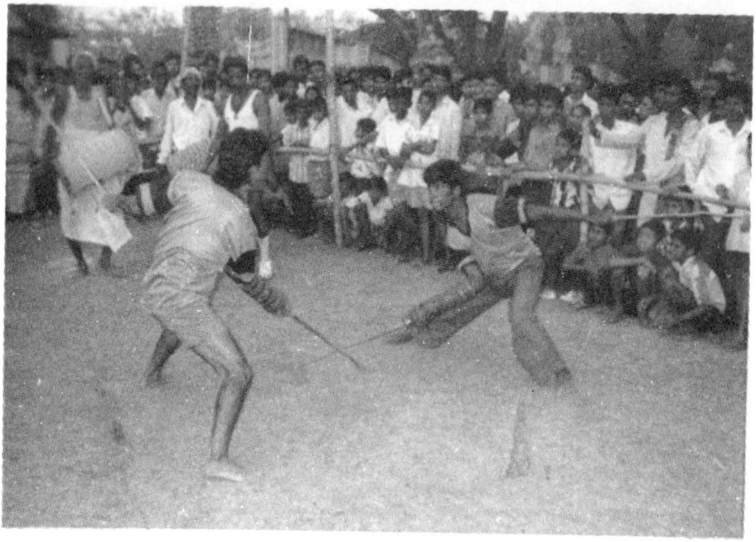

Fig. 25. Patta (Hastavara Khanda) fighting

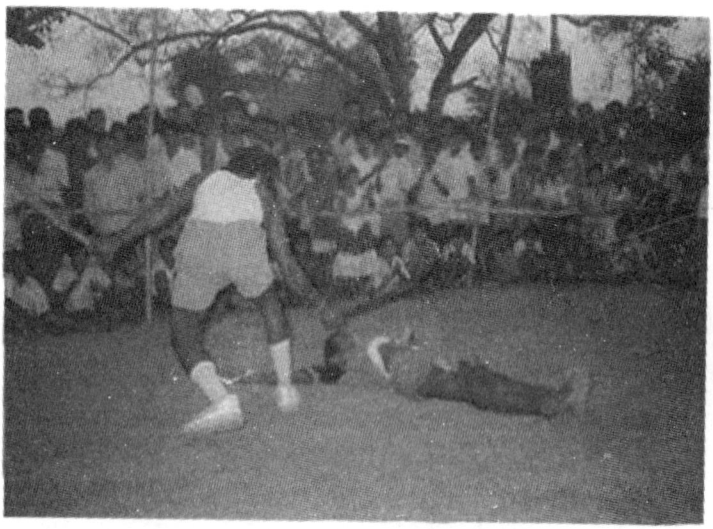

Fig. 26. Kadalikata scene.

Plate–1

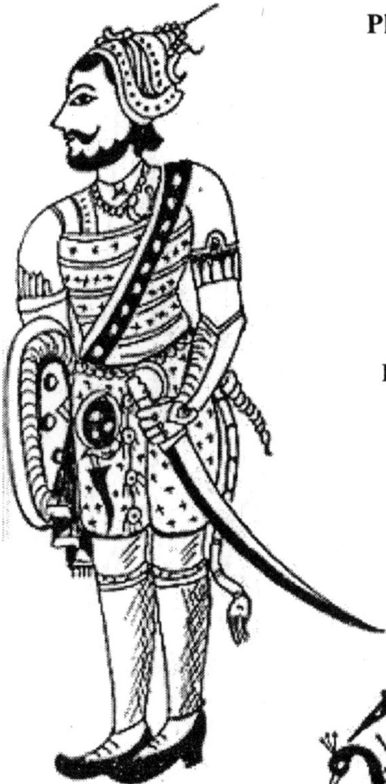

Fig. 27. Uniform and Weapons used by Paika after Paika Kheda.

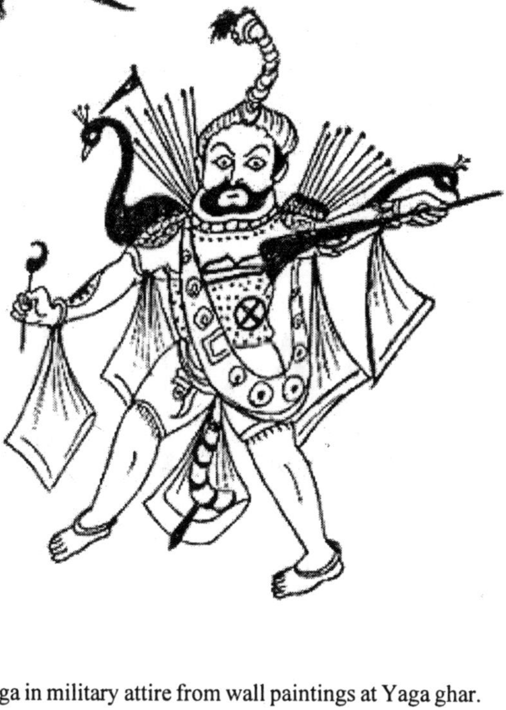

Fig. 28. Naga in military attire from wall paintings at Yaga ghar.

Plate–2

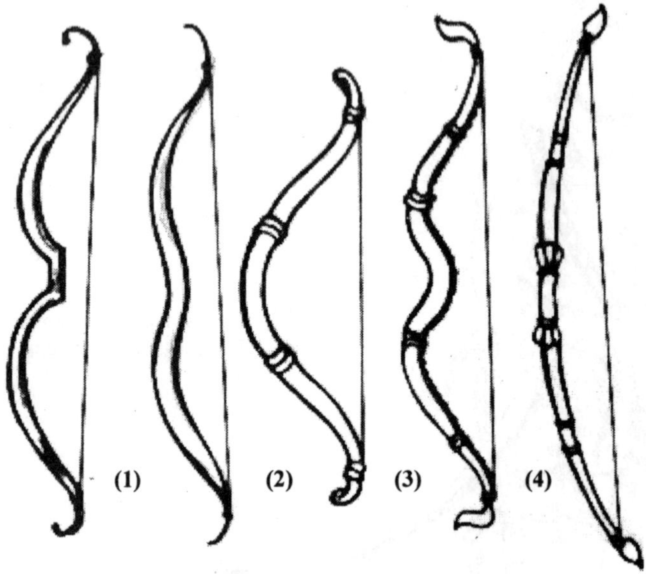

1. Bows from 10th century A.D. (Sculptures : From Mukteswar Temple, Bhubaneshwar,)., **2.** From Brahmeshwar Temple, Bhubaneshwar, 11th Century A.D. **3.** From a bronze image, Achutarajapur, Puri District (Orissa State Museum) 11th century A.D., **4.** From a Loose sculture, Jeypore, Koraput District 11th Century A.D. **5.** Bow Made of Bamboo. Contemporay, Orrisa.

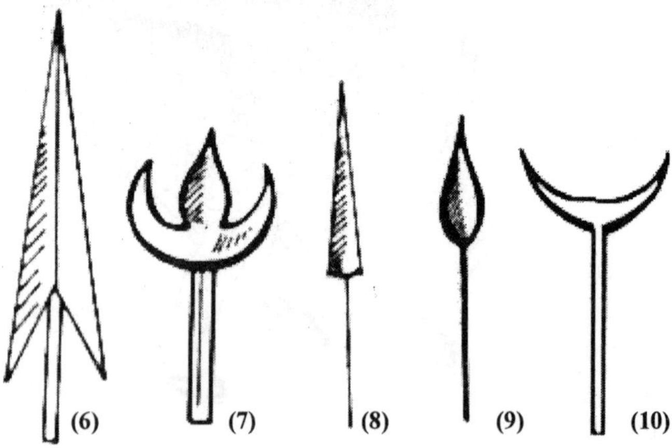

6. Karnika, **7.** Kakatunda, **8.** Suchimukha, **9.** Gopucha, **10.** Ardha-Chandra.
6-10 Vedic Arrow Points, After G.N. Pant (Conjectural)

Plate–3

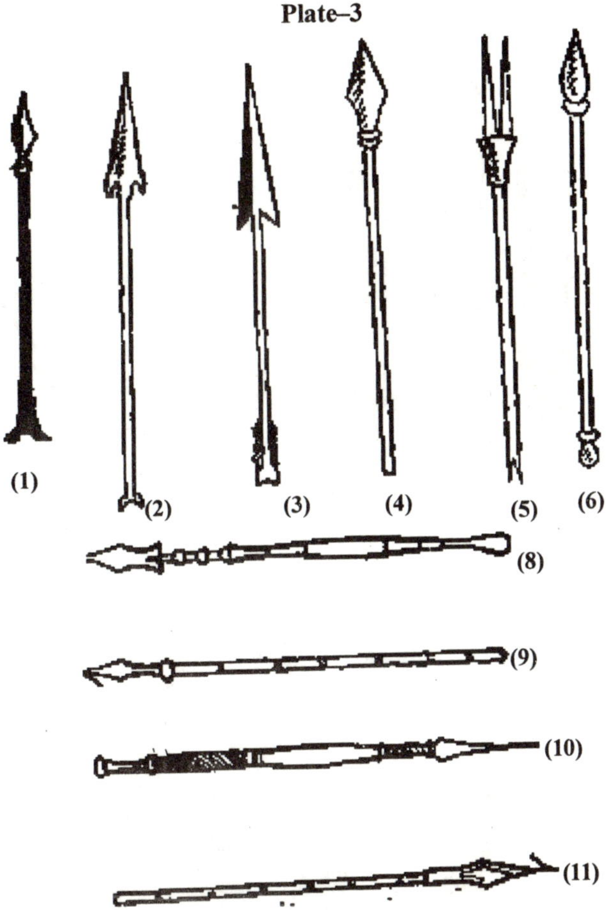

1. Spears from Sculptures, Orissa : (From Vaital Temple, Bhubaneshwar, 8th Century A.D.)

2,3,5. Tribal Arrows preserved in the Orissa State Museum, Bhubaneswar (with Iron Ani) Wooden Tips

6,7. From Sculptures of the Orissa State Meseum, Bhubaneswar 11th Century A.D.

4. From Parasuramawar Temple, Bhubaneswar, 7th Century A.D.

9-11. Bhala "Spears of different categories (Mughal)"

Plate–4

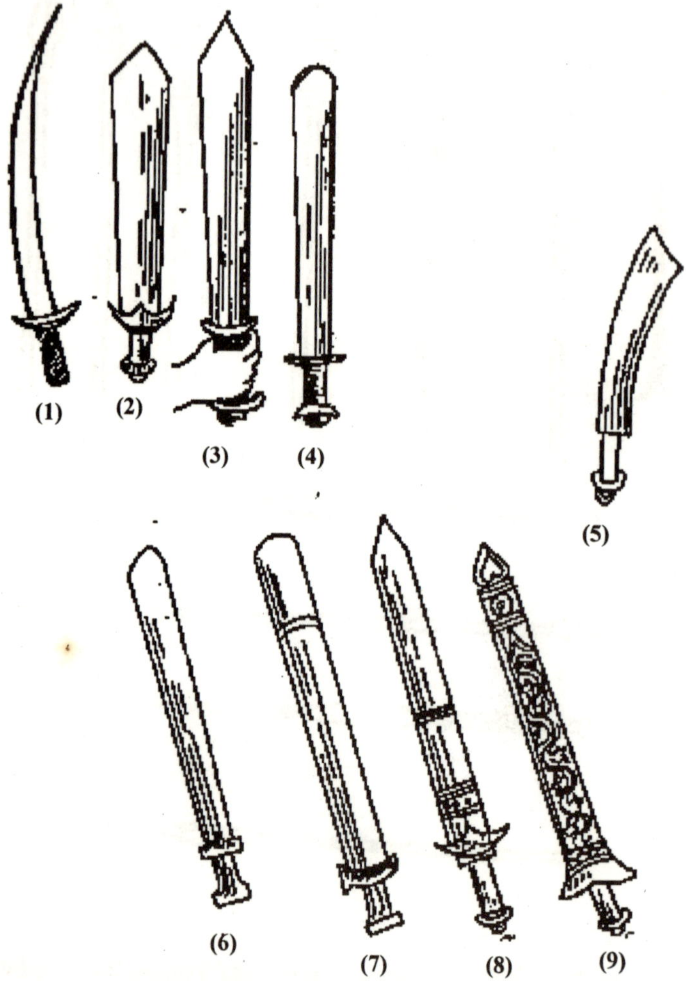

1. Sword of Paika in Orissa.

2,3,4. Sword from Orissan Sculptures: (From Vaital Temple, Bhubaneswar, 8th Century A.D.)

5. From Sun Temple Konarka, Puri District, 13th Century A.D.

6-9. From Lingaraj Temple, Bhubaneswar. 11th Century A.D.

Plate–5

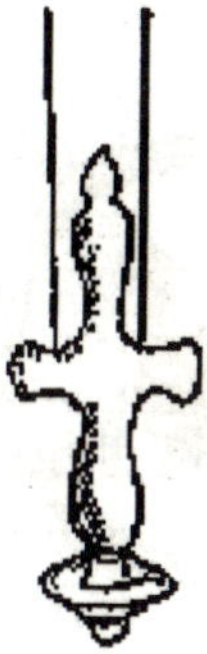

(1)

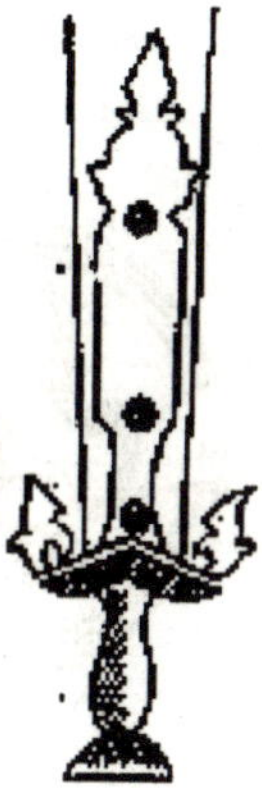

(2)

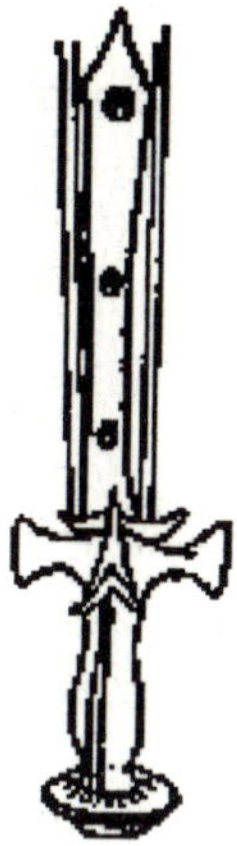

(3)

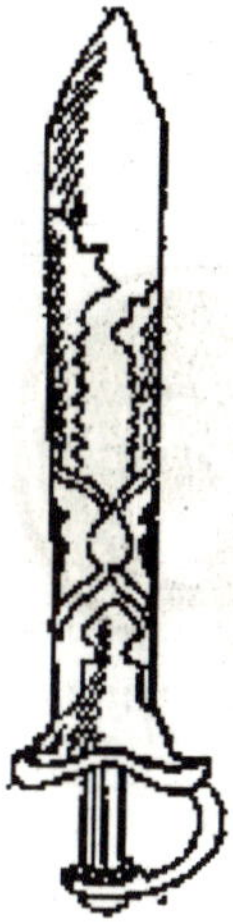

(4)

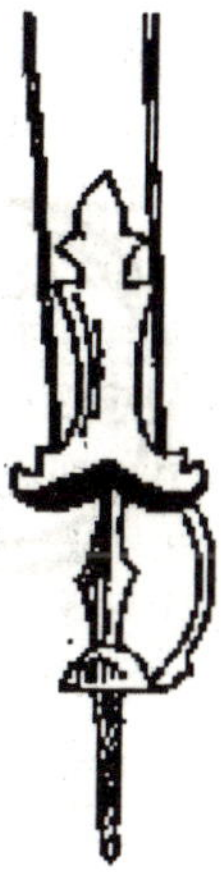

(5)

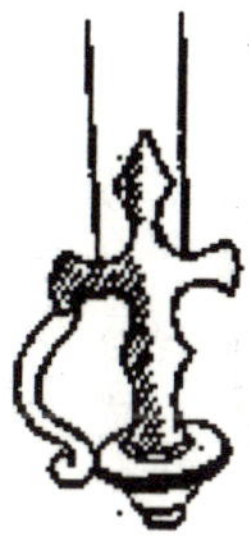

(6)

1-6. Sword and Swoard Hilts of Orissa. During Mughal, Maratha and British Periods preserved in the Orissa State Museum, Bhubaneshwar.

Plate–6

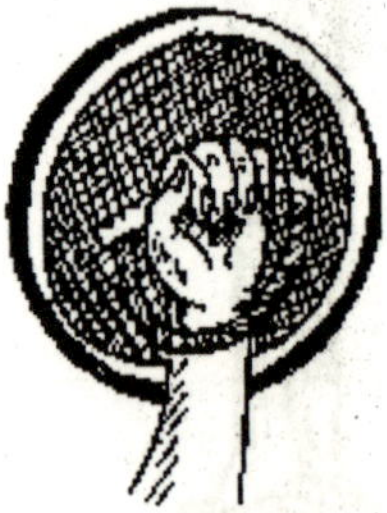

(1)

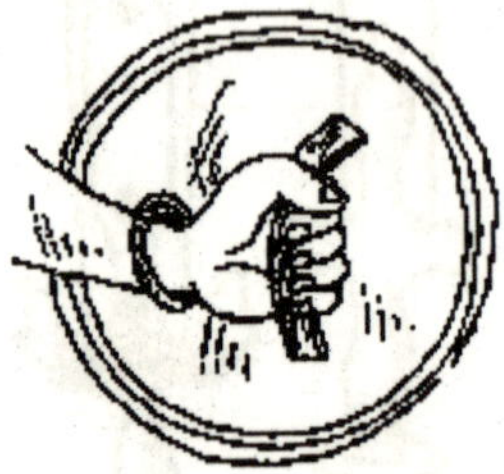

(2)

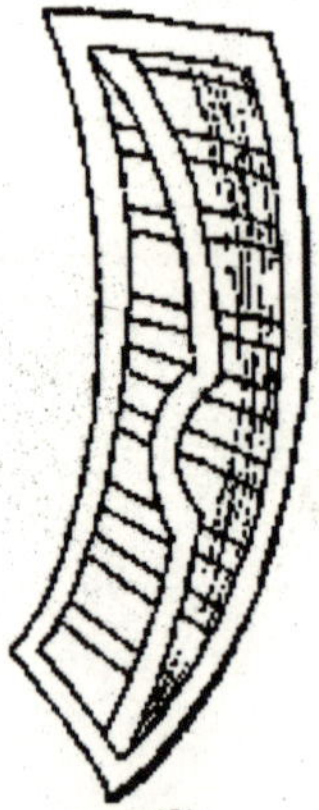

(3)

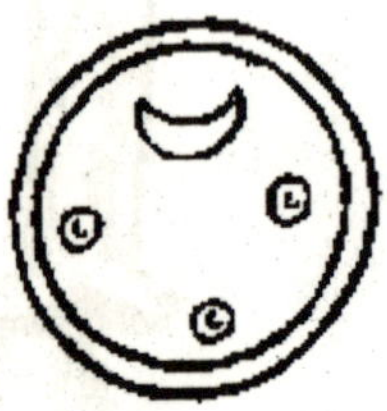

(4)

1. Shield from Orissa Sculptures. From Sisireswar Temple, Bhubaneshwar, 8th Century A.D.

2-3. Shield from Sun Templesof Konarka, Puri District, 13th Century A.D.

4. Shield (Muslim Period)

Plate–7

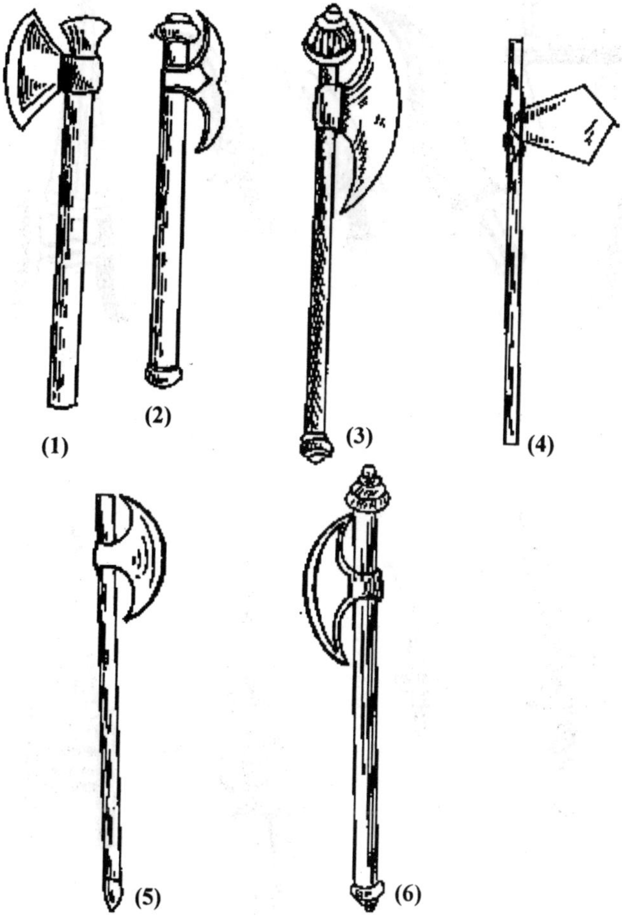

1-6. Axes and Battle-Axes from Orissan Sculptures.

Plate–8

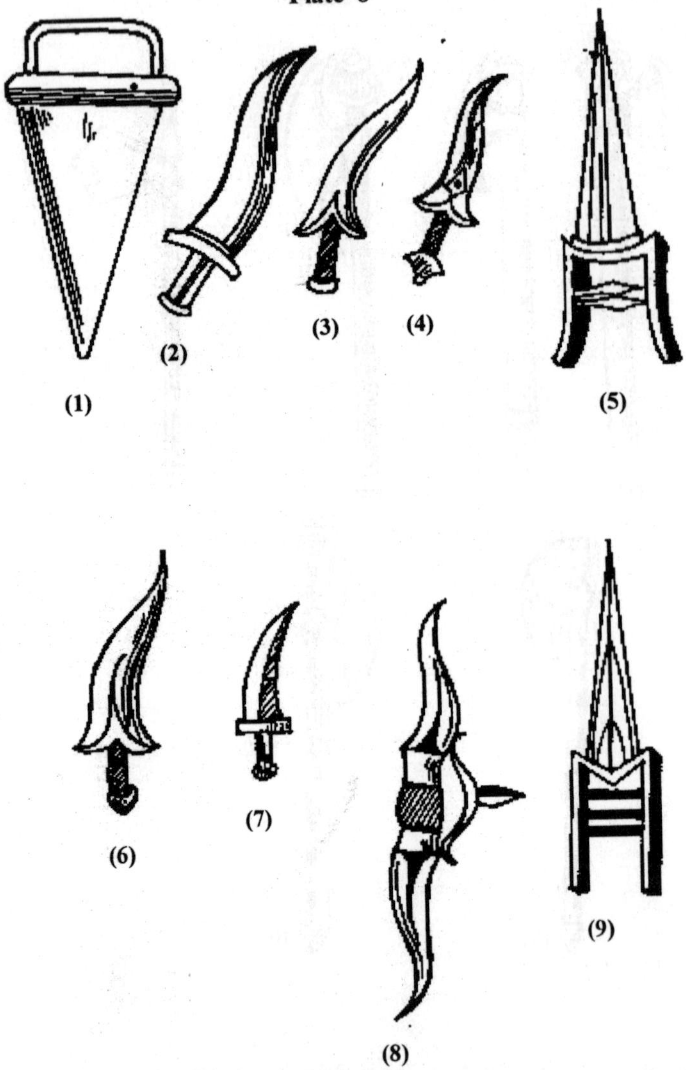

1-4. Draggers from Orissan Sculptures.

5&8. Yamadhara (Mughal Period)

6&7. Bankachuri.

9. Katari (Mughal Period)

Plate–9

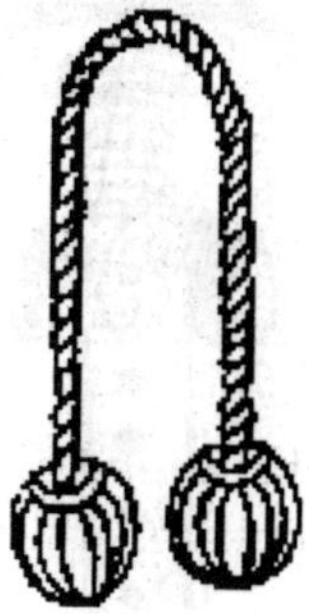

(1)

(2)

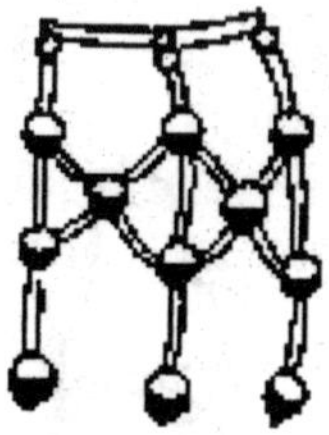

(3)

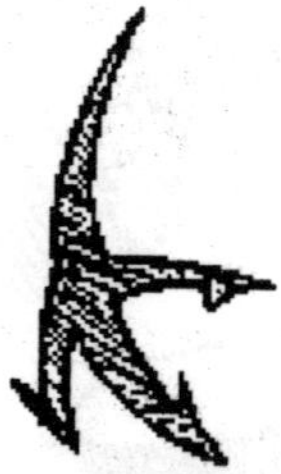

(4)

1. Banati
2. Baghankkhi
3. Body armour of a soldier after Paika Kheda
4. Caltrop, Recovered from Sisupalagarh Excavation, 1st Century B.C.

Plate–10

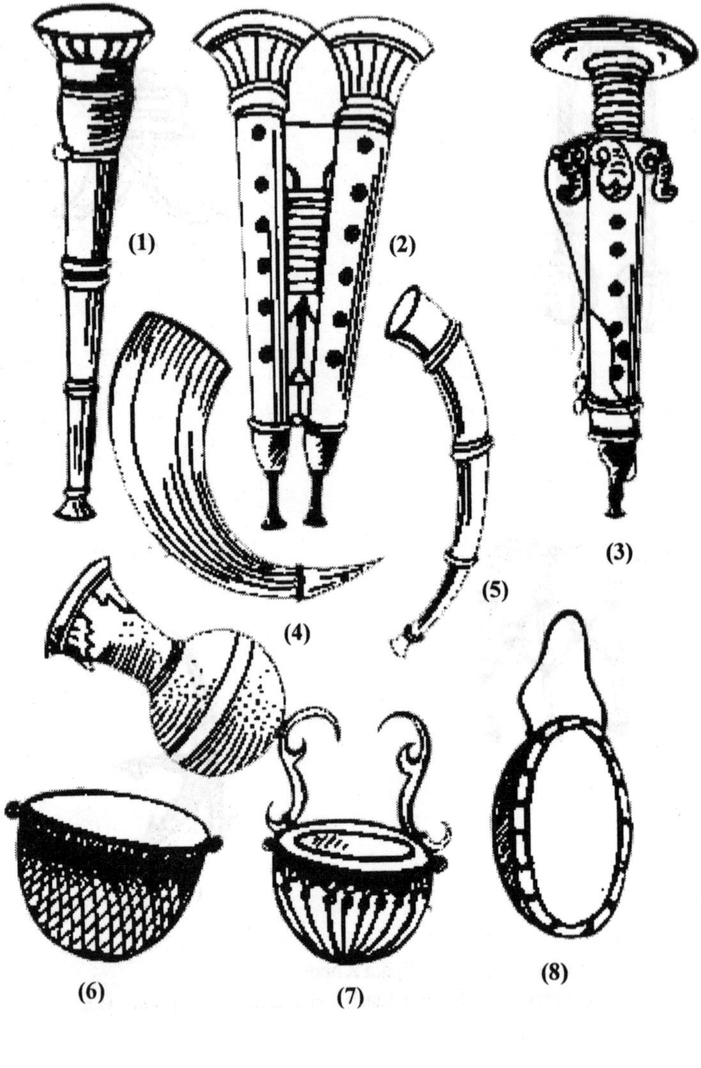

1. Turi, **2.** Jodi Mahuri, **3.** Mahuri, **4.** Singha, **5.** Vira Kahala, **6.** Nagara **7.** Danpha Nagara **8.** Nagara (Other Variety).

Plate–11

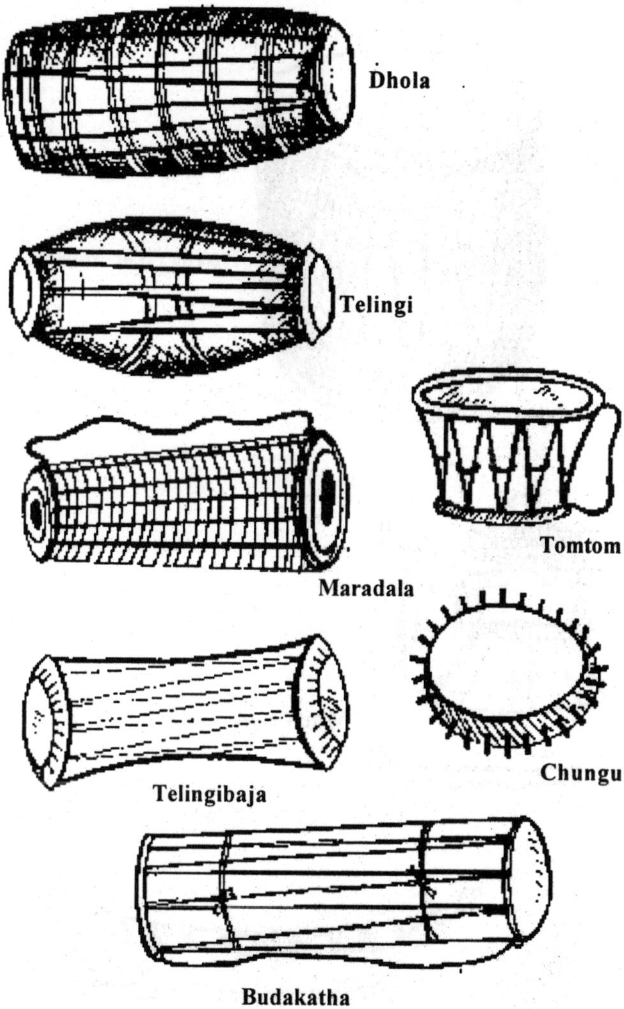
Dhola
Telingi
Tomtom
Maradala
Chungu
Telingibaja
Budakatha

Plate–12

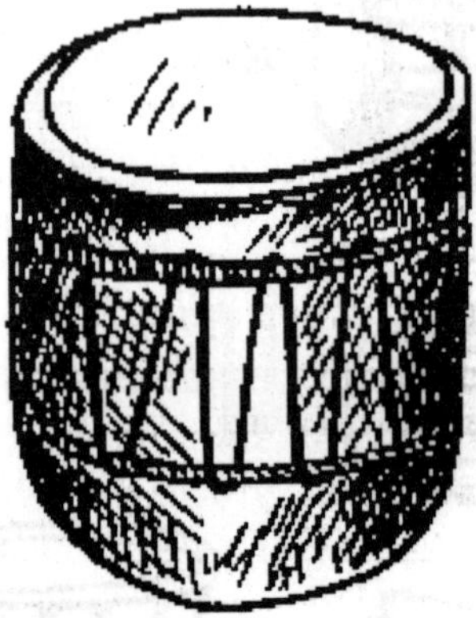

Nisana (War Music)

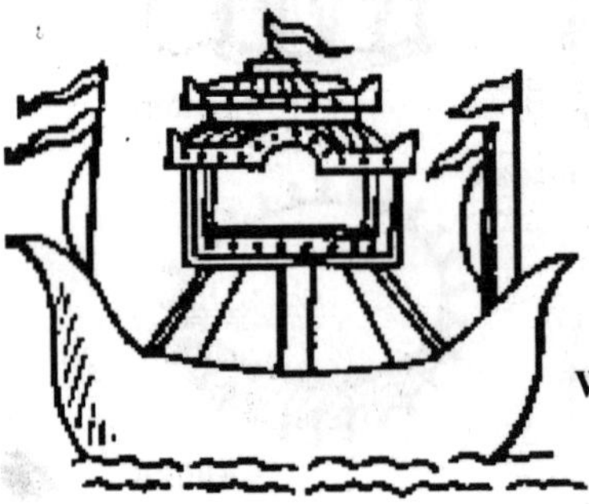

War Vessel

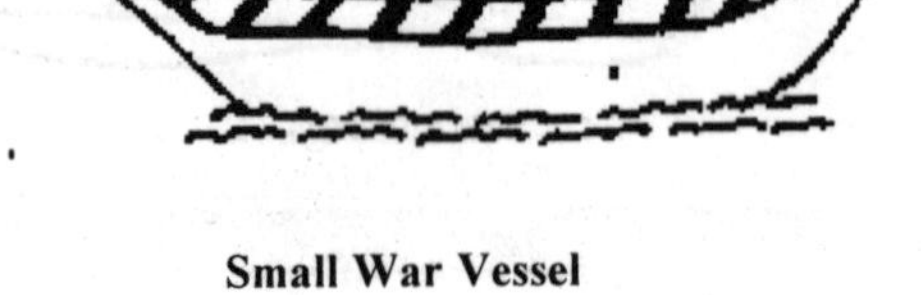

Small War Vessel

Plate–13

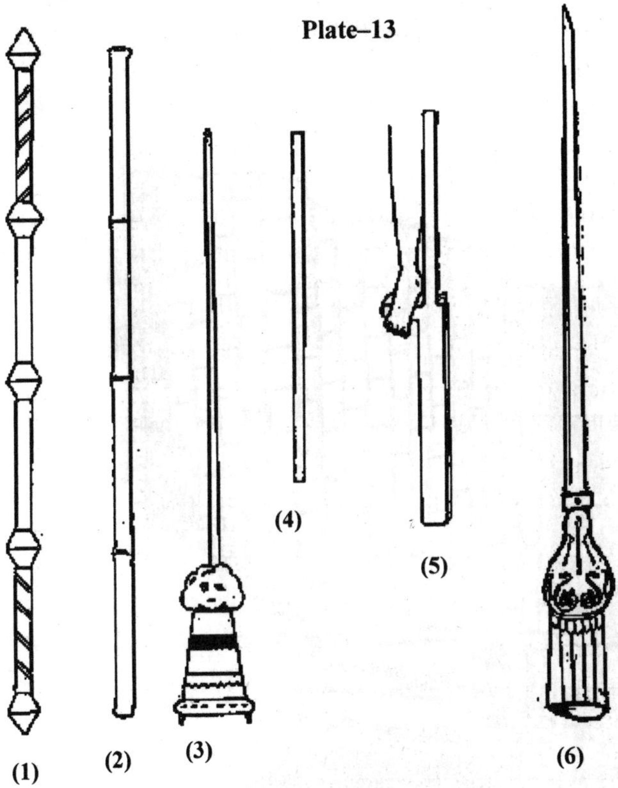

1. Decorated Lathi, **2.** Lathi, **3.** Patta (Wooden Stick Attached), **4.** Pasara, **5.** Ranapa, **6.** Patta (Sword is Attached on the Top)

Plate–14

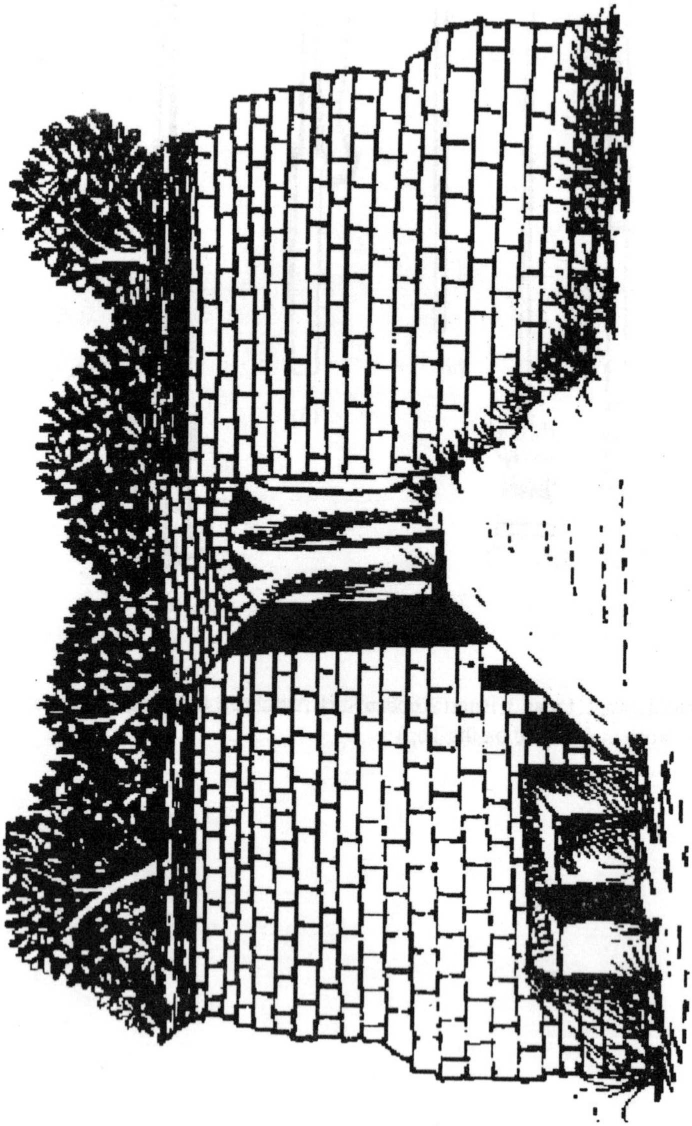

Main Entrance, Barabati Fort, Cuttack.

4
Analysis of Data

Survey

The purpose of Survey was to enlighten the number of paika akhedas and their location, the number of paikas and girl's participation, the existing facilities available for the paika akhedas in Orissa. The data collected from the questionnaire were broadly divided into the following phases for easy and systematic analysis.

1. Akhedas and their location.
2. List of the responded paika akheda teams.
3. Involvment of paikas and gurus in their respective akhedas.
4. Equipments available at responded akhedas.
5. Activities practised by paikas at their akhedas.
6. Musical equipments used by the drummers of there akhedas.
7. Provision for conducting martial arts programme at akhedas.
8. Financial condition of the akhedas.
9. Organisational set up.

Table – 1

Location of Paika Akhedas in Different Districts of Orissa

Sl.No.	*District*	*Number of Akheda*	*Percentage*
1.	Anugul	3	2.58%
2.	Balasore	4	3.44%
3.	Bolangir	1	0.86%
4.	Cuttack	3	2.58%
5.	Dhenkanal	48	41.37%
6.	Ganjam	3	2.58%
7.	Kalahandi	1	0.86%
8.	Khurda	25	21.55%
9.	Koraput	1	0.86%
10.	Nayagarh	2	1.72%
11.	Puri	23	19.82%
12.	Rayagada	1	0.86%
13	Sambalpur	1	0.86%

Location of Paika Akheda in different district of Orissa

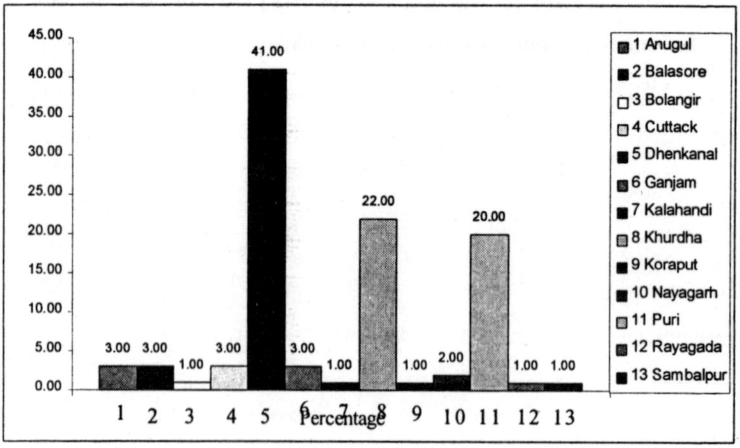

The surveys of the first area of enquiring were concerned with the acquisition of information from Director of Sports and Youth Services and Surapratap Smurtipitha, Dhenkanal, about the location of akhedas. The total number of paika akhedas are shown in Table-1.

Out of 116 akhedas 3 akhedas (2.58%) were located in Anugul district. 4 akhedas (3.44%) in Balasore district, 1 akheda (0.86%) in Bolangir district, 3 akhedas (3.48%) in Cuttack district, 48 akhedas (41.37%) in Dhenkanal district, 3 akhedas (2.58%) in Ganjam district, 1 akheda (0.86%) in Kalahandi district, 25 akhedas (21.55%) in Khurda district, 1 akheda (0.86%) in Koraput district, 23 akhedas (19.82%) in Puri district, 1 akheda (0.86%) in Rayagada, 1 akheda (0.86%) in Sambalpur district are located.

Table--2

List of the Responded Akhedas

Sl.No.	*Name of the district*	*Number of Akhedas*	*Percentage*
1.	Anugul	1	1.23
2.	Balesore	2	2.46
3.	Bolangir	1	1.23
4.	Cuttack	2	2.46
5.	Dhenkanal	33	40.74
6.	Ganjam	2	2.46
7.	Khurdha	19	23.45
8.	Nayagarh	1	1.23
9.	Puri	18	22.22
10.	Rayagada	1	1.23
11.	Sambalpur	1	1.23

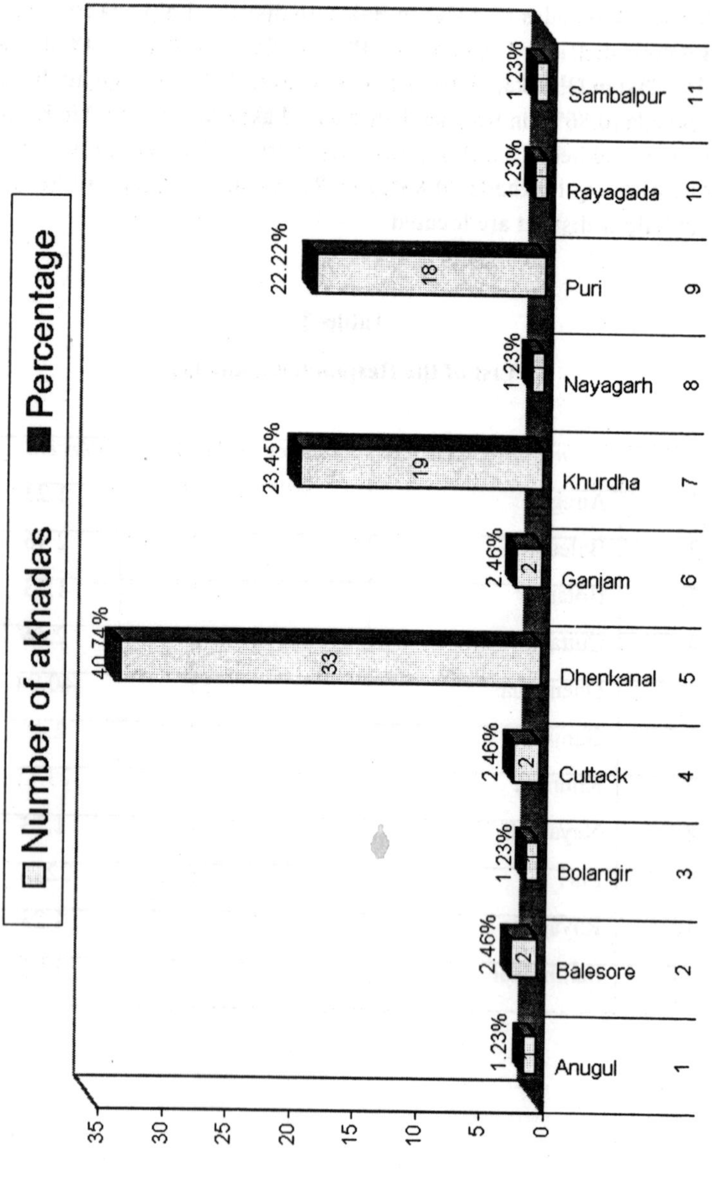
Number of akhadas
Percentage
35
30
25
20
15
10
5
0
1.23%
Anugul
1
2.46%
2
Balesore
2
1.23%
Bolangir
3
2.46%
2
Cuttack
4
40.74%
33
Dhenkanal
5
2.46%
2
Ganjam
6
23.45%
19
Khurdha
7
1.23%
Nayagarh
8
22.22%
18
Puri
9
1.23%
Rayagada
10
1.23%
Sambalpur
11

The questionnair send to 116 paika akhedas of Orissa. Out of 116 akhedas, only 48 akhedas sent their questionnaire in time. Again they were sent a sample questionnaire with self-addressed and stamped envelop and requested to send their filled up questionnaire. Another 33 questionnaire receved from the different akhedas. The total 81 akhedas sent their questionnaire. Out of 81 responded akhedas, 1 akheda (1.23%) belongs to Anugul district, 2 akhedas (2.46%) belongs to Balasore district, 1 akheda (1.23%) belongs to Bolangir district, 2 akhedas (2.46%) Cuttack district, 33 akhedas (40.74%) belong to Dhenkanal district, 2 akhedas (2.46%) Ganjam district, 19 akhedas (23.45%) belong to Kshurda district, 1 akheda (1.23%) belongs to Nayagarh district, 18 akhedas (22.22%) belong to Puri district, 1 akheda (1.23%) belongs to Rayagada district and 1 akheda (1.23%) belongs to Sambalpur district.

Table–3

Involvement of paikas and gurus in their respective akhedas.

Sl. No	*District*	*Number of Akhedas*	*Number of paikas involved in akheadas*	*Number of gurus involved in akhedas*	*Ratio between paikas and gurus*
1.	Anugul	01	16	01	1:16
2.	Balasore	02	44	05	1:9
3.	Bolangir	01	14	01	1:14
4.	Cuttack	02	38	03	1:13
5.	Dhenkanal	33	668	43	1:16
6.	Ganjam	02	36	03	1:12
7.	Khurda	19	410	29	1:14
8.	Nayagarh	01	21	02	1:11
9.	Puri	18	376	25	1:15
10.	Rayagada	01	18	01	1:18
11.	Sambalpur	01	13	01	1:13

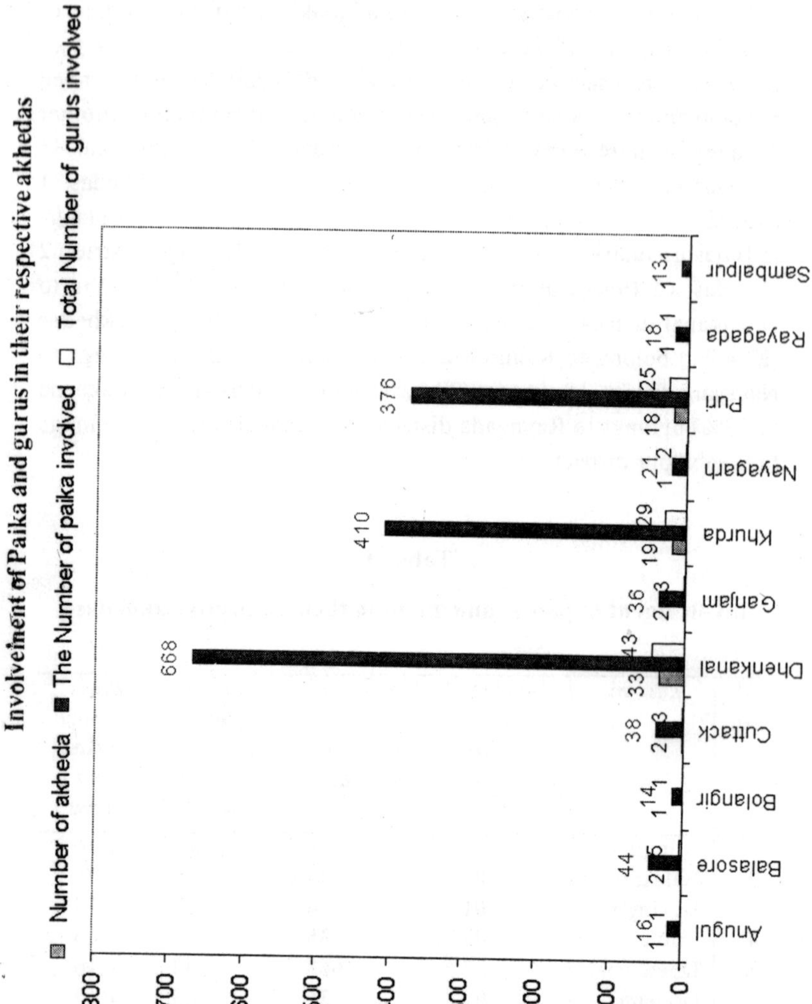

The strength of the akhedas and paika gurus in different akhedas and ratio between the paikas and gurus are shown in Table 3. The minimum paika strength was 12 numbers and maximum was 28 numbers. The total paika strength of the responded akhedas was 1654 numbers. The total numbers of the paika gurus of all the responded akhedas were 114. It was observed that, there were more than one gurus in 33 akhedas. The ratio between paikas and gurus ranges from 1:9 to 1: 18.

Table–4

Equipments available at different akhedas

Sl.No.	*Name of the equipments*	*Number of akhedas*	*Percentage*
1.	Sword and shield	81	100
2.	Patta	77	95.06
3.	Banka chhuri	59	72.83
4.	Lathi	81	100
5.	Gada mudgara	71	88
6.	Banati	53	65.43
7.	Nagafasa	07	8.64
8.	Nijham	20	24.69
9.	Singhata	03	3.70
10.	Bana	57	70.37
11.	Dhupa	43	53.08
12.	Gupti	12	14.81
13.	Bows and arrows	03	3.70
14.	Ranapa	41	50.61
15.	Bhala	26	32.09
16.	Tenta	20	24.69
17.	Trisulla	04	4.93
18.	Pharsha	17	21
19.	Akalana	12	14.81
20.	Jamadhara	5	6.17

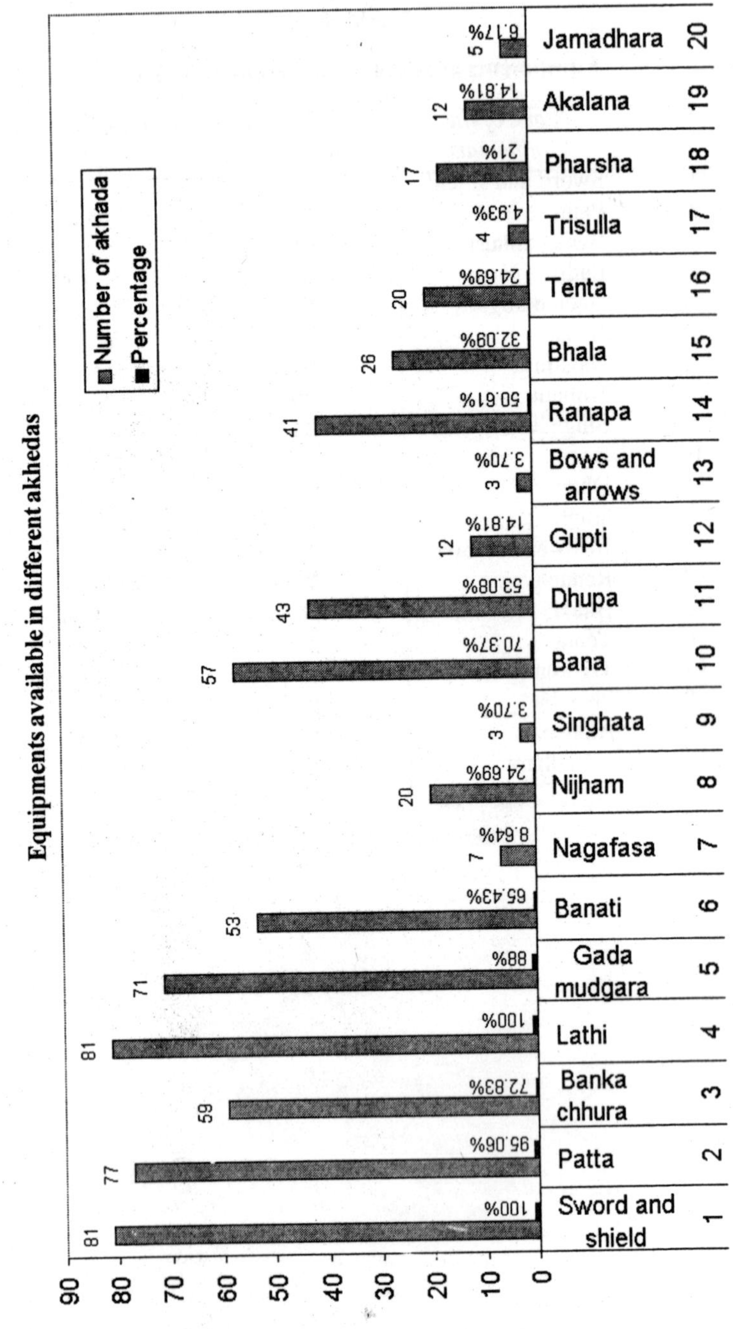
Equipments available in different akhedas
Number of akhada
Percentage
1 Sword and shield 81 100%
2 Patta 77 95.06%
3 Banka chhura 59 72.83%
4 Lathi 81 100%
5 Gada mudgara 71 88%
6 Banati 53 65.43%
7 Nagafasa 7 8.64%
8 Nijham 20 24.69%
9 Singhata 3 3.70%
10 Bana 57 70.37%
11 Dhupa 43 53.08%
12 Gupti 12 14.81%
13 Bows and arrows 3 3.70%
14 Ranapa 41 50.61%
15 Bhala 26 32.09%
16 Tenta 20 24.69%
17 Trisulla 4 4.93%
18 Pharsha 17 21%
19 Akalana 12 14.81%
20 Jamadhara 5 6.17%
0
10
20
30
40
50
60
70
80
90

In this table the various types of equipments, available in akhedas one depicted. Out of 81-responded akheda, all the akhedas possess sword, shield and lathi. The total 77 akhedas (95%) possess Patta, 59 akhedas (73%) possess Bankachuri, 71 akhedas (88%) possess Gada mudugara, 53 akhedas (65%) possess Banatti, only 7 akhedas (9%) possess Nagaphasa, 20 akhedas (25%) possess Nizham, only 3 akhedas (4%) possess Singhat, 57 akhedas (70%) possess Bana, 43 akhedas (53%) possess Dhupa, 12 akhedas (15%) possess Gupti, 3 akhedas (4%) possess bows and arrows, 41 akhedas (51%) possess Ranapa, 26 akhedas (32%) possess Bhala, 20 akhedas (25%) possess Tenta, 4 akhedas (5%) possess Trisulla, 12 akhedas (15%) possess Akalana and 5 akhedas (6%) possess Jamadhara.

Table 5

Practice of Martial arts at different akhedas.

Sl.No.	*Activities*	*Number of akhedas*	*Percentage*
1.	Dhala and Khanda (Sword and Shield)	81	100
2.	Patta	77	95.06
3.	Banka chhuri	53	65.43
4.	Lathi	81	100
5.	Ranapa	41	50.61
6.	Gada mudgara	71	87.65
7.	Bhuinghar bidya	67	82.71
8.	Banati	53	65
9.	Mati kusti	---	0
10.	Nagafasa	7	8.64
11.	Nijham	12	14.81
	Exceptional activities (traditional weight lifting like Akalana and sagadachaka)	04	5

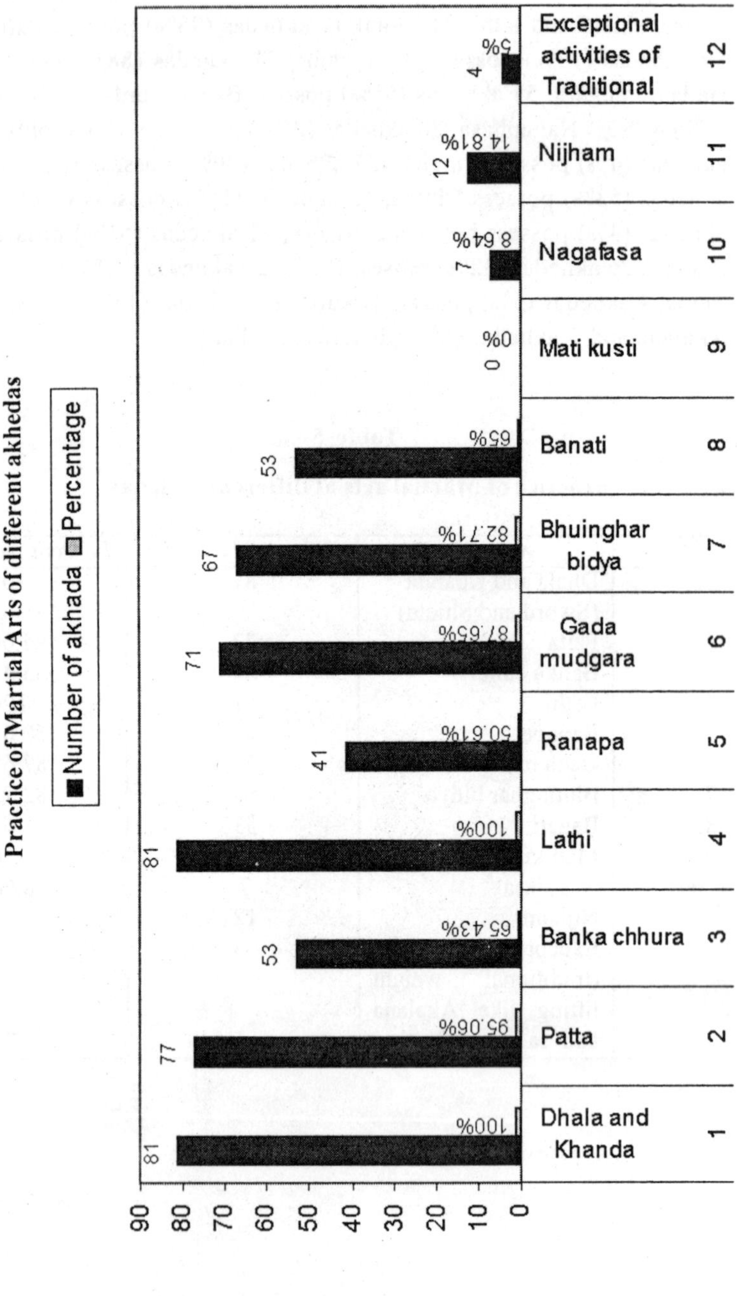
Practice of Martial Arts of different akhedas
Number of akhada
Percentage
Dhala and Khanda 81 100%
Patta 77 95.06%
Banka chhura 53 65.43%
Lathi 81 100%
Ranapa 41 50.61%
Gada mudgara 71 87.65%
Bhuinghar bidya 67 82.71%
Banati 53 65%
Mati kusti 0 0%
Nagafasa 7 8.64%
Nijham 12 14.81%
Exceptional activities of Traditional 4 5%
1 2 3 4 5 6 7 8 9 10 11 12
0 10 20 30 40 50 60 70 80 90

Various types of activities are practised by the paika at there respective akhedas are explained in this table. The sword and shield and lathi were the common activities practised by all the akhedas. Out of 81 responded akheda, the paiks of 77 akhedas (95%) practised patta, 53 akhedas (65%) practised Banatti, 41 akhedas (51%) practised Rannapa, 71 akhedas (88%) practised Gada mudgara, 67 akhedas (83%) practised Bhuinghar bidya, 7 akhedas (9%) practised Nagaphasa, 12 akhedas (15%) practised Nizham and exceptional demonstration activities like Akalana and Sagadachaka were practiced by only 4 akhedas (5%). It has been observed that many paikas of their akhedas did not practice the activities though their akhedas possessed the equipments. Only 12 akhedas practised Nizham though 20 akhedas possessed the said equipment. Similarly, Trisula, Farsha, Tenta etc, were possessed by few akhedas but the paikas and gurus of the said akhedas did not use the equipments. However, paika gurus and their students demonstrated weapons like Bhala, Bana, and Jamadhara. The paiks who were proficient in sword, Lathi could demonstrate these weapons.

It has been observed that no paika and guru of their respective akhedas practise *Mati Kusti* (Indian style of Wrestling) where as *Mati Kusti* is very popular at all the Jaga Ghars in Puri town.

Table–6

Musical equipments available at akhedas.

Sl. No.	*Musical equipments*	*Number of Akhedas*	*Percentage*
1.	Dhola	81	100
2.	Changu	55	68
3.	Mahuri	81	100
4.	Nagera	67	83
5.	Nishana	09	11
6.	Turi	05	6
7.	Singha	07	9
8.	Telingibaja	18	22
9.	Jodimahuri	07	9
10.	Phunka	02	2

Musical equipments available at akhedas.

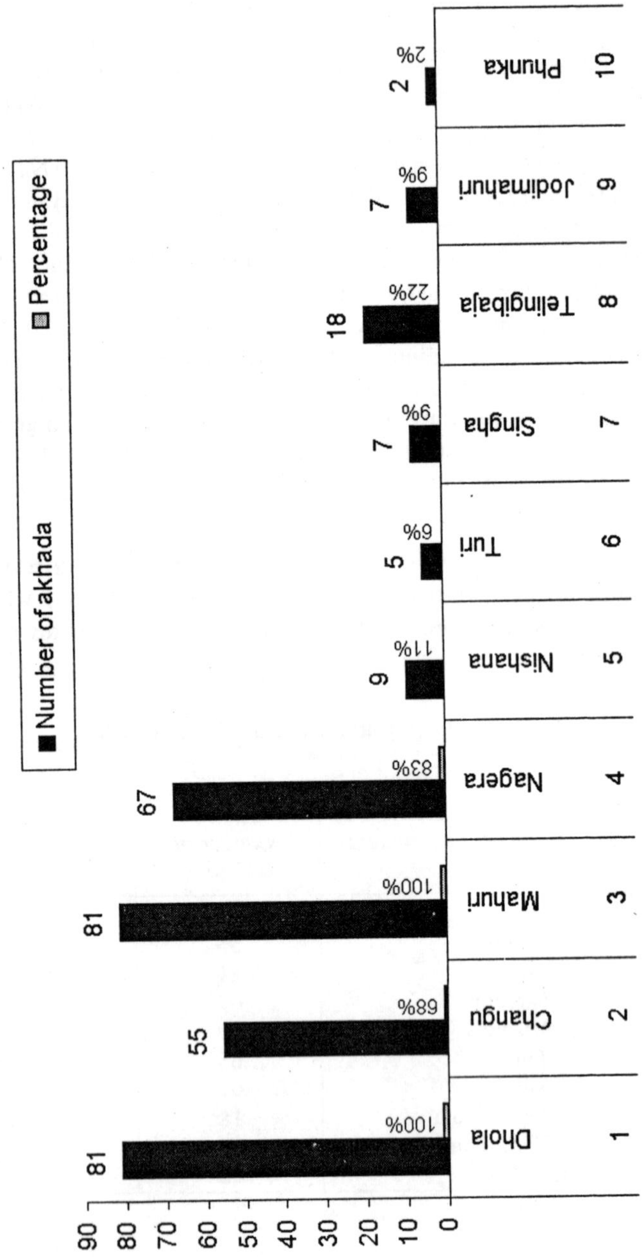

The musical equipments used by the Palika in different akhedas are mentioned. In ancient period, the music was used in the time of war. Nowadays the paikas are encouraged with the music at the time of demonstration. Out of 81 responded akhedas, all the akhedas used Dhola and Kahali which were very common musical equipments. 58 akhedas (68%) used changu, 67 akhedas (83%) used Nagera, only 9 akhedas (11%) used Nishana, 5 akhedas (6%) had possessed Turi, 7 akhedas (9%) possessed Singha, 18 akhedas (22%) possessed Telingibaja, 7 akhedas (9%) possessed Jodimahuri, 2 akhedas (2%) possessed Phunka. The research scholar observed that the Neshan is only used at Dhenkanal district. The musical beats of Gajapati Samarakala Pratisthana of Paralakhemundi were very popular.

Table–7

Premises Provision for conducting martial arts programme in akhedas

Sl. No.	*Provision*	*Number of Akhedas*	*Percentage*
1.	Permanent building	22	27.16
2.	One room	19	23.45
3.	More than one room	03	3.70
4.	Field facilities	37	45.67
5.	Fulka	03	3.70

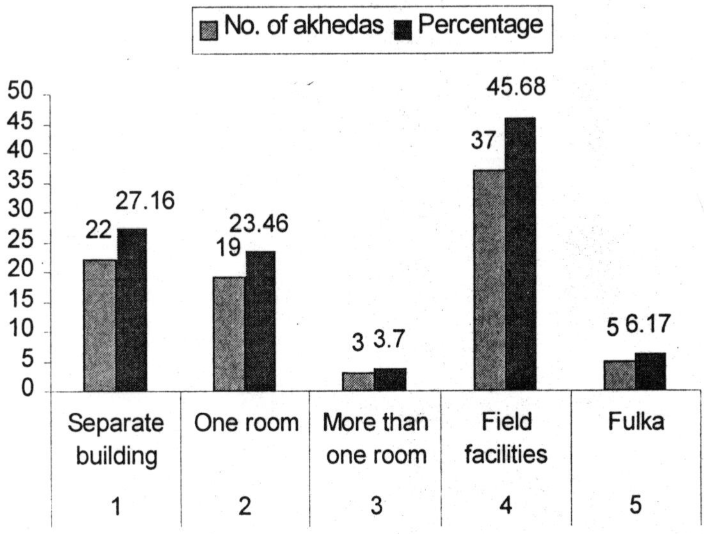

The Provisioin for conducting Martial art Programme in different akhedas are analysed. Out of 81-responded akhedas only 22 akhedas (27%) possess there own building. Out of these 22 akhedas, 19 akhedas (23%) possess only one room and 3 akhedas (4%) had possess more than one room. The total 59 akhedas (73%) have building of their own. Only 37 akhedas (46%) have there own fields. The other akhedas had not possessed their own fields but they practice their martial art in their village fields. Only 3 akhedas (4%) possess fulka.

Financial conditions and organisational set up of the akhedas— It has been found that almost all the akhedas have no adequate funds to meet the minimum needs. There is no government grant to meet the minimum requirements and preserve the ancient martial art. The contributions of villagers towards the development of the akhedas are very low. The cost of equipments of the martial arts is very high. No akheda is maintaining its annual budget. The main sources of income are only donations collected from the villagers at the time of various festivals. The managing committee of the akhedas does not provide any financial support to their gurus. The senior, most person having proficiency in martial arts of the concerned akheda is regarded as guru. It is observed that every year the villagers nominated their president, secretary, treasurer and other office bearer to their akhedas. In some akhedas they nominated them for two or four years. Since their financial condition is very poor, it is very difficult on their part to organise the martial arts competitions. More than 90% akhedas are registered under the social registration act.

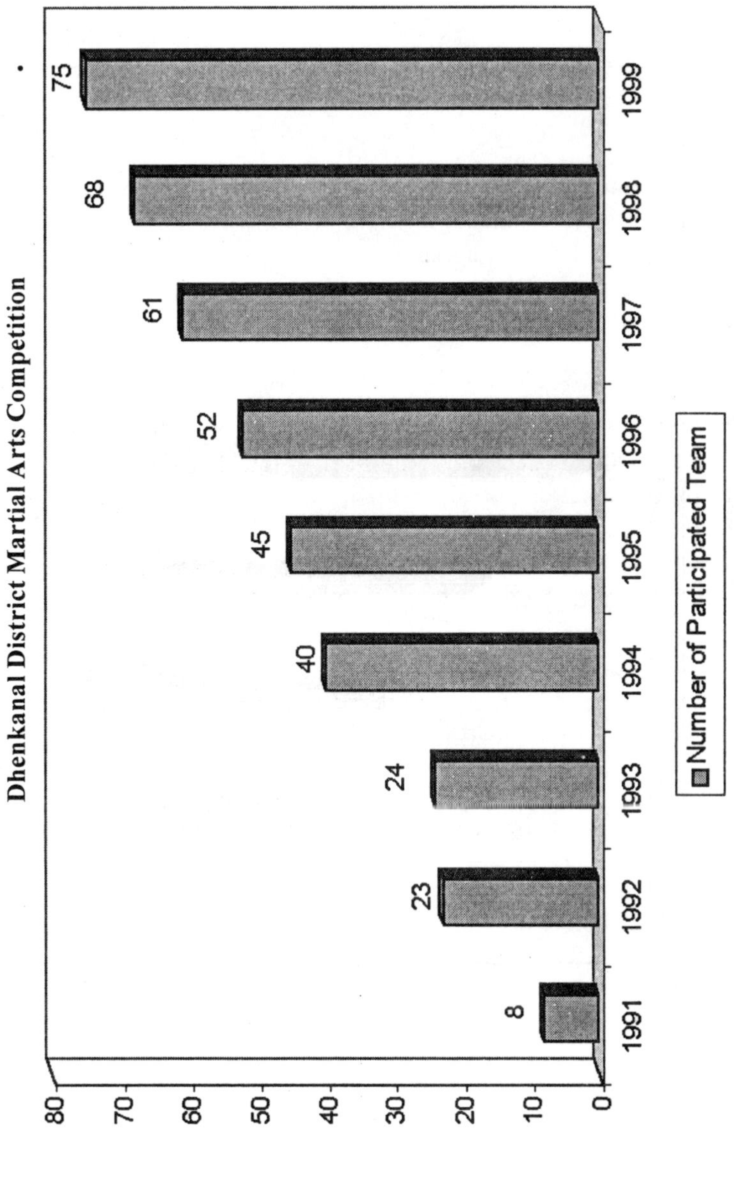
Dhenkanal District Martial Arts Competition
80
70
60
50
40
30
20
10
0
8
23
24
40
45
52
61
68
75
1991
1992
1993
1994
1995
1996
1997
1998
1999
Number of Participated Team

State Level Paika Akheda Competition

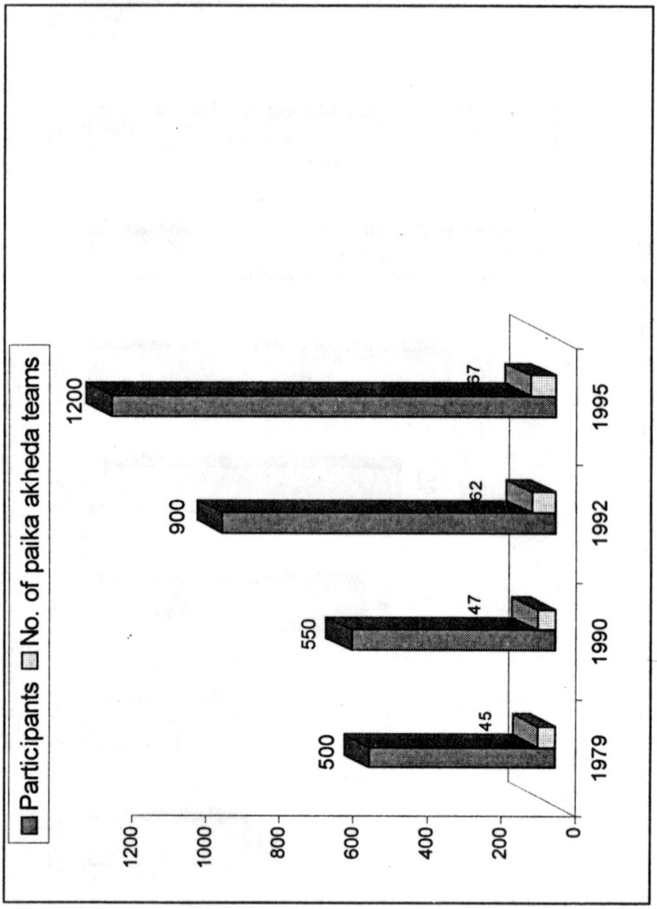

5

Summary, Conclusion and Recommendation

Summary

In ancient and medieval times, Orissa passed under the names of Kalinga, Utkal, and Odra Desa. Ancient Kalinga was a powerful state and extends its boundary from the river Ganges to the river Godavari. The history of Kalinga goes by its own significance. But the past has no connection with their present history. The military glory of Kalinga is marked from the time of Ashok (3rd century B.C.) the Mauryan Emperor of Magadha. The economic prosperity of the Kalinga people vested mainly on its maritime and inland trade, agriculture and natural products. The war booties brought from time to time by the emperors and his soldiers from other kingdoms raised the economic standard of the country. The personality of the Monarchs counted considerably in shaping the military character of the people. A powerful army is a basic necessity of monarchical state. Kalinga all through the phases of its history maintained a vast army consisting of infantry, cavalry, elephant and in the early period the chariots. In consideration of numerous forts, the remains of which are still in existence built by the monarchs right for the time of Ashok till the 16th century reveals that the entire Kalinga empire of the past was honey-combed with forts and military stronghold for defensive and offensive purpose. Kalinga had the distinction of possessing all types of forts prescribed in the *Arthasastra* and Puranas. The militant and chivalrous characters of Kalingans were reflected in numerous wars fought against the enemies over the ages. Their powers, bravery, strength and quality to shoulder risk are of special type.

After the period of Kalinga war, the famous dynasty, which rose to power, is called as Chedi or Chiti Dynasty. Mahameghavahana

Kharavela was the famous ruler of the Chedi Dynasty. He organised a vast army with four-fold division. Kharavela was a great conqueror and his military achievements are incomparable to other dynasty during that period. After the period of Kharavela, the notable dynasties, which ruled over the territory, were the Mathara, the Bhauma-Kara, the Somavamsi, the Gangas and the Suryas. Every powerful dynasty and several of their great kings have left their permanent monuments like forts and temples etc. It was the reign of Raja Raja III of the Ganga dynasty that of Muslims of Bengal invaded Orissa for the first time in A.D. 1205. This was the beginning of Muslim invasions, which continued to endanger Orissa throughout the Ganga and Suryavamsi dynasties till her final conquest in A.D. 1568. Kings under the Ganga dynasty were brave and their administrative ability was superb. Among the Monarch of Ganga Dynasty, Narasingha Deva I was exceptionally brilliant. The greatest monument of the reign of Narasingha Deva I was the Sun Temple of Konarak. The artistic needlework on stone was unique in our country. The Orissan architecture, art, literature, administration and military achievements were also reached its zenith during this period. They mentioned the four-fold division of army. The military expeditions and the army were rare. The person bearing titles is the indicative of their social, official and military status. The military scenes of the various temples signify the military proficiency and martial race of the land.

The Suryavamsi dynasty gave to Orissa three famous rulers Kapilendra Deva, Purusottam Deva and Prataprudra Deva. From political point of view, by second quarter of fifteenth century, the Orissan kingdom was surrounded on all sides by formidable powers, such as, the Bengal Sultantates, Bahamani Kingdom, and Vijayanagar Empire. Kapilendra Deva took necessary steps against all his neighbouring powers to safeguard his territory. His army was a rare, and the last example of Orissa's military traditions. This monarch is usually compared with the great Kharavela of ancient times for the military expeditions and the martial vigour he showed. His elephant force was invincible in India. His military title of Gajapati or Lord of elephant force is an evidence of his big elephant force. The third Surya Monarch Prataprudra was the last in the long line of Orissa's great rulers of ancient and medieval times from the days of Kharavela. Repeated invasions from Vijayanagar Empire and sultanates of Bengal disturbed him a lot. He lost most of his ancestral dominions in the peninsular India. The reduced Orissa had by then approximated its present day size. Even the name Kalinga that signified much of her ancient and medieval glory vanished.

When the Surya Dynasty was thus extinguished Govinda Vidyadhar ascended the throne and proclaimed himself as the Gajapati King. During his brief rule, Orissa was disintegrated speedily with independent small principalities coming into existence in the inaccessible hill tracts of Orissa. His worthless successors were removed from the scene and a brave general named Mukunda Harichandan ascended the throne to try desperately to save a dying kingdom. Mukunda Deva was killed in an internal battle in the year 1568, which at once paved path for Muslim conquest of Orissa. Again Orissan prestige was doomed and local Kings became more puppets in the hands of Muslim Governors. It is no doubt adds glory of Orissa that although the Muslim rule was established in India by the end of twelfth century A.D., Orissa could defend herself from the onslaught of the Muslim invasion for more than three hundred years.

Orissa lost her independence in 1568. For long 379 years, the Afghans, the Mughals, the Marathas and the British ruled Orissa. During Mughals and the Maratha period, the feudatory chiefs enjoyed the semi-independent status. The semi-independent princes of Orissa revolted against the Mughal Government whenever they got opportunity. These feudatory chiefs had their own standing militia called paika. During British period a notable event called "Paika Rebellion" spread in Khurda and various other parts of Orissa. The British authority resumed the service lands of the paikas, which they enjoyed in the days of Hindu kings. There faulty revenue system was the main cause of paika rebellion. Soon after the event, the martial law was proclaimed in the affected areas. Many weapons like sword, shield, patta, bana, jamadhara etc were sized and practice of martial arts was banned at akheda ghar. Many weapons of Orissa got influenced under the Muslim and Maratha rules. During this period the term patta was used instead of Hasthavara khanda. Gupti the weapons of Muslim period was hugely used in Orissa.

The presently Orissan martial arts, though popularly known as paika akheda has some literary meaning. There is no doubt this famous martial arts have been derived from ancient war skills exhibited by the Kalingan soldiers from time to time. The term 'paika' derived from the Sanskrit word 'padatika' which means foot soldiers. They were requited from all the classes and castes. The paika enjoyed the cultivation lands, as cash for their military services, which was called Paika Jagire, did not pay them. The paikas of Orissa used sixteen types of weapons. The most important thing is that, at the age of twenty they are eligible to join in the army. They retired from their military services at the age of forty. However, after their retirement they can work as a watchman at palace, treasury, and fort. Some of them also utilize their service as paika guru and trained young at their village akheda. Further the elder son of the family was bound to join in the army and the younger son look after the cultivation and their family. The single son of the family is not entitled to join the army. From this we can very well understand the equipment process of the Kalingan army. The famous Joy Javan and Joy Kisan slogan of our late Prime Minister Sri Lal Bahadur Sastri was practically implemented in long back in the state of Orissa.

The various war dances of Orissa like *Naga Nacha*, *Paika Nacha*, *Ranapa Nacha* etc, are associated with martial traditions of Orissa. With the help of drumbeats and other war music they perform the dance, which recalls our past military glories. The stories of the dances are usually borrowed from the Indian mythology and puranas. Some stories are also related to ancient war stories of Orissa. The military literature of Orissa like Paika Kheda, Samara Taranga, Rana Taranga, Phiringikali Bharata, Khalikota Rajanka Yasa, Virsarvasva, Viraparakrama, Bhudapanka Yudha, Yudhagita, etc, describe the military glory and the war that was conducted by various Rajas with the formidable British power. In many manuscripts, the author described the principle of warfare, systems of constructing forts, organization of army, use of war drums, recital of mantras and puja before joining the war, use of medicine, etc.

The martial arts of other states in our country and different other countries were analysed in details. Few martial arts like Filipino art of Kali, Bersilat of Malaysia were originated in 15th century. The Japan's Samurai system was originated 1185A.D. The Zen archery of Japan is an ancient system of martial arts came from a battlefield skill. The Korean martial arts also was originated prior to the fifth century. The Chinese system is also an ancient one. So, comparable to other martial arts of the different countries of the world, the Orissan martial arts was originated from the ancient war skill and also it was one of the oldest martial arts in the world.

The various types of activities of Orissan martial arts like Dhala Tarabari, Patta, Banatti, Lathi, Banka Churi etc, are still practised by the paika gurus in most of the akhedas. In Bijayadasami days they worship their remained weapons and goddess Durga and demonstrate their skills in their villages. The list of the paika akheda teams (total 116) is collected from the department of Sports and Youth Services, Bhubaneswar and Surapratap Smurtipitha of Dhenkanal district. The state level martial arts competitions were arranged by the sports and culture department of Orissa for four times. It has been noticed that most of the akhedas are located in Dhenkanal, Puri and Khurda districts of Orissa. Every year paika akheda teams of Dhenkanal district got the opportunities to participate in the district level competition. The gurus and paikas are felicitated by the organising committee.

From the time of Kharavela to present days the paikas of Orissa showed their caliber as a martial race through generations and centuries. Social customs, festivals, ceremonies, rites, and rituals, art, music, crafts etc, all in their traditional forms need some amount of social patronage. The four time State level Martial arts competitions and sports persons pension implemented by the Government are not quite sufficient to revive this arts. Even if, the present days do not need their continuance for any valid material benefit, yet they are trying their level best to retain their traditional art for the sake of mental pleasure as memories of bygone days. In between hundreds of years passed and political and economic scenario have been changed but there great ceremonies during the period of Dashara did not change their martial spirit. It is said the art and artist never die. The martial spirit among the paikas and gurus of Orissa will continue to remain from generation to generation.

Conclusion

The Origin of the Orissan martial arts is traced at the time of Ashoka and Kharabela, even though the terms paika and akheda were used during the period of Ganga dynasty 12th century A.D.

The Orissan Martial Arts had been used in warfare by the different dynasties of Orissa. At present it has found a place in the recreational programme. The paikas and gurus demonstrate these activities in some festive occasions at their village. Viewing it critically, one can very well see that the culture of Orissan martial arts might have been the soul factor of finding Orissa as an Ideal State.

Long ago Plato, one of the greatest possible intellectuals of the world wanted that every individual of one Ideal State should be a trained soldier and should be sound both physically and mentally. A sick or physically unsound human being should not be allowed to marry to avoid weak offsprings. Such a desire of Plato, to provide compulsory military training to everyone, was found to be in practice in Orissa. Due to socio-political and financial conditions of the state, the tradition and culture of Orissan warfare activities are almost paralysed.

However, there is nothing to become more panic or pessimistic about it. Even though the martial arts culture was going to die but it is not dead. It is a matter of great pleasure that now, the Orissan martial arts and paika akheda teams are reviving with a good spirit. In our survey, it is found that at present 116 teams are participating in martial arts competitions. The State Government have organised State level competitions four times. Every year Surapratap Smurtipitha of Dhenkanal District is organising such competition. The districts such as Khurda, Dhenkanal, Puri, Nayagarh, Ganjam and Balasore are the places where it is popular in these days. Besides the 116 teams, there are many other places (the then feudetory States) where small groups of youths are found to practise martial arts. If this trend continues then we can expect a bright future of martial arts in our state.

Further, in this present society, where social crimes like robbery, murder, snatching away costly items from persons are increasing day by day, the practise of martial culture would be of a great help to the Oriyas. Moreover, every individual should be mentally sound and physically fit. The akhedas and jaga gharas of Orissa play as health clubs and gymnasiums and offer the youth varieties of activities to keep them fit. Our ancient Paika Gurus were very much acquainted with warming up and conditioning exercises and their training process was systematic.

The techniques of the various activities involved various kinds of swings with different parts of the body. Defence, on the part of the player involves quick footwork in advancing, retreating, stepping etc, so as to make it impossible for the opponent or his weapons to reach him. The mock fighting is arranged in the events like sword, patta, lathi etc, in dual and group basis. They demonstrate it as if, they fight seriously. Before the start of the contest, the paika salutes to his guru, opponent and audience with opposite movements. It is also called *Salami*. The term *Salami* was used in Muslim periods. The research scholar came to know from the observation and interview that many skills and techniques of sword, patta, Banka churi are still in practice by the gurus. Many of the difficult skills are not practiced.

From the survey of 116 akhedas, 81 akhedas responded the questionnaire. The Dhenkanal district possesses highest number of akhedas. Most of the akhedas possess more than one gurus. The weapon arts like sword and shield, lathi are common and found in all the akheda. Out of 81 akhedas, 77 akhedas (95%) possess Patta and 71 akhedas (88%) possess Gada Mudugara, 59 akheda (73%) possess Banka Churi, 57 akhedas (70%) possess Bana, 43 akhedas (53%) possess Dhupa and few akhedas (4%) possess Bows and Arrows, Singhat.

All the Paikas and Gurus of their respective akhedas practise Dhala and Khanda (sword and Shield) and Lathi. Out of 81 responded akheda 77 akhedas (95%) practise Patta, 53 akhedas (65%) practise Banka Churi, 41 akhedas (51%) practise Ranapa, 67 akhedas (83%) practise Bhuinghar Bidya and 53 akhedas (65%) practise Banatti. No akheda ghar practise Mati Kusti. Whereas all the young members of yaga ghar practises matikusti. This event is very popular in every yaga ghar of Puri town. Only 7 akhedas (9%) practise nagaphasa, 12 akhedas (15%) practise Nijham though twenty akhedas possess the equipments. Exceptional activities like Sagadachaka, Akalana etc, are practised by 4 akhedas (5%). The musical equipments like Dhola and Kahali are common in every akheda. Out of 81 responded akhedas 67 akhedas (83%) possess Nagara, 55 akhedas (68%) possess Changu, 9 akhedas (11%) possess Nisana, 5 akhedas (6%) possess Turi, 18 akhedas (22%) possess Telingibaja, 7 akhedas (9%) possess Jodimahuri, 2 akhedas (2%) possess Phunka. Among these musical equipments Dhola and Kahali play significant role in present days.

It is observed that out of 81 responded akhedas only 22 akhedas (77%) possess permanent building whereas all the jaga ghars of the Puri town are having their own buildings. Only 37 akhedas (46%) are having their permanent fields. Other akhedas practise the martial arts in their village fields. Only 3 akhedas (4%) possess Fulka. The term Fulka is used as Khel-jaga at jaga ghars in Puri town.

After 32 years of independence of our country, the State Government, through Orissa Council of Sports organised a State level martial arts competition in the year 1979. After 11 years gap, the State Government again conducted martial arts competition in the year 1990. The third and fourth State level competition was held in the year 1992 and 1996. The gap was only two and four years. These four times martial arts competitions motivated paika and Gurus in al most all the akhedas. To revive this art, the state level competition should be organised in every two years. The districts level competition at Dhenkanal motivates the Guru, organising secretaries and paikas. Now, many new paika teams are formed at Dhenkanal. In the first district competition, which was held in the year 1991, only 8 teams participated. In the last competition 75 teams participated in the competition. The participated teams increased from 8 to 75 within nine years.

It is worth appreciating that the Government have started providing Sports persons pension to paika gurus. It is also the responsibility of those old gurus, not to forget their art, rather should revitalise the old and valuable techniques, which are going to be given less importance in our present culture. The government, voluntary agencies and other associations should take proper attention towards the development of these martial arts.

Recommendations

On the basis of conclusion drawn in this study, the following recommendation may deserve attention.

1. For a common goal, adequate attention should be given for forming a universal pattern of movements of the Orissan martial arts. All the senior gurus of the different akhedas should be invited for the workshop. The common techniques of various activities of all the gurus should be kept on record and an uniform type of all the activities shouid be formed for competition and demonstration programme.

2. The directorate of Sports and Youth Services or the Department of Culture, Government of Orissa should organise a state level martial arts competition at least once in every two years. So almost all the gurus and paikas will be motivated towards the martial arts. At the end of the competition, apart from merit certificates and first, second and third prizes, a best paika guru and a best paika should be felicitiated and special award should be given to them. The district level competition is also highly essential.

3. The events for competition are suggested below.

   I. Sword and shield demonstration (Individual event)

   II. Sword and shield (dual fighting)

   III. Patta (dual fighting)

   IV. Patta (group fighting not less than four)

   V. Banati (Individual demonstration)

   VI. Lathi (Individual demonstration)

   VII. Lathi (dual fighting)

   VIII. Lathi (group fighting not less than four)

   IX. Gada Mudgara (individual demonstration)

   X. Banka Chhuri (dual fighting)

   XI. Banka Chhuri (group fighting not less than four)

   XII. Ranapa (individual)

   XIII. Ranapa (dual fighting with sword and shield)

   XIV. Bhuinghar Bidya (Floor exercises) individual and group

   XV. Exceptional Martial arts demonstration programme like heavy traditional weight lifting (Sagadachaka, akalana) or event like chandan pochha, singhat chalana etc. should be encouraged.

It depends open the organizing committee to choose the events from the above. According to the feasibility like financial factors, area or space for the accommodation, competition arena etc the committee should invite the necessary teams for the competition.

4. Minimum three and maximum five judges (among seniormost gurus from different districts) should be judges in the competition. Five juries should be present and observe the competition properly. If any dispute arises among the judges, the decision of jury is final.

5. A match referee or steward should be selected. The main duties of the steward are to send the teams and individual competitors to the arena as per the order of events.
6. The juries and judges should carefully discuss the rules and regulations of the competition framed by the organising committee. The rules and regulations should be properly communicated to all the team managers and gurus before the competition.
7. A timekeeper and announcer should be present for the smooth conduct of the competition. The score sheet should be properly framed. The judges should evaluate the performance impartially. The judges should observe five important points like (a) the traditional paika dress, paika boli, kuhata and stepping (b) attacking techniques (c) defensive techniques (d) exceptional activities and (e) physical fitness.
8. Since there is no actual fighting practised by the paika in different akhedas, provision of standard equipment is a must for the successful demonstration of Orissan martial arts.
9. The seniormost paika gurus of the different akhedas should get monthly pension from the government for their life long contribution and dedication in promoting the Orissan martial arts.
10. The paikas those got special award and first position in the state level martial arts competition should get scholarship from the government.
11. The martial activities of all the senior and talented gurus should be video filmed and their interview should be kept in record for documentation.
12. The local authority and government should take up steps to provide a separate building for the akheda. A fulka should be constructed in each akheda for the practice purpose of the martial arts.
13. Without finance no work can be successfully implemented. The Govt. of Orissa should frame a special budget for promoting the martial arts.
14. Almost all the akhedas should get financial aid for purchasing and making their equipments.
15. Provision of extra financial aid should be implemented to akhedas producing more number of champions in state level martial arts competition in order to encourage more participants in the competition.

16. The government may take steps to provide separate open space to the akhedas available in the locality through appropriate legislation.
17. All the gurus and secretaries of the concerned akhedas should take necessary steps to display their old equipments, weapons, photographs of their gurus etc at their akheda rooms for museum purpose. The research scholar from various parts will get the opportunities to observe it.
18. Additional facilities like a demonstration halls for various activities may please be made in every akheda.
19. Available of play area may please be utilized in a planned way. The maintenance of fulka, fields etc are very important from the hygienic point of view.
20. For proper development and promotion of this art, it is felt necessary that a governing body be established to regulate contests with universal rules, to prevent injuries and to produce popular and scientific literature on the subject. Special attention should also be given to conduct research on physiological, kine-anthropometrical and bio-mechanical analysis of various motor movements of Orissan martial arts.
21. The Orissan Martial arts Academy that was established in the year 1995-96 sessions under the financial assistance from the Directorate of Sports and Youth Services, Government of Orissa is now defunct. The same organization should be re-established. The students of the academy should visit other states like Kerala, Manipur, Tamil Nadu to observe their martial arts and also demonstrate our martial arts as a cultural exchange programme. Even they should visit other countries to demonstrate our martial arts.
22. The Government should take necessary steps to organise State level seminar, workshop among the paika gurus to revive and preserve various techniques and tactics of martial arts.

Glossary

Abhiseka–	coronation ceremony. When the prince's coronation takes places, he attains the status of a king.
Adalat–	court of Justice.
Adhya	chapter.
Akheda–	a club house where paika practice all sorts of physical activities.
Alankar–	ornament
Allah–	Muslim God
Amali–	a title of revenue era prevailing in Orissa since the mughal rule.
Amla–	Government officer of a judicial or a revenue court.
Anka–	a special year from which the rule of the Orissan king are calculate.
Ardhachandra–	half–moon.
Astragara–	arsenal where all kinds of arms and ammunitions are stored.
Badyakara–	drummer.
Baghachahani–	aggressive facial action like a tiger while performing danda.
Bagha chata–	eating action of a tiger while performing a danda.
Baghasingha–	who braves like a tiger in a war, a title conferred by the Raga of Khurda.
Bahalia–	singer.
Bahitra–	war vessels.
Bahubadia–	beating to the arm wlile performing danda.

Bahujhinka–	action shows like pulling the opponent towards own body.
Bahuvalendra–	a title denoting physical strength.
Bahuti–	an ornament for the arm.
Baithak–	free hand squat with arm swing.
Bakshi–	military commander.
Bala–	an ornament for the wrist.
Balabantaray–	chief among the strongest; title conferred by the king to those who noted for their physical strength.
Baliarsingh–	one who is strong as lion.
Baliamukha–	a weapon used by paika.
Bana–	big sword with edge in both side.
Banua–	person in charge of fire arm.
Barcha–	spear.
Bari Durga–	fort or stronghold surrounded by water.
Baruda kumpa–	a weapon used in war by paika.
Benta bhaunri–	circle movement while performing danda.
Behera–	servant attached to paikas.
Bhagabata Gita–	sacred book oh Hindu.
Bhakti–	devotion.
Bhoee–	an infirior village officer entrusted with the task of collection cowries (used as coin).
Bhoeemul–	high offcial in charge of accounts of the kingdom.
Bhiana–	Seventy dalas (group) make one bhiana; each dala comprising 27 paika; a bhiana comprises 27×70=1890 paika.
Boli–	various types of war songs used by paik to their opponent.
Brahmin–	high class Hindu.
Campus martius–	physical education schools of Rome.
Chakra–	wheel.
Chalatalia–	the name of a danda.

Chamaka–	fake or dogging action while performing danda.
Chamupati/ champati–	title
Chatibadia–	danda performed with swinging action of the hand beating in the Chest.
Dagar–	carrier of message.
Dak–	post.
Dakhinakabat–	in charge of southern front group.
Dala–	troop.
Dalapati–	leader of the troop.
Dalabehera–	in charge of a Zilla with one or more forts or garhs but with a principal Fort which was the local military and revenue headquarters of the Zilla.
Dalei–	subordinate to dulbehera. He usually resides in a fort and commands the service of a number of paikas.
Danda–	Indian styles of physical exercises to strengthen the arms. It is like dips with swinging action of the upper body.
Durbar–	royal court.
Daroga–	subordinate officer in charge of police station or of a revenue or excise office.
Dena–	wing.
Dhala–	shild.
Dhana–	desert.
Dhanu–	bow.
Dhaniki–	archer.
Dhupa–	big sword used by paika in the front at the time of marching.
Digvijya–	conquest of regims.
Diwan–	minister of finance and revenue.
Diwani adalat–	civil court.
Fauzdar–	a district officer under the Muslims and Marathas exercising civil Military powers.

Gajapati– Lord of elephants. the king of Orissa styled themselves as gajapati. this title indicated their sovereign status.

Gala– neck.

Gangaprasad– name of a war vessel used in war during the war period.

Garuda viyuha– battle array like eagle.

Ghagudi– an ornament used by the paika.

Ghats– a landing place near river bank for loading and unloading of goods From boats.

Giri– hill.

Gantimala– an ornament for the neck.

Gaya– singer.

Guru– teacher.

Gurjhat– feudatory states.

Harichandan– a title conferred by the king of Khurda.

Harikatha– imprisonment.

Hatigumpha– elephant cave located Udyagiri, Bhubaneswar.

Haveli vana– fire arm used by the paika in the war.

Itikara– lancer.

Jagir– revenue free land in lieu of payment of service.

Jagirdar– an official.

Jamadhara– big sword.

Jatra/ Yatra festival

Jala– water.

Jena– fort official in charg of receiving complaints of the people and bringing it to the notice of the king.

Jhanja– musical instrument.

Jhaptasingh– a title conferred by the king.

Jhulakata– a weapon used by the paika in the war.

Kandha– of aboriginal tribe in Orissa.

Kathaia– one who provides entertainment to the paika while marching to battlefield.

Kali–	Goddess
Karana–	writer class
Katari–	a weapon.
Kandi–	lane.
Kantia–	a weapon.
Kenchuamoda–	movement like roundworm.
Khanda–	National sword of Orissa.
Kavya–	long poem.
Khadga–	long sword.
Khandayat–	person carrying a sword.
Kolajhinka–	action shows like pulling the opponent towards waist while performing danda.
Ketra–	place.
Kshatrias–	warrior class people.
Khapar–	a weapon used by paika in the war.
Khas–	managed by the government.
Khasmahal–	district held in the management of the government.
Killa/quilla–	a fort or fortress.
Kimbhiria–	one who provides entertainment to the paikas while on the march.
Kimbhiria–	a danda performed in crocodile action.
Kothi–	palace.
Kuhata–	sort loud voice used by paika.
Lahadia–	waves.
Madala panji–	chronicle written in bundless of palm leaves.
Mahal–	territory of a tributary Raja, an estate.
Mahi–	forest.
Mana–	a measure of land.
Mauza–	a village or a group of village.
Munsiff–	officer in charge of administration of justice under British.
Manusya–	people.

Mughal bandee– portions of Orissa (the costal district of Baleswar, Cuttack, and Puri)

Formerly under mughal rule and hence, the name as distinguished

Garhjat or hill estate.

Naib– deputy.

Naik– subordinate to bisoee.

Nali– a weapon.

Nawab– a viceroy or governor of a province.

Padatika– foot soldier.

Padhikara– swordman.

Pahari– watchman.

Paikaray– chief among the paika. They are responsible for maintaince of discipline In the army.

Panchaghara– technique used in patta(Weapon).

Panda– priest of the temple.

Panduraya– physicians in the army.

Parvata durga– fort situated on the top of the mountain.

Pasara– stick.

Pragana– a tract of country comprising many village.

Pattanaik– a title, chief muhariir whose duty was to assist the diwanin keeping the accounts of the kingdom. His duty was also to enforce discipline in the army.

Pithichhat– handspring movement while performing danda.

Purana– religious litrature.

Quiladar– In–charge of the fort.

Raisingha– chief among the lions, a title conferred by king.

Rajguru— religious preceptor of the king.

Rajput– inhabitants of old Rajputana (now Rajastan).

Ranapa– warfoot.

Rani– queen.

Rashi– rope.

Ratha– chariot.

Rupachandra– an ornament used by paika

Royt/raiyat– a cultivator or a farmer.

Sada– simple or plain.

Sahi– habitat.

Sardar– leader.

Saka– an era current in India.

Samanta– a title means nobles.

Samar– war.

Salamee/mi– a present to a superior officer, saluting to the superior officer.

Samrat– emperor.

Samhita– Hindu religious texts.

Sangramsingh– one who is like a lion in war; a title conferred by king.

Sarbarakar– a trustee, manager, collector of rent in a revenue circle.

Sardar– a headman or a chief; a leader.

Sarkar– a division of the country.

Sataghara– technique used in patta (weapon).

Sava parva– one part of the Epic, Mahavarat.

Savara– an aboriginal tribe.

Sena– army.

Sevayatas– priests of the Lord Jaganath temple of Puri.

Subhadar– the governor of a province, a viceroy under the mughal government.

Suchi byuha– needle–array.

Sudra– low caste Hindu.

Suli– gallows.

Suryanamaskara–sun salutation; it is performed by combinations of various types of Asana in sequence manner.

Swayamvara– selection of the king by the queen before the marriage ceremony.

Tahasil– a division of a district.

Tahasildar– collector of the revenue for the cultivators.

Taluka– a division of a province.

Thana– police station.

Telugu– persons of Andhra Pradesh.

Thani– facial appearance shown by paika.

Vajra– thunder.

Ugalsingha– one who is in charge of collecting medicinal herbs.

Upanayana– thread ceremony of Brahmin.

Uttar kabata– in charge of northern front.

Vaikuntha bhavana– heaven.

Vaisya– third main caste in Hindu society.

Vansa– dynasty.

Veda– holi scripture of the Hindu.

Vira vadya– war music.

Vyayam– exercise.

Yudha– war.

Zamindar– landlord

Zamindari– pertaining to a Zamindar.

Appendix–A

List of the Paika Akheda Team

Anugal

1. Maa Barunei Paika Association, At- Haripur, Po-Anugul.
2. Maa Kalapat Paika Sangha, Madhyagarh Sahi, Balaram Prasad, At/Po- Anugul.
3. Birabhanu Paika Sangha, Anugul.

Balasore

1. Mahavir Lathi Khela Dala, Vil/Po- Chhanua, Via- Haladiapada, Balasore, Pin-756027.
2. Bira Bajaranga Bayam Nagar, Balasore, Pin-756003.
3. Mahavira Paika Sangha, Gopal Gaon, Balasore.
4. Aprna Yubak Sangha, Manikhumb, Balasore.

Bolangir

1. Maa Samaleswari Paika Sangha, At/Po-Bolangir.

Cuttack

1. Mahavir Akheda, At/Po.- Athagarh, Cuttack.
2. Khairapanga Paika Sangha, Baramba, Cuttack.
3. Mahendra Kumar Singh Paika Akheda, Po-Lalitagiri, Cuttack.

Dhenkhanal

1. Jayadurga Paika Sangha, Gadapalasuni, Po-Gadapalasuni, Via-Parajanga.
2. Mahisha Mangala Paika Sangha, Ganga Dhara Prasad, Po-Ganga Dhar Prasad, Via.-Bhapur.

3. Maa Kalapaika Sangha, Balaram Prasad, Po-Balaram Prasad.
4. Jayadurga Paika Sangha, At/Po- Chandrasekhar Prasad.
5. Jayadurga Paika Sangha, At-Baniapada, Po- Khandiapatana.
6. Somanath Singha Jagadeb Paika Sangha, At/Po-Budhapanka.
7. Chandra Sekhara Paika Sangha, At-Chandrasekharpur, Po-Neulapoi, Via-Mahimagadi.
8. Birabhanu Paika Akheda Sangha, At/Po- Bhudapanka.
9. National Youth Club, Vil-Bhudapanka, Po-Bhudapanka.
10. Nilamadhab Paika Sangha, At/Po- Bhudapanka.
11. Adi Anadi Paika Sangha, Giridhari Prasad, Po-Dudurkot.
12. Jayadurga Paika Akheda Baniapada, Po-Gadiapatna.
13. Jaymaa Mangala Balika Paika Sangha, At/Po-Basulei.
14. Baruneswar Balika Paika Akheda, At/Po-Basulei.
15. Kamadhenu Kote Paika Sangha, Kamadhenu Kote, Po/Via-Bhapur.
16. Dudurkote Paika Akheda Dala, At/Po-Dudurkote.
17. Pidhasahi Paika Sangha, Gadasanta, Po-Santree.
18. Jamusahi Paika Sangha, Khadasantri, Po-Santri.
19. Satyanarayan Balika Paika Sangha, Gadasantri, Po-Santri.
20. Satyanarayan Paika Sangha, Gadasantri, Po-Santri.
21. Bhudapanka Dasahra Parisada, At/Po-Bhudapanka.
22. Satyanarayan Paika Yubak Dala, Gadasantri, Po-Santri.
23. Siddha Ramachandi Paika Sangha, At/Po-Talabarkote.
24. Siddha Ramachandi Balaka Paika Sangha, At/Po-Talabarkote.
25. Siddha Kameswari Paika Akheda, At-Simin, Po-Gadasila.
26. Siddha Kameswari Balaka Paika Akheda, At-Siminei, Po-Gadasila.
27. Siddha Kameswari Balika Paika Akheda, At-Simin, Po-Gadasila.
28. Basusabar Paika Akheda, At/Po-Gundichapada.
29. Birahanuman Paika Sangha, At/Po-Gundichapada.
30. Maa Mangla Paika Sangha, At-Krusnaprasad,Po-Bhapur.
31. Malaluhakabat Balika Paika Akheda, At/Po-Kandabindha.
32. Malaluhakabat Paika Akheda, At/Po-Khandabindha.
33. Jayadurga Paika Akheda, At/Po-Neulapoi.

34. Sangram Paika Parisad At/Po-Mota.
35. Dileswar Paika Akheda, At/Po-Kulei.
36. Dileswar Balak Paika Akheda, At/Po-Kulei.
37. Bhujabala Paika Sangha, At/Po-Bhudapanka.
38. Jayasree Yubaka Sangha, At/Po-Bahada.
39. Mahanayak Kulamani Khatriya Sangha, At/Po-Bhudapanka.
40. Satyanarayan Paika Sangha, At-Biradia, Po-Kaimati.
41. Brahumanamaru Paika Sangha, Dudurkote, Hindola, Dhenkanal.
42. Gada Parajanga Paika Akheda, At/Po-Parajanga.
43. Gurile Paika Akheda, At-Dudurkote, Via-Blimi.
44. Kishor Club, Po-Talcher.
45. Kalinga Keshari Khetariya Sangha, Kasturipod, Banrapal.
46. Gajapati Birabara Samanta Paika Sangha, Talcher.
47. Maa Dasabhuja Paika Bahini, Tilapada.
48. Krusna Harichandan Singh Paika Sangha, Nachhipura, Dhenkanal.

Ganjam

1. Gajapati Samar Vidya Sangha, At/Po-Paralakhemundi, Ganjam.
2. Friends Physical Institute, Brahampur, Ganjam.
3. Phulla Sundari Surtipitha, Samujhia Sahi, Paralakhemundi, Ganjam.

Kalahandi

1. Mahabir Paika Akheda Cultural Organisation, Bhabanipatna, Kalahandi,766001.

Khurda

1. Narayan Baliar Singh Bira Bajaranga Paika Akheda Club, At-Rasala, Po- Senapadar, Khurda.
2. Mahabir Youth Club, At/Po-Narayanipada, via-Begunia, Khurda.
3. Satyam Shivam Sundaram Cultural Association, At- Saha-Paika Sahi, Po-Tangi, Khurda.
4. Keranga Paika Akheda Sangha, At/Po-Keranga, Khurda.
5. Jairajguru Paika Akheda, At/Po- Keranga, Khurda.

6. Swapneswar Dev Paika Akheda, At-Kumbhila, Po-Keranga, Khurda.
7. Nayakata Paika Akheda Sangha, At-Nayakata, Po-Nachuni, Khurda.
8. Manikya Athletic Association, At/Po- Manikyagada, Khurda.
9. Champila Paika Akheda, At-Champila, Po-Pichukoli, Khurda.
10. Gadamanetri Paika Akheda, At/Po-Gadamanitri, Khurda.
11. Prativaguna Paika Akheda Parisad, At/Po-Gadamanitri, Khurda.
12. Dalabehera Memorial Paika Akheda, At-Gadamenitri, Khurda.
13. Paika Akheda Dala, Sundarpada, Old Town, Bhubaneswar, Khurda.
14. Kapila Prasad Paika Party, At/Po- Kapila Prasad, Old Town, Bhubaneswar, Khurda.
15. Baxi Jagabandhu Paika Akheda, At/Po- Gurujanga, Khurda.
16. Jogamaya Paika Sangha, Bacharapatna, Jatani, Khurda.
17. Gadibhrahma Darunsun Thakurani Paika Akheda, Gambhari Nuagaon, Khurda.
18. Ranaranka Paika Nacha Pratisthana, At/Po-Gadamanitri, Khurda.
19. Maa Paduki Paika Akheda Sangha, Ranipada, Po- Kumaraja, Via-Banapur.
20. Bhimpur Paika Akheda At/Po- Bhimpur, Khurda.
21. Tinikudi Khetrapal Sangha, At-Tinikudi, Po-Rahasmal, Khurda.
22. Suliadevi Paika Akheda Sangha, At/Po-Pratap, Via-Banapur, Khurda.
23. Maa Ugratara Paika Akheda Dala, Gobardhanpur, Bhusandapur, Khurda.
24. Sipai Paika Sangha, Balugaon, Khurda.
25. Nandighosh Paika Akheda, At/Po- Bolagarh, Khurda.

Koraput

1. Srikrishna Chitanya Paika Akheda, At/Po-Jaipur, Koraput,764001.

Nayagarh

1. Bira Hanuman Paika Akheda, Lathipada, Nayagarh.

2. Maa Bhairab Paika Sangha, Lathipada, Nayagada.

Puri

1. Puri Paika Sangha, Bimanbadu Sahi, Puri.
2. Maa Jageswari Paika Akheda Sangha, Damodarpur, Puri.
3. Pingaleswar Paika Akheda Sangha, At/Po-Damodarpur, Puri.
4. Dibya Singha Prasad Paika Akheda Sangha, At-Dibya Singha Prasad, Po- Keranga, Puri.
5. Bari Brahma Juharasweri Paika Akheda, At/Po-Gamahari, Puri.
6. Ramachandi Thakurani Paika Akheda, At/Po-Bashui, Puri.
7. Netar Paika Akheda, At/Po-Netar, Puri.
8. Hinjeliganga Panchayat Samit, Po/Dist-Puri.
9. Bhaktabandhu Paika Akheda Parisad, At-Dekanda, Po-Kanas, Puri.
10. Radha Krishna Paika Akheda Parisad, At-Aliaput, Po-Rebena Neuagaon, Puri.
11. Ratia Paika Akheda, At/Po-Bentapur, Puri.
12. Narayan Baliar Singh Bira Bajaranga Paika Akheda Club, At-Rasala, Po-Sanapadar, Puri.
13. Palankeswari Sanskrutika Anusthana, At/Po- Goruala, Puri.
14. Bramha Bihar Pratistan Paika Akheda, At/Po-Bramhagiri, Puri.
15. Rabi Sankar Paika Bahini, At-Kathuaredi, Po-Bentapur, Via-Brahmagiri, Puri.
16. Srikethra Paika Akheda, Lions Gate, Puri.
17. Kanaka Durga Paika Sangha, At/Po-Maluda, Via-Balugaon, Puri.
18. Maa Rudrani Paika Akheda Youth Club, Bhatapur Behera Sahi, Po- Barala, Via- Sakhigopal, Puri.
19. Gajapati Paika Akheda Sangha, At-Dokanda, Po-Kanasa, Puri.
20. Neheru Paika Akheda Seva Sangha, Bramhan, Po-Ramalenka, Puri.
21. Mahavir Paika Akheda, At-Kotakana, Po-Kodalasasana, Puri.
22. Trinath Dev Paika Sangha, At-Patapur, Po-Siala, Krushna Prasad, Puri.

23. Mahavir Paika Sangha, Ora, Po-Siala, Krusnaprasad, Puri.

Rayagada

1. Sri Majigani Paika Akheda, Rayagada.

Sambalpur

1. Toreswari Yuva Krida and Sanskrutika Parisada,Tora.

Appendix-B

Introductory Letter

From

Shyam Sundar Rath

(Research scholar)

To

The Secretary,

____

____

Dear Sir,

With due respect I want to bring the matter into your kind notice that I am doing research on Orissan Martial Arts (Paika Akheda).

In this connection, I request your good self to fill up the questionnaire sent herewith for collecting necessary data for my study and send to me at your earliest convenience.

The replies will be kept confidential and it is only for academic analysis and conclusion.

Your co-operation will go a longway in making the study meaningful and it will also help to revive the Orissan Martial Art in our State.

With regards,

Yours faithfully,

(Shyam Sundar Rath)

N.B. You are requested to send the filled up questionnaire within 15 days from the date of receipt.

Appendix-C

Questionnaires

Topic of the study: A critical analysis of the orissan martial arts.

Instruction: (a) Please answer the all questions.

(b) Add additional sheets, if space provided for answers insufficient.

1. Name of the paika guru in your akheda.
2. Educational qualification.
3. Did he participate in any paika akheda competition, organised by Directorate of Sports and Youth Services of Orissa?

   Yes/No

   (If yes, mention the name of the competition and year)
4. Has he got any prize or award from the Government?

   Yes/No
5. How many students are learning martial art in your akheda?
6. Age group of the students.

   Minimum ....

   Maximum...............
7. Please mark (√) on the list of the equipments used in your akheda.

   (a) Sword and shield, (b) Patta, (c) Banka Chhuri,
   (d) Lathi, (e) Ranapa, (f) Mudugara,
   (g) Nagaphasa, (h) Banati, (i) Nizham,
   (j) Singhata, (k) Bana, (l) Jamadhara,
   (m) Gupti, (n) Bow and Arrow,

   if any other, Please mention.

8. Please mark (√) on the list of the musical equipments used at your akheda.

   (a) Dhola, (b) Changu, (c) Mahuri,
   (d) Nagera, (e) Nisana, (f) Turi,
   (g) Singha, (h) Telingibaja, (i) Jodimahuri,
   (j) Phunka.

   if any other, please mention.

9. Do you feel the facilities your akheda possesses is adequate for the students? Yes/No

   (If no, please write the deficiency in details)

10. Does your akheda possess separate building? Yes/No

11. Does your akheda possess one room or more than one room? (One room, two rooms, more than two rooms)

12. Does your akheda have field facilities? Yes/No

13. Please mark (✓) on the list of the martial activities practised at your akheda.

    (a) Dhala Tarabari, (b) Patta, (c) Banka Chhuri,
    (d) Lathi, (e) Ranapa, (f) Mudugara,
    (g) Bhuinghar Bidya, (h) Banatti,
    (i) Mati Kusti (wrestling), (j) Nagaphasa,
    (k) Nizham,
    (l) Exceptional activities like Sagada Chaka, Akalana etc.

    If any other activities practised, please mention.

14. Whether the students of your akheda practise everyday or during Dashara or any other festivals?

15. Does your akheda organise any competition at village or district level? Yes/No

16. Are the village youth interested to learn this martial arts? Yes/No

17. Is your akheda registered under government socialisation act? Yes/No

18. Does your akheda possess a girl team? Yes/No

19. Do you support the idea of organising a state level competition every year for the development and revival of Orissan martial arts? Yes/No

20. Are the guardians interested or motivated to send their children to participate in the akheda? Yes/No

21. Are you in favour that the paika akheda competition should be organised with proper rules and regulations and in a modified manner? Yes/No

22. Do the students of your akheda belong to all classes?

23. Does your akheda provide any finance or other thing to your guru? Yes/No

    (Please mention the details of your provision)

24. Does your akheda get any financial grant from the Government? Yes/No

    (If yes, give details)

25. (a) Please mention your annual budget for the year concerned.

    (b) List down the source of income of the budget.

    Please give your suggestion, if any, regarding the development of the Orissan martial arts.

Appendix-D

Interview

Name Age

1. At what age had you learnt the martial arts?
2. Why did you want to learn the martial arts?
3. How many years did you take to learn all the techniques and tactics of martial art?
4. During the time of king's rule it was highly essential for the defence purpose but in modern days how does it help the village youth and society?
5. Is it a fact that day-by-day the standard of our martial arts is deteriorated and many gurus are not much interested to be involved in paika akheda?
6. Are you of opinion that few activities of Orissan martial arts like sword and shield; banatti, patta etc. should be included in school games and sports?
7. Do you agree that every year a state lavel competition is highly essential for the revival and development of martial arts?
8. Is it a fact that many activities and traditional equipments are not used, not even seen in the competition.
9. How do you arrange the traditional equipments of the martial arts?
10. Name the activities of the martial arts, which are not practised due to non-availability of equipments and extra space in your akheda?
11. Whether the youth of your village are interested to learn the martial arts?

12. How will the youth of your village be motivated towards this martial arts?
13. War music was an essential factor during those days. Do you or your team face any problem during the competition or practice period for want of musicians?
14. Do you face any problem regarding officiating in the competition etc.?
15. Do you face any major problems during your training period like injury, shortage of equipments etc.?
16. What difference do you find when you teach your students compare to your youth times?
17. Tell me the name of the techniques you have used in sword fighting patta, banati etc.?
18. As a paika guru, are you really interested to involve the traditional martial art in modern days?
19. Are you getting any financial support from your akheda?
20. As a guru, have you got any award or incentive from the Government or any social organisation?
21. Are the parents are interested to send their children to learn the martial arts?
22. Can you give your opinion about the state level martial arts competitions organised by Directorate of Sports and Youth Services during recent past?
23. In which way did you train a beginner? Please tell your method of training.
24. Are your trainees contributing financially to you or your akheda to learn the martial art?
25. Last, not the least; please tell your opinion regarding the development of the Orissan martial arts?

Bibliography

Books

Acharya, P. *Studies in Orissan History Archaeology and Archives*. Cuttack: Cuttack Student Store, 1969.

Acharya, P. *Mayurbhanja Gazette*. Cuttack: Government press, 1934.

Altekar, A.S. *Education in Ancient India.* Varanasi: Nandakishor Bros, 1964.

Ayangar, S.K. *Social and Political Life of Vijayanagar Empire*. Karaikudi: South India Press, 1975.

Banarjee, R.D. *History of Orissa*. Vol. II, Calcutta: Pravati Press, 1931.

Barker, E, *Greek Political Theory*. London: Mackenzie Publishing Ltd, 1971.

Basu, Dipak Kumar. *The Magnificent Fort of Barabati*. Cuttack: Nalanda, 1972.

Basu, N.N. *Archaeological Survey of Mayurbhanja*. Delhi: Rare Reprints, 1981.

Beal, S. *The Romantic Legend of Sakya Budha*. London: Turban and Co., 1875.

Bhandarkar, D.R. *Comprehensive History of India*. Varanasi: Motilal Banarasidas, 1956.

Blochmann, H. *Ani-I-Akbari*. translated, Calcutta: Royal Asiatic Society of Bengal, Vol. VI. No. I, 1939.

Chakravarti, P.C. *The Art of War in Ancient India*. Calcutta: Abinas Press, 1941.

Chaplin, Sturut. *New Trends in Research.* quoted by Young. London: Scientific Surveys and Research, Asia Publishing House, 1954.

Dasgupta, D.C. *Educational Psychology of Ancient Hindus*. Calcutta: University Press, 1949.

Das, K.D. *A Study of Orissan Folklare.* Cuttack: Nalanda, 1953.

Das, S.N. *Physical Education Games and Recreation in Early India.* Lucknow: The Upper India Publishing House, 1985.

Das, H.C. *Military History of India.* Calcutta: Farma K C M Pvt. Ltd., 1980.

Das, H.C. *Military History of Kalinga.* Calcutta: Punthi Pustak, 1986.

Das, M.N. *Indian History.* Cuttack: Vidyapuri, 1981.

Das, Sivaprasad. *Glorious of Ancient Orissa.* Sambalpur: Saraswata Pustak Bhandar, 1964.

Dasgupta, D.C. *Jain System of Education.* Calcutta: Sri Bhart Press, 1942.

Dash, Srivatsa. *Baramba Itihasa.* (Oriya) Cuttack: Saraswata Press, 1940.

De, S.E. Guide to Orissa Records III. Cuttack: Government Press, 1972.

Deobold, B, Van Dalen and Bruce L.Bennentt. *A World History of Physical Education.* New Jersey: Englewood Cliffs, N.J: Prentice Hall, 1971.

Dikshitar, V.R.R. *War in Ancient India.* Madras: Macmillan and Co. Ltd., 1948.

Finn Michael, *Martial Arts a Complete Illustrated History.* London: Mackenzie Publishing Ltd, 1988.

Gardiner, E.N. *Athletics of the Ancient World.* London: Oxford Clarendon Press, 1930.

Goode, W.J.and Halt, P.K. *Methods in Social Research.* New York: M.C. Grow Hill Book Co, 1952.

Gyani, S.D. *Agni Purana: A study.* Varanasi: Chowkhamba Publication, 1964.

Haque, M.A., *Muslim Adminstration in Orissa.* Calcutta: Punthi Pustak, 1980.

Hota, Damodara. *Orissi as a form of Classical Music.* Ed. by M.N. Das, History and Culture of Orissa, Cuttack: Vidyapuri, 1977.

Johnson, H.M., *Trsastisalaka- Purusacarita*, translated by Hemacandra, Vol. II, Baroda: Baroda Oriental Institute, 1931.

John N. Drowatzky and Charles W. Armstrong. *Physical Education Career Perspectives and Professional Foundations*. New Jersey: Prentice Hall, Inc. Englewood Cliffs, 1984.

Jowetl. *Political Thought*. Translated Republic of Plato, Book III, New York: Alpine Publishing, 1967.

Kar, H.C. *Military History of India*. Calcutta: KCM Pvt. Ltd, 1980.

Keay, F. E. *Ancient Indian Education*. London: Oxford University Press, 1918.

Khan, Eraj Ahamad. *History of Physical Education*. Varanasi: Narendra Bhargava, 1964.

Laurie, S.S. *Historical Survey of Pre-Christian Education*. New York: Longmans Green and Co., 1900.

Lewis, Peter. *The Way to the Martial Arts*. London: Cavendish Books Ltd, 1986.

Marie, Natalire. *Foundations and Principles of Physical Education*. New York: Ronald Press Company, 1960.

Maltby, J.J. *Ganjam District Manual*. Cuttack: Government Press, 1968.

Mahatab H.K History of Orissa, Cuttack: Prajatantra Prachara Samiti, 1960.

Majumdar, B.K. *Military system in Ancient India*. Calcutta: World Press, 1955.

Majumdar R.C and Pusalkar, A.D., *The Vedic Age*. London: George Allen and Union Ltd., 1957.

Maxmuller, F. *Chandogya Upanisad*. Vol. I Varanasi: Motilal Banarasidas, 1969.

Maxmuller, F. *Mundika Upanisad*. Vol. XV, Part II, Varanasi: Motilal Banarasidas, 1969.

Monroe, Paul. *Cyclopedia of Education*. New York: The Macmillan Co., 1919.

Mishra. B. *Orissa Under Bhauma King*. Calcutta: Viswamitra Press, 1934.

Mishra, P.K Last days of Oriya Militia, Bhubaneswar: S.S Printers and Publishers, 1999.

Mishra, P.K. *Freedom Struggle in Orissa*. Ed. by M.N. Das, History and Culture of Orissa, Cuttack: Vidyapuri, 1977.

Mitra, R.L. *Antiquities of Orissa*. Vol. II, Calcutta: Indian Studies Past and Present, 1963.

Mohapatra, S. M. *The Princely States of Orissa in Retrospect*. Edited by M.N. Das, History and Culture of Orissa, Cuttack: Vidyapuri, 1977.

Mohapatra, R.P. *Military History of Orissa*. Delhi: Cosmo Publication, 1986.

Mohapatra, C.D. *Utkal Itihasara Eka Agyanta Adhyaya*. Cuttack: Kitab Mahal, 1970.

Mohapatra, Gopinath. *Jaganath During the Role of Gangas and Suryas*, Ed. by, M.N. Das, History and Culture of Orissa, Cuttack: Vidyapuri, 1977.

Mukherji, R.K. *Ancient Indian Education*. Varanasi: Motilal Banarasidas, 1960.

Mukherji, P. *The Gajapati Kings of Orissa and their Success*. Calcutta: General Trading Co., 1953.

Panda, H.C. *Military History of Orissa*, Ed. by P.K Mishra, *Comprehensive History and Culture of Orissa*, New Delhi: Kaveri books, 1997.

Panigrahi, K.C. *History of Orissa*. Cuttack: Kitab Mahal, 1981.

Pant, G.N. *Indian Arms and Armour*. Vol. I, New Delhi: Army Educational Store, 1978.

Pattanaik, P.K. *A Forgotten Chapter of Orissan History*. Calcutta: Punthi Pustak, 1979.

Patra, K.M., *Orissa Under East India Company*. New Delhi: Munshiram Monoharlal, 1971.

Pradhan, A.C. *A Study of History of Orissa*. Bhubaneswar: Panchashila Publishers, 1984.

Prasad, S.N. *A study of work done on the Military History of India*. Calcutta: K.P.Bagchi and Company, 1976.

Rai Chaudhry, H.C. *Political History of Ancient India*. Calcutta: Punthi Pustak, 1959.

Rajagopalan, K. *A Brief History of Physical Education in India*. Delhi: Army Publishers, 1962.

Rao, Ramachandra C.V. *Administrative And Society in Medieval Andhra (1033-1538)*. Nellore: Manasa Publications, 1972.

Rathasarma, Sadasiva. *Paika Kheda* (Ed). Puri: Bharati Press, 1956.

Ray, B.C. *Foundation of British Orissa*. Cuttack: New Student Store, 1960.

Ray, B.C. *Orissa Under Maratha 1751-1803*. Allahabad: Kitab Mahal, 1960.

Sahoo, N.K. *History of Orissa*. Bhubaneswar: Utkal University, 1964.

Sahu, N.K. *History of Orissa*. Calcutta: Nabajiban Press, 1980.

Sensharma, P. *Kurukshetra War: A Military Study*. Ganganagar: Darbari Udjog, 1975.

Shamasastry, R. Tr. *Kautilya's Arthasastra*. 7th Ed, Mysore: Mysore Printing and Publishing House, 1961.

Singhdeo, S.P. and Singhdeo G.P. *War Waves*. Calcutta: Punthi Pustak, 1980.

Sitaramiah, V. *Valmik Ramayan*. New Delhi: Sahitya Akademi, 1972.

Sports Authority of India, *Indian Traditional Folk Culture and Martial Art*. Delhi: Cosmo Publication, 1988.

Tawney C. H., *Somadevas Kathasaritsagar*. Varanasi: Motilal Banarasidas, 1968.

Tirunarayanan C. and Hariharasarma S. *An Analytical History of Physical Education*. Karaikudi: South India Press, 1985.

Tripathy, R.S. *History of Ancient India*. Varanasi: Motilal Banarasidas, 1960.

Vaidya P.L. *Lalita-Vastara*. Buddhist Sanskrit Text, No 1, Darbhanga: Mithila Institute, 1958.

Vuillier, Gaston. *A History of Dancing From the Earliest Ages to our own times*. New York: Appleton and Co., 1878.

Wilson Jim. *An Illustrated Introduction to the Martial Arts*. London: Marshall, Cavendish Ltd., 1988.

Thesis

Raj, Manuel David. *Silambam Technique and Evaluation*. Unpublished thesis, Gwalior: Jiwaji University, 1967.

Raysingh, L.N. *Oriya Samara Sahitya*. Unpublished thesis, Bhubaneswar: Utkal University, 1991.

Journal and Periodicals

Barala, P. Paika Akheda Competition of the year 1993 and Statement of the Judges. *Souvenir of Orissan Martial Arts*, Dhenkanal, 1994.

Basu, D.K. The Magnificent Fort of Barabati. Souvenir, Seminar on *Utkaliya Paramparika Paika Akheda* Competition and Martial Tradition of Oriyas, Bhubaneswar: 27th to 30th may,1979.

Bisoi, K.K. *Orissa Historical Research Journal*. Vol. XVI No. 1-2.

Gochhikar, Baidyanath. *Sahi Yatra Re Sanyashi*. Souvenir on *Utkaliya Paramparika Sanskurtika Mahautusava*, (Oriya) Puri: Srikhetra Hanuman Jayanti Committee, 1988.

Mohapatra, K.C. *Anti British Movements of Paika, 1776-1836*. Souvenir, Seminar on *Utkaliya Paramparika Paika Akheda* Competition and Martial Tradition of Oriyas, Bhubaneswar: 27th to 30th May, 1979.

Orissa Historical Research Journal. Vol. IX no. 3-4.

Orissa Historical Research Journal. Vol. XXVII no. 1-4.

Paikaray, D.J. *Oriya Samarabigyana Kabya Paika Kheda Re Aitihasika Bibarani*. Souvenir, 1993.

Pattanaik, Jagannath. *Role of Orissa in the National Movement*. Souvenir on Utkal at a Glance, Bhubaneswar: Sikhya Vikash Samitti, 1998.

Pattanaik, Jagannath.*Orissara Paika Sampradaya Eka Aitihashika Anusilana, Prajatantra Saptahiki*. July, 19-25,1992.

Pradhan, Nagendranath. *Rise and fall of a Powerful Hindu Kingdom of India*. Souvenir, Bhubaneswar: Sikhya Vikash Samiti, 1988.

Rathsarma, Sadasiva. *Jaga and Akheda Relation*. Souvenir on Utkaliya Paramparika Sanskurtika Mahautusava, (Oriya) Puri: Srikhetra Hanuman Jayanti Committee, 1983.

Samantasinghar, D. *Srikhetra Sanskrutika Pranakendra Jagaghar*, Souvenir on Utkaliya Paramparika Sanskurtika Mahautusava, (Oriya) Puri: Srikhetra Hanuman Jayanti Committee, 1983.

Toynbee, G. A Sketch of the History of Orissa, *Orissa Historical Research Journal*. IX, 1962.

Index

F

G

H

I

J

K

L

M

N

O

T

U

V

W

Y

Z